THE TAMING
OF THE PRESS

THE TAMING
OF THE PRESS

Cohen v. Cowles Media Company

Elliot C. Rothenberg

 PRAEGER

Westport, Connecticut
London

Library of Congress Cataloging-in-Publication Data

Rothenberg, Elliot C., 1939–
   The taming of the press : Cohen v. Cowles Media Company / Elliot
C. Rothenberg.
      p.   cm.
   Includes bibliographical references and index.
   ISBN 0–275–96601–1 (alk. paper)
   1. Cohen, Dan, 1936–   —Trials, litigation, etc.   2. Cowles Media
Company—Trials, litigation, etc.   3. Press law—United States.
4. Confidential communications—Press—United States.   5. Minnesota—
Politics and government—1951–   6. Leaks (Disclosure of
information)—Minnesota.   I. Title.
KF228.C633R68   1999
343.7309'98—dc21   99–13431

British Library Cataloguing in Publication Data is available.

Library of Congress Catalog Card Number: 99–13431
ISBN: 0–275–96601–1

First published in 1999

Praeger Publishers, 88 Post Road West, Westport, CT 06881
An imprint of Greenwood Publishing Group, Inc.
www.praeger.com

Printed in the United States of America

The paper used in this book complies with the
Permanent Paper Standard issued by the National
Information Standards Organization (Z39.48–1984).

10 9 8 7 6 5 4 3 2 1

Copyright Acknowledgments

The author and publisher gratefully acknowledge permission for use of the following material:

Excerpts from Lili Levi, "Dangerous Liaisons: Seduction and Betrayal in Confidential
Press-Source Relations," originally published at 43 *Rutgers Law Review* 609 (1991).
Reprinted by permission of *Rutgers Law Review*.

To my wife, Sally, and our children
and to the memory of my parents, Claire and Sam Rothenberg.

Contents

Acknowledgments

Heather Ruland Staines, Praeger's legal studies editor, was an indefatigable advocate of *The Taming of the Press* from the time she received the original manuscript. I am grateful for her considerable editorial skills and enthusiasm, which brought this project to publication.

I also thank Gillian von Nieda Beebe, the book's production editor, for her similar commitment and for her leadership and good humor in expeditiously converting the manuscript to a published book.

No author could ask for finer editors. I am fortunate to have had the opportunity to work with both.

I wish to thank my mother-in-law, Lyda M. Smayling, for her idea of *The Taming of the Press* as a title.

My final gratitude is to my family for its support during the many years of litigating *Cohen v. Cowles Media Company* and the additional years of writing this book.

CHAPTER 1 —————————————————————————————————

Hanging Cohen Out to Dry

IT DID NOT have, at first blush, the ingredients of a landmark Supreme Court case. It began as a routine transaction among politicians and journalists in the coverage of the waning days of a not very exciting campaign for governor. Just another day at the politicians' office, or so it seemed.

A group of prominent businessmen, lawyers, and academicians who were leaders of Wheelock Whitney's campaign for governor in Minnesota met early one morning in the last week of October 1982 at the Whitney headquarters to discuss newly discovered information about Marlene Johnson, the Democratic candidate for lieutenant governor. One of the participants, a former state legislator and Hennepin County (Minneapolis) attorney, had photocopied some public court records at the St. Paul courthouse. The chairman of this group, a former head of the Minnesota Republican party, had learned of the court documents a couple of days earlier. The three pages of court files revealed that in 1970 Ms. Johnson had been convicted of an unspecified offense of "petit theft" and had also been arrested for unlawful assembly at a construction site. The petit theft document contained an entry indicating that the conviction was vacated in 1971. The election would be held the following week, and Whitney and other Republican candidates were trailing in opinion polls. The group debated whether and how the documents should be shared with the media. After arguing about whether the disclosures would make any difference at that late date, the participants decided to give the media the documents, but only in return for assurances that the source would not be revealed.

Such an arrangement is the typical way in which journalists obtain derogatory information about candidates that the candidates themselves obviously do not volunteer and would do everything possible to cover up.

The group drafted Dan Cohen to disseminate the documents because of his experience in dealing with the media. Cohen had been active in politics. More than a decade before, he had been president of the Minneapolis City Council. Earlier in 1982, he had been a candidate for Hennepin County commissioner but did not survive the September primary. Cohen also had written many guest editorial features for the *Star Tribune* newspaper in Minneapolis. Along with all his other accomplishments, he was a graduate of Harvard Law School and Stanford University.

Cohen had learned about the meeting only an hour before. He almost didn't make it because his car broke down on the way. Cohen was lukewarm about the idea but accepted the draft because his father had been a friend and business associate of Whitney. Whitney's media adviser, journalism professor and later journalism school dean Arnold Ismach, instructed Cohen on how to obtain promises of anonymity. Cohen spent the next hour or so at the Whitney office, setting up appointments with various news outlets.

Armed with several unaltered copies of the complete documents, Dan Cohen that day met separately with reporters from four different media organizations: the Associated Press, the Minneapolis television affiliate of CBS (WCCO-TV), the Minneapolis *Star Tribune*, and the St. Paul *Pioneer Press*. So there would be no misunderstanding about his condition for giving the documents, he went through a prepared litany to each:

I have some documents which may or may not relate to a candidate in the upcoming election, and if you will give me a promise of confidentiality—that is, that I will be treated as an anonymous source, that my name will not appear in any material in connection with this, and you will also agree that you're not going to pursue with me a question of who my source is—then I'll furnish you with the documents.

Cohen's information did not seem to approach the level of interest of that dispensed by "Deep Throat" of Watergate fame, and Cohen's formality of language seemed excessive. In the event, each reporter agreed and had no doubt that he or she was promising Cohen confidentiality in return for the documents. Cohen gave the documents to each one without commenting on their contents.

None were shocked or offended at the nature of the materials. On the contrary, they were glad to get them. *Star Tribune* reporter Lori Sturdevant asked Cohen for more of the same. "This is the sort of thing," she said, "that I'd like to have you bring by again if you have anything like it." If anything, *Pioneer Press* reporter Bill Salisbury was even more enthusiastic. He gushingly told Cohen the documents were "political dynamite."

Later that day, Cohen went back to his office at Martin-Williams, an advertising and public relations agency, which was billing and collecting fees from the Whitney campaign for Cohen's work. Cohen told company officers about his contacts with the press and alerted them that the newspapers would likely publish articles on Johnson the following day. No one batted an eye. It was nothing out of the ordinary, after all, and more money for the company.

As political shenanigans go, this was pretty innocuous stuff. Neither Cohen nor the Whitney office fabricated anything about Ms. Johnson's past. No one trespassed on Johnson's property, no one stole her papers, no one eavesdropped, no one tapped her phone, and no one otherwise invaded her privacy. Cohen did not doctor the documents, nor did he make any comments about them to the reporters. The court records were public documents that anyone could have obtained at the courthouse. The wonder is that no reporter for any newspaper or radio or television station in the state had bothered to do so before. Perhaps they were not encouraged by their editors. The *Star Tribune* earlier had enthusiastically endorsed Johnson to be the state's first woman lieutenant governor. The *Pioneer Press* had endorsed Whitney but still had kind things to say about Johnson. The newspaper reporters nevertheless warmly received Cohen's documents.

As the appreciative comments of the reporters indicated, encouraging disclosures of the variegated skullduggeries of politicians by their opponents is a tradition in media coverage of political campaigns. Unlike Cohen's court documents, the "revelations" are often outright fabrications. Minnesota, with its supposedly high ground politics, is no exception to the rule. Quite the contrary. In one notorious example twenty years, almost to the day, before Cohen's meetings with the reporters, unsubstantiated "revelations" of supposed wrongdoing brought about the defeat of a Republican governor running for reelection.

Less than two weeks before the 1962 election, an informant, who later turned out to be the brother of a worker for the Democratic gubernatorial candidate, made sensational charges of graft and substandard construction of a highway project in northern Minnesota. Gov. Elmer L. Andersen denounced the charges as a "last minute desperation maneuver by cheap, dirty politicians." Investigations after the election cleared Andersen of any wrongdoing, but the findings came too late for the governor. Andersen was defeated by only 91 votes out of more than 1.2 million cast. A recount commission took until March 1963 to decide which candidate won.[1]

Despite the manifest injustice of it all, the Minneapolis and St. Paul newspapers did not vilify Andersen's accuser and his cohorts. After all, politics is politics.

For Cohen, everything went smoothly as far as the Associated Press and the television channel were concerned. The TV station decided that it was not much of a story and did not broadcast anything on the Johnson court documents. AP prepared a short article for its affiliates about Johnson's court records that, in accord with the promise to Cohen, did not identify him as the source.

The newspaper reporters went back to their papers and gave their stories to their editors for publication the next day. They did not identify Cohen in their drafts and told their supervisors about their promises of confidentiality. Unfortunately, they did not keep the name of their source secret from their editors.

The executive editor of the *Pioneer Press* quickly decided to identify Cohen. "Honestly, I don't think that we ever considered doing it another way other than using his name." He did not ask for Salisbury's opinion.

Star Tribune editors met and also decided to identify Cohen. Sturdevant was not present at the meeting, and the editors did not consult her about the decision. Editors of the two newspapers denied that each had determined to identify Cohen in response to what the other newspaper decided.

Both reporters were angry that their editors had decided to dishonor their promises. Sturdevant demanded that her byline not appear on the story to be published in the next day's paper.

From the outset, the *Star Tribune* recognized that Cohen could have a valid legal claim. They instructed Sturdevant to try to persuade Cohen to release the newspaper from what they called "their agreement." She called Cohen several times in the afternoon and evening. Each time Cohen refused to allow his name to be published. That did not change the editors' decision.

The Associated Press story published in several Minnesota newspapers did not identify Cohen but reported that the court documents "were slipped to reporters Wednesday."

The *Pioneer Press* article on Johnson's court records appeared in section D of the newspaper. It reported that Cohen gave the newspaper the documents "but asked that his name not be used." It did not mention that Cohen demanded and received a promise of confidentiality.

The *Star Tribune* lowered the boom on Cohen and made him, rather than Johnson's record, the focus of its story. Its long article, "Marlene Johnson arrests disclosed by Whitney ally," appeared prominently on the newspaper's front page and included a photo of Cohen alongside one of Johnson. The article not only named Cohen himself but gratuitously named Cohen's employer, Martin-Williams, as well.

The article portrayed Johnson sympathetically as "a leader in small-business and women's organizations" and listed several awards she had received. It quoted her as claiming that the conviction was for shoplifting $6 in sewing supplies when she was upset over the death of her father. The court documents themselves did not disclose the nature or amount of Johnson's theft, and Johnson's claims have never been independently corroborated.

After deciding to break their promises, the newspapers dispatched reporters to seek out all the major players of both political parties, in a frenzied effort to solicit derogatory remarks about Cohen.

When reporters questioned them, Whitney and his campaign abandoned Cohen, leaving him to twist in the wind. Whitney told the press that he had not spoken with Cohen for two months. He and his campaign manager claimed that Cohen had acted without the knowledge or permission of anyone on the campaign staff. They said that they would not mention Johnson's record in the remaining days of the campaign. They claimed that Cohen was not on the campaign payroll and was not on any leadership committee of the campaign. The very people who had dragooned Cohen into going to the press for the supposed good of the candidate insisted to the same media organizations that Cohen was on a frolic of his own. No one would own up to the simple truth that Cohen was only the messenger for the big shots of the Whitney campaign who deputized him in the candidate's own headquarters.

The same article that expressed such revulsion over the revelation of candidate Johnson's criminal record made a point of telling readers that Cohen, unlike Johnson not then a candidate for any office, had been arrested three years earlier for scalping a ticket at the Kentucky Derby.

The *Star Tribune* article did not reveal that the paper had given a promise of confidentiality in return for Cohen's documents and, unlike the *Pioneer Press*, did not inform readers that it had even discussed confidentiality. The *Star Tribune* also did not disclose that because of the violation of the promises to Cohen, its reporter had refused to allow her name to be used as writer of the story.

The consequences of the disclosure of the court records and their source were minimal or nil for Johnson and gubernatorial candidate Rudy Perpich, who won handily. They were devastating for Cohen and eventually for the two newspapers and the entire media industry.

Cohen's employer fired him the day the newspaper articles appeared. The president of Martin-Williams told him to get out within twenty-four hours. The company did not want to jeopardize prospective business from a Perpich-Johnson administration.

Over the next weeks, the *Star Tribune* did not let the matter rest but continued to assault Cohen. The day after Martin-Williams fired him, the *Star Tribune* published a column-length snarl at Cohen for the offense of giving the newspaper the court documents. "Dan Cohen comes to us in those most improbable robes of all for the political partisan and publicist: The Conscience of the Community. It is not an easy role switch to bring off, standing there slipping a pair of white gloves over soiled fingernails. This is the sham of a partisan personality taking what everybody can understand as a piece of campaign hardball, sleazy as it is, and trying to elevate it as a public service. It is the shabbiest kind of a late-thrown kidney punch. Alongside other cases of human fallibility on the ballot, Marlene Johnson's is mild."

The author of this tirade was an influential columnist and Perpich pal named Jim Klobuchar. Klobuchar did not inform readers that Cohen had supplied these documents to his newspaper in exchange for an agreement of confidentiality.

Not only that, Klobuchar did not disclose that at the same time he was editorializing about the political campaign in this and other columns, he was secretly writing speeches for Johnson's running mate Perpich. Much later, when someone other than the columnist revealed this information, the newspaper briefly and quietly suspended Klobuchar for this transgression. It then reinstated him without further ado and no public criticism. It was Klobuchar's second suspension. The first one came in 1981, for deliberately fabricating a quotation from the subject of one of his stories.

The day after Klobuchar's column, the *Star Tribune* published an editorial page cartoon depicting a squat and sinister Cohen as a garbage can with slanted beady eyes peering out of the top of the can, which was labeled "last minute campaign smears." The garbage can was juxtaposed next to a tall and benign Rudy Perpich. Needless to say, again there was no mention of the newspaper's promise to Cohen.

While *Star Tribune* columnists and cartoonists were piling on Cohen, the *Pioneer Press* published an editorial on October 29 entitled "Relevant Disclosures," which offered an entirely different perspective. "Too much is being made by supporters of Rudy Perpich about Republican finger-prints on documents leaked to the press showing his running mate was convicted of shoplifting 12 years ago. . . . To focus on how the informa-tion got to the public's attention is to overlook a larger issue. That is, the information about Marlene Johnson is something the voting public de-serves to know. It is legitimate to examine her past as part of an assessment of her fitness for public office. . . . The last-minute disclosure could have been avoided if Mr. Perpich and Miss Johnson had informed the public themselves earlier and confronted the issue squarely." There was no crit-icism of Cohen or mention of his name. The editorial indicated that at least some within the newspapers questioned the wisdom of identifying Cohen. This editorial, lost among the barrage of attacks on Cohen, later would become a potent weapon against both newspapers.

On October 31 and November 1, both newspapers published yet more criticism of Cohen, this time attributed to his former employer. If Cohen had stayed, Martin-Williams Executive Vice President David Floren said, "our clients would view us as offering less than fully professional services. That's something we don't want to put our clients in the position of accepting from us." Still, there was no disclosure of the promises by the newspapers. The *Star Tribune* published yet another attack on Cohen, from a woman named Helen Yates, without disclosing that Yates was a political ally of Johnson and a Democratic candidate for the state legis-lature. In what was now the politically correct convolution on Johnson's crime and Cohen's disclosures, Yates said, "The release of information regarding Marlene Johnson's mistaken exit of a store with unpaid items is the absolute bottom of the barrel."

For the *Star Tribune* especially, Cohen became the big story of what until then had been a boring election campaign. The nonstop attacks were a veritable media riot. Never mind that the newspapers were pun-ishing a source of information for relying upon their own promises.

The election on November 2 gave Cohen small respite. Both papers were filled with articles about the election of Marlene Johnson and Rudy Perpich. Even so, another columnist pilloried Cohen: "Every state has its stinkballs (or do I mean gunkheads) and there have been instances of name-calling and nasty, 11th-hour leaking in Minnesota this year that I would definitely put in this category."

The *Star Tribune* continued to hound Cohen even after the election of its favored candidates. A long article in its editorial page of November 7 discussed the circumstances in which the newspaper had promised Cohen confidentiality and how the editors had decided to dishonor their reporter's promises. It was the first time the newspaper disclosed that it had made and broken promises to Cohen.

To no one's surprise the commentary, by an editor whom the newspaper called the "reader's representative," excused the newspapers' conduct and again criticized Cohen. According to the newspaper, violation of its promise "is justified by an unspoken standard of journalism that defines the substance of Cohen's tip as beneath the threshold of acceptable, unattributable information." The commentary did not define this supposed "unspoken standard of journalism." The "standard" was so "unspoken" that Sturdevant and Salisbury were unaware of it when they made their promises to Cohen.

Indeed, until a week earlier, the widely trumpeted and not unspoken "standard of journalism" of the *Star Tribune* and the media industry in general was that journalists must never break promises of confidentiality even if it meant violating a court order and going to jail.

The *Star Tribune* editorial concluded on a note of self-congratulation. The newspaper's treatment of Cohen, it said, "served a purpose" by "contributing to the cleansing of political campaigning."

In the meantime, despite all the newspapers' condemnation, Cohen had found new employment with the University of Minnesota, producing recruiting brochures for athletes. But the *Star Tribune* still did not let up on Cohen. On November 20, the newspaper published another attack on Cohen by columnist Doug Grow, who ridiculed the university for hiring "such a controversial political figure."

Grow did not stop there. He personally called and berated the university's athletic director and other university officials for daring to do business with Cohen. Grow lectured them that it was "politically unwise" and "inexpedient" for the university or any government agency to hire Cohen, regardless of the quality of his work. It would antagonize the governor and lieutenant governor. Cohen quickly lost his job at the university.

Ironically, Grow found out about Cohen's short-lived employment from a source to whom he promised confidentiality. Neither Grow nor the *Star Tribune* has ever disclosed the name of this person.

The day after Grow's column, the *Star Tribune* published another commentary piece by the "reader's representative" that contained yet more criticism of Cohen, this time by journalists around the country. For example, the associate director of the National News Council, himself a former editor of the *Star Tribune*, said the newspapers did the right thing in breaking their promises to Cohen. Cohen had thrown a "curve ball. The real story was the political dirty trick and not the two-bit shoplifting business." Although again supporting his newspaper's decision to break its promise to Cohen, the "reader's representative" did grant that the original article naming Cohen should have explained that the *Star Tribune*'s reporter promised him confidentiality.

The venom of the newspapers, particularly the *Star Tribune*, shocked other local journalists. Dave Nimmer, whose station honored his promise to Cohen and who had formerly worked as an editor at the *Star Tribune*, said that the newspapers "hung him out to dry" because they did not like Cohen.

Cohen entered a professional wilderness. No one would hire him. The next month, he sued the newspapers. Cohen hired Charles Hvass to handle his case. Hvass was a local king of torts who had won many large jury verdicts as a personal injury trial lawyer. He hit the newspapers with a lawsuit in December 1982.

For the next three years, little of any consequence went on. The lawyers took depositions from Cohen and the newspaper reporters, and written interrogatories went back and forth. The newspapers made no move to dismiss on First Amendment grounds, the usual response of media organizations to suits against them. Neither side pushed for a trial date.

Note

1. On the Andersen defeat, see Ronald F. Stinnett and Charles H. Backstrom, *Recount* (Washington, D.C.: National Document Publishers, 1964).

No Way to Treat a Tipster

I FIRST GOT to know Cohen in 1982, when I was in the state legislature and running for Minnesota attorney general. After leaving politics, I returned to the practice of law both privately and as president of a public interest legal foundation I had begun in 1983. I also published several articles in newspapers, magazines, and law reviews on legal, public affairs, and foreign policy issues. The foreign policy interest came from my service with the U.S. State Department in the late 1960s and early 1970s in Vietnam and the U.S. Mission to the United Nations.

A favorite subject of mine was the flouting of the law and the rights of ordinary people by pampered individuals and groups currently fashionable with media and political elites. For example, my December 1983 *Wall Street Journal* article, "Heat's on Honeywell but the Public Gets Burned," discussed the semiannual blockades for many years in the 1970s and 1980s of Honeywell's Minneapolis headquarters by thousands of "peace" protesters. These actions were clear violations of the law and the rights of Honeywell employees who were prevented from getting to their work. That did not bother Minneapolis officials and the local chief of police, Tony Bouza, and his wife. Chief Bouza regularly delivered coffee and doughnuts to the hungry and thirsty demonstrators. Mrs. Bouza regularly manned the barricades.

In the next couple of years I ran into Cohen occasionally on the bus we took to work in downtown Minneapolis. We talked about politics and current issues in the news, but he never brought up his litigation with the *Star Tribune* and *Pioneer Press*. I was not sure that he had even started a suit but assumed that by now he had resolved or dropped any dispute he had.

"You'll like this joint," Cohen said. It was right after the Fourth of July 1985. Cohen was taking me to lunch. The joint was the now defunct Fountain Room on the fourth floor of a splendid old department store building. The store started as Maurice L. Rothschild and Co. and then became Young-Quinlan, names suitably evoking the upscale and rather haughty nature of the place. As a little boy, my mother bought clothes for me there, but only on sale. I felt uncomfortable walking in even then. But it had its charms. The building had the only human elevator operators left in Minneapolis, a group of engaging ladies who were young women in my youth and had grown old with the structure.

I had not been to the restaurant before. It boasted budget prices but was frequented mainly by society matrons. Cohen and I were the only males in the establishment and the only ones of any gender under sixty. We also were the only patrons not stylishly dressed. We stuck out like sore thumbs. Neither of us worried much about social convention.

As soon as we sat down, Cohen wanted to talk about his case. To my surprise, it still was in court. Cohen had read some of my editorial commentary articles. The suit had received no coverage except for sketchy articles, buried in inner sections, in the Minneapolis and St. Paul newspapers in December 1982, when Cohen's attorney filed the complaint.

No one in the national media, or in journalism or law reviews, had picked up on the Cohen litigation. Even locally, no one was paying any attention to it. To me, it seemed a potential landmark First Amendment case that had U.S. Supreme Court written all over it.

Cohen's suit looked like a good subject for an article. For the next couple of months, I studied the court files of the Cohen case and the current judicial interpretations of the First Amendment. Aside from the attorneys for Cohen and the newspapers, I probably became the expert on the Cohen litigation. There was, to be sure, not much competition.

Although I sympathized with Cohen, I wanted to write an objective article presenting the positions of both sides. The article did not spare Cohen; it quoted the criticism of Cohen's conduct by editors of the newspapers. It reprinted the *Star Tribune* editorial cartoon depicting Cohen as a garbage can with the sign: "Last minute campaign smears."

Tim Ferguson, editorial features editor of the *Wall Street Journal*, which had published other articles of mine, thought the case was not important enough to give it space: "Sure, it has some technical interest for us in the press. But it won't go anywhere in court."

The *Columbia Journalism Review's* editor, Spencer Klaw, saw more potential to Cohen's case when he called me in early October 1985. He was interested in the article and offered to publish it by December 1985. Klaw had one big concern, however. He wanted my assurance that I was not involved in the case as a lawyer for either side. I told him that I was not.

In my submitted manuscript I predicted that the case eventually would reach the U.S. Supreme Court and that, when that happened, the Court could be a lot less willing to expand the privileges of the press than it had been in the past couple of decades. "By the time the case is ready for its review," I wrote, "the Supreme Court may well have one or more Reagan appointees which could tip its ideological balance. In considering an appeal, the high court would have the opportunity to clearly demarcate those exemptions from the civil and criminal law which are essential to enable the media to properly fulfill the function of collecting and interpreting the news for the public from those which merely serve to aggrandize the powers of the press. Previous courts have not enunciated any such comprehensive principle with the result that the First Amendment has been used to steadily expand the privileges of the media with inadequate analysis of and regard for the underlying purposes of the constitutional guarantee of freedom of the press.

"While doctors and lawyers and even clergymen and weather forecasters are becoming more vulnerable to the general public for real or supposed malpractice, the journalistic profession has won increasing immunity from liability.

"The Minnesota newspapers have made no showing that performing their work of informing the public or exercising their right to express their opinions requires that they in effect be above the laws of contract and tort.

"The central question for the judges considering the Cohen case in its trial and inevitable appeals is how much freedom of the press, at the expense of the rule of law and its own rights, can the public afford."

The last four paragraphs did not get past the editors of the *Columbia Journalism Review*.

The published article concluded: "The newspapers' ultimate defense is their claim that the First Amendment gives them the right to print anything factual regardless of any prior agreements or representations to the contrary. This argument—that the First Amendment supersedes the laws of contract and tort—has not been the subject of any previously reported judicial decision. Unless the parties settle out of court, the litigation could produce another landmark ruling on what powers are permitted the news media by the First Amendment."

In the meantime, the lawyers for Cohen and the newspapers were attempting to negotiate a settlement of the case. Even three years after the event, the newspapers could have settled the case for a trivial cost if only they would have apologized to Cohen or at least acknowledged that they had made and broken an agreement with him. Such an admission would have vindicated Cohen and would have limited his injuries from lost income. It would have avoided a potential trial and multiple appeals that at the very least would involve enormous legal fees for the newspapers even if they eventually won the case. Still, the newspapers refused to apologize or admit that they had done anything wrong.

The lawyers sent numerous letters to each other, arguing about the wording of articles to be published by the newspapers that would announce to the public that the litigation was over. The newspapers at first did not want to pay Cohen anything. Eventually, they offered a paltry $4,000.

At that time, though, the money dispute was secondary. To Cohen, public admissions without excuses that the newspapers had broken agreements with him would have been more important than a money payment in restoring his ability to earn a living in his profession.

The newspapers were adamant that the articles not portray them unfavorably. The *Star Tribune* in its proposed article would not mention that it had made and had broken a promise to Cohen. The *Pioneer Press* wanted to publish that it was paying no money to Cohen to settle the case even though it was proposing to do just that. Neither article would even hint at an apology to Cohen or would admit to any wrongdoing. The negotiations broke down.

The newspapers could have ended the case then by a simple and unconvoluted apology. They might suffer some wounded pride for a while, and then everyone would have forgotten about it. That would be far better than risking a debacle by letting the case continue.

If the newspapers did not want to admit any wrongdoing, they still might have been able to get rid of the suit but would have had to put a lot more money on the table. It beggars credulity that they could have seriously expected that three years after the broken promises, with all the rancor and all the injuries, Cohen would have let them off the hook for just $4,000.

Their obstinacy was not all that misplaced. What with the state of U.S. Supreme Court First Amendment interpretation at the time, they and their lawyers were confident that they would rid themselves of Cohen's case as soon as a judge looked at it.

The *Columbia Journalism Review* published my article in its January–

February 1986 issue under the title "No Way to Treat a Tipster." Around the same time, Cohen and Hvass decided to part company after more than three years of working together.

The timing of publication was fortuitous indeed. Cohen liked the article. He asked me to become his new lawyer. To say that I was excited would be an understatement. This was simply a great constitutional law case.

There were a couple of things to take care of beforehand, however. First, I had to get in touch with Klaw. I could not very well be suing the newspapers for breach of contract if I in turn could be accused of violating an agreement of my own with the *Columbia Journalism Review* about the same case. I asked Klaw if he would object to my becoming Cohen's lawyer. To my relief, he responded that he had no problem because Cohen had hired me after publication of the article.

That wasn't so bad at all.

The real fun was about to begin.

Rothenberg v. Rothenberg

I HAD ONE other call to make. It was a lot tougher than the call to the *Columbia Journalism Review*. My former wife, Patricia Hirl, was the associate general counsel for the *Star Tribune*. More to the point, she was the newspaper's attorney in the Cohen case. I would be confronting her in the courtroom. It would be a lot better for her to hear from me rather than someone else that we would be on opposite sides of the most important case of our lives. I had not spoken to her for years. Both of us had remarried. It took a couple of days to screw up my courage, as if I were a teenager asking a girl for a date.

I tried to be nonchalant.

"Pat Hirl," she answered.

"Hello, Pat, this is Elliot Rothenberg." (After the divorce, whenever we called one another, we always identified ourselves with our last names.)

"Yeah."

"Dan Cohen has asked me to take over as his lawyer in his case with you."

"I already heard about it."

"I hope you will not take this personally. I don't want to cause you any problems with the newspaper. If it will hurt you there, I'll ask Cohen to try and find another lawyer. I would like to do this because it's a really interesting case."

"It's okay with me. It's just a professional matter."

Pat's cordiality was a relief. She seemed to relish the thought of opposing me in court. Whatever she told me then, though, she later demonstrated that she did not like my participation in the case one bit.

Pat and I had met when we both were attorneys for the Minnesota Public Interest Research Group (MPIRG). In fact, I hired her.

It was 1976, and the organization, which was on the cutting edge of political correctness, was on a mission to hire women. I had no problem with that, because Pat was the brightest and most attractive of the candidates.

As the legal director, I handled litigation, especially environmental and public utility rate cases. Pat did lobbying at the Minnesota legislature.

We began dating soon after she began her work at MPIRG. No one in the organization knew about our relationship. It was Pat's idea to throw a party for the whole staff in the spring of 1977 and, at a propitious moment, casually announce our engagement. There was dead silence from the jaws on the floor. We were an unlikely couple. Pat was considered sophisticated, socially adroit, and ambitious. Some detractors, and even friends, saw me as a gangling and less than socially adept cross between Ichabod Crane and Mr. Magoo who accidentally wandered in from an ivory tower at the nearby University of Minnesota.

After we married later that year, Pat and I left MPIRG and formed a law firm in downtown Minneapolis. Pat was developing a media law practice, having studied journalism before going to law school. She became the counsel for the Minnesota Newspaper Association and developed an active practice representing smaller newspapers throughout Minnesota in various types of litigation. She also lobbied at the legislature. She was good at her work and attracted clients. One *Star Tribune* editorial column called her a "crack media attorney." She loved her work and was fond of saying that she was doing exactly the type of work that she wanted to do.

Pat's biggest ambition was to argue a constitutional law case before the U.S. Supreme Court that would expand the First Amendment rights of the media. The case Pat talked about most was *New York Times* v. *Sullivan*, a March 1964 U.S. Supreme Court decision. The ruling was too recent to be covered in my constitutional law courses at Harvard Law School (I graduated in June 1964). At the time, I vaguely recalled the case as establishing new privileges for newspapers that made it difficult or impossible for politicians to sue for libel. It had never come up in any legal work I had done. For Pat, however, the decision was holy writ.

Before meeting Pat, I had little knowledge of, and less interest in, media law in general. All that changed. It was a fascinating subject, I learned.

Nevertheless, I did not share Pat's reverence for the press, particularly her support of what I thought were extravagant claims by the media to be exempt from laws governing everyone else. It was a matter on which we agreed to disagree.

Until I took over Cohen's case, my only litigation experience in the subject was assisting Pat on a case that, ironically, sought to compel the disclosure of names of persons who wanted anonymity. Shortly after we formed our firm, the Minnesota Newspaper Association hired Pat to oppose a suit by the Minnesota Medical Association demanding a court order to prohibit the Minnesota Department of Welfare from disclosing the names of doctors who had received state funds to perform abortions. The Medical Association claimed that the publicity would subject the doctors to harassment and worse. *The Catholic Bulletin*, a weekly newspaper published in St. Paul, entered the litigation on our side. We won the case, *Minnesota Medical Association* v. *State of Minnesota et al.* During our marriage I went with Pat to several Minnesota Newspaper Association conventions. After our divorce, Pat gave up her private practice and went to work for the *Star Tribune*. Pat's favorite periodical was the *Columbia Journalism Review*.

In February 1986 I became Dan Cohen's lawyer. Taking on the two largest Minnesota newspapers in a case where both would rely upon the many privileges that the Supreme Court had given the media in the name of protecting the First Amendment, was not something to be done lightly. As an attorney in private practice with no associates or assistants or even a secretary, it would be a full-time task for me for years.

The legal challenge was daunting, to say the least. It is hard enough to prevail in a libel suit against a newspaper when it has lied. Here, it was undisputed that the newspapers told the truth that Cohen had distributed the documents about Johnson. No one since the adoption of the Constitution had ever succeeded in holding any U.S. newspaper liable for publishing true information about a political campaign. Would broken promises make the newspapers liable even though they told the truth? That was the question it would take a decade to answer.

Making matters worse was the power of the two newspapers Cohen was suing. The *Star Tribune* of Minneapolis not only was the largest newspaper in Minnesota but also was the most powerful political institution in the state. Its zeal for savaging the positions and even the character of politicians and others not meeting the approval of its editors and columnists had terrified even the state's most aggressive politicians for years. The columns and editorial cartoon excoriating Cohen were typical but more vituperative than most.

As it happened, I had incurred the wrath of the newspaper at the same time as Cohen's tribulations. In October 1982, when I was running for attorney general, I held a news conference at which I demanded stiffer penalties for violent crimes, including capital punishment for particularly heinous murders. The *Star Tribune* was viscerally opposed to the death penalty.

A couple of days later, Arne Carlson, running for reelection as Minnesota state auditor, grabbed me at a campaign stop. Carlson for decades had been notorious for his brutal campaign style. At the time, he was hammering his challenger, college professor Paul Wellstone, for a supposed learning disability affecting his capacity to read graphs.[1] Wherever he went, Arne bellowed, "How can a guy who cannot even read numbers on a chart run for auditor?" When it came to challenging the state's biggest newspaper, and not just another hapless politician who got in his way, Carlson was a lot more circumspect.

"The death penalty!?!" Arne snorted. "You'll turn the *Star Tribune* against you. They will destroy your political future. You'll never get to be a judge."

"What's wrong with the idea?" I asked.

"Who cares about right and wrong? What counts is that the *Star Tribune* will go nuts. It'll hurt me too."

The *Star Tribune* endorsed Carlson. Unlike the newspaper's outrage over the disclosure of Ms. Johnson's court records, its editorial promoting Carlson had no complaints about his exposure of Wellstone's alleged handicap.

Just before launching its assaults on Cohen, the *Star Tribune* published a lengthy editorial condemning my candidacy and positions on crime and punishment. Almost as an afterthought it endorsed my opponent, Hubert Humphrey III. It also published the predictably derogatory cartoon that depicted me as crosseyed and paunchy, hanging myself with my necktie. I was not paunchy. The humor of it eluded me, but humor never was the strong suit of the newspaper's political cartoons.

Carlson won his election, and I lost.

It was bad enough to espouse positions deemed incorrect on general political issues. Far worse in the editors' eyes was criticism of the newspaper itself, especially where the corporate financial well-being was threatened. Although the paper's editors delight in attacking others, they have thin skins when it comes to others expressing disapproval of their own conduct.

Four months after my article, the *Columbia Journalism Review* published a letter signed by the *Star Tribune*'s executive editor, Joel Kramer. Kramer was not working for the newspaper when its editors decided to break its reporter's promise to Cohen. He was not even in Minnesota at the time; he was executive editor of the *Buffalo Courier Express*. Kramer could not be accused of any personal responsibility for the newspaper's conduct toward Cohen. There was no personal animosity between him and me; we had never even met. Kramer had no reason to respond. Anyway, he should have had more important things to do. But respond Kramer did, in a ferocious ad hominem attack. It was a harbinger of how the Cohen case would proceed.

Kramer's letter began, "A dart to CJR editors for allowing Elliot Rothenberg to write, 'No way to treat a tipster' (January/February), an article that portrays political consultant Dan Cohen in a favorable light and the two Twin Cities dailies unfavorably." Kramer gave no examples of such supposed disparate portrayal. Instead, he continued, "Far from a disinterested observer, Rothenberg was an unsuccessful candidate for state office on the same ticket which Cohen was trying to aid. He is also the divorced husband of the *Star and Tribune* [sic] counsel who has been handling this case from the beginning. The article made no mention of these connections. In fact, since the article appeared, Rothenberg has become counsel for Cohen."

Before publishing Kramer's letter, CJR editor Spencer Klaw sent it to me and offered me an opportunity to reply. In his letter to me, Klaw said that "we certainly see no need to disclose the job held by your former wife." As for the rest of Kramer's letter, Klaw observed, "From the tortuous syntax employed by Kramer, I suspect there may be a catch."

The *Columbia Journalism Review* published two replies to Kramer's letter, its editors' and mine. The editors' response was twice as long as Kramer's letter. Regarding the substance of the article, the editors said, "We find Mr. Kramer's assertion that our article portrayed Dan Cohen 'in a favorable light' puzzling, inasmuch as the piece quoted unflattering references to him by local columnists and was accompanied by a cartoon showing Cohen in the guise of a garbage can." As for my ex-wife's work, "it would not have occurred to us that this disqualified Rothenberg from writing the article." The editors referred readers to my response about my past political activity and declared, "For our part, we don't see a problem here." Finally, the editors told Kramer that "before accepting Cohen as a client, Rothenberg called us to ask if we would object to his taking the case. If we did, he said, he would turn Cohen down. We replied that, since the article had already been published, he was free to do whatever he pleased."

In my reply, I pointed out that neither Cohen nor his gubernatorial candidate, Wheelock Whitney, gave any assistance or support whatsoever to my campaign. On the contrary, Whitney emphasized his independence and his distance from other Republican campaigns. I concluded, "Mr. Kramer's statement that I was 'on the same ticket which Cohen was trying to aid' is more than just tortuous syntax. Neither Whitney nor his campaign supporters regarded their efforts as supporting any candidacy other than Whitney's and certainly not a 'ticket' of Republican candidates."

That was the last word on the *Columbia Journalism Review* imbroglio. An outsider could be excused for viewing the intensity of charge and countercharge as almost comical.

Note

1. Betty Wilson, "Auditor Says Opponent 'Can't Read Graphs,' " *Star Tribune*, August 26, 1982, 1A.

CHAPTER 4 _____

Taking on City Hall

"YOU'RE CRAZY TO do this. Sure Cohen got screwed. But you're taking on city hall." That was what a journalist friend, a former business and financial editor of the *Pioneer Press* who now has his own business newsletter, said to me when I told him that I was Cohen's new lawyer.

To the experts, even those who recognized the injustice of the newspapers' conduct, Cohen had no chance. For one thing, the *Star Tribune* and *Pioneer Press* had unlimited funds to hire armies of the best legal talent. Far more important, the law itself was skewed in their favor. Courts had granted media organizations special constitutional privileges to injure persons with their reporting.

The purpose of the framers of the First Amendment was to protect newspapers from interference and censorship by government. Nothing in the wording of the Bill of Rights gives the press any special privilege to harm private citizens. Even so, at least one of our Founding Fathers warned of the dangers of adopting any constitutional protection for the press.

In *The Federalist* no. 84 (May 1788), Alexander Hamilton argued against including in the Constitution a guarantee of freedom of the press. "Why should it be said, that the liberty of the press shall not be restrained, when no power is given by which restrictions may be imposed? . . . It is evident that it would furnish, to men disposed to usurp, a plausible pretense for claiming that power. . . . What is the liberty of the press? Who can give it any definition which would not leave the utmost latitude for evasion?"

Hamilton was prescient. But it took a while for the press to convince the courts to permit it to use the constitutional guarantee of freedom of the press not only as a shield against government but also as a sword against the very citizens who were supposed to be the beneficiaries of the Bill of Rights.

In the event, Supreme Court decisions going back two decades before Cohen sued the newspapers interpreted the First Amendment to create a virtually unlimited right for media organizations to inflict injury on ordinary citizens with impunity.

It began with New York Times v. Sullivan (1964), which established special privileges for the media in libel litigation. Until then, newspapers were subject to the same law of defamation as any other business or in- dividual. Liability had existed for newspapers and everyone else for the dissemination of false charges regardless of whether they were made in- nocently, with no intent to lie about the victim of the defamation, and even if there was no negligence. When a plaintiff claimed defamation, the defendant had to prove that the charges were true rather than the other way around.

New York Times v. Sullivan and later cases ruled that a public official or "public figure" (a concept courts defined very broadly) suing a media organization, rather than any other business or individual, for defamation must prove that the report was false. Not only that, he or she must also prove what the Court called "actual malice," that is, that the media or- ganization knew that the report was false or that it published with reckless disregard for truth or falsity, a much tougher burden than just negligence. Needless to say, the new rule made it extremely difficult, if not impossible, to prevail on a claim of defamation against a newspaper.

In the years following, the Supreme Court applied the New York Times v. Sullivan standard to suits alleging other wrongdoing by the media. Time, Inc. v. Hill, a 1967 decision, was particularly egregious. There a family who had never sought publicity went to court for violation of their right to privacy under a New York statute. They sued the publisher of Life magazine for a graphic article in 1955 about their ordeal of being held prisoners for nineteen hours in their home by three escaped convicts. Except for the confinement, the prisoners actually treated the family cour- teously. Still, the family wanted no publicity because of the fear of retal- iation. The Life article, however, not only publicized the event but fictionalized it by including staged photos of the convicts supposedly beating and sexually molesting the family, conduct that never occurred. Family members suffered severe psychological damage as a result of the article. After two trials, a court awarded the Hills $30,000 in damages. Time, Inc. appealed, and the case eventually reached the Supreme Court.

In 1966 Richard Nixon, at the time a Wall Street lawyer, argued the case for the Hill family in the Supreme Court. It was Nixon's only case before the Supreme Court, and he took it very seriously. Nixon had moved to New York after his catastrophic defeat in the 1962 California gubernatorial campaign. He recognized *Time, Inc. v. Hill* as an important First Amendment case. He also saw the case as a vehicle for his personal and political vindication. The subject matter was perfect, too; Nixon did not like the press. Beginning in 1965, Nixon immersed himself in *Time, Inc. v. Hill* with exhaustive research and preparation of arguments.

The case was the subject of heated controversy within the Supreme Court. At first, Nixon appeared to have won. A tentative decision, written by Justice Abe Fortas, initially ruled in favor of the Hills and minced no words about its view of *Life* magazine's behavior:

Needless, heedless, wanton and deliberate injury of the sort inflicted by *Life's* picture story is not an essential instrument of responsible journalism. Magazine writers and editors are not, by reason of their high office, relieved of the common obligation to avoid inflicting wanton and unnecessary injury. The prerogatives of the press . . . do not confer a license for pointless assault.

In a dissent to Justice Fortas's opinion, Justice Byron White, never regarded as a strong supporter of the press, declared that "the Court should make it unmistakably clear that the First Amendment will not permit the imposition of liability for publishing a truthful account of the news of general public interest." Regardless of whether this statement was germane to the *Hill* case, its applicability to the *Cohen* case was painfully obvious.

The draft by Fortas never became the final decision of the Court. Justices began to switch their votes. When the dust cleared, the Court ruled in favor of Time, Inc. The ultimate decision, written by Justice William Brennan, held that anyone suing the press for invasion of privacy must prove that the story was false. Even that would not be enough. Applying the *New York Times* rule, he or she must also prove that the newspaper or magazine knew that the story was false or acted in reckless disregard of the truth. The Hills lost their damages award.

Nixon told a law partner, "I always knew I wouldn't be permitted to win a big appeal against the press."[1]

Hustler Magazine v. *Falwell* in 1988 applied the *New York Times* v. *Sullivan* standard to yet another tort for the benefit of a "media organization" of rather less repute than the *New York Times* or *Life* magazine. There Jerry Falwell sued Larry Flynt and *Hustler* magazine over a cartoon that depicted Falwell having sex with his mother in an outhouse. A jury found that *Hustler* and Flynt intentionally inflicted emotional distress and awarded Falwell $200,000. Falwell lost the judgment in a unanimous decision written by Chief Justice Rehnquist. The Court ruled that any public figure seeking to recover on a claim of emotional distress must prove that a media organization knowingly or recklessly published a false report. No one, said the Court, would take the Falwell cartoon as anything but a parody.

It would be hard enough for Cohen to win a suit against the *Star Tribune* and *Pioneer Press* if they had lied about him. Here, no one could dispute that the newspapers told the truth: Cohen was the source of the information about Marlene Johnson's criminal record. The newspapers admitted that they had broken promises to Cohen. But there simply was no precedent for compelling a newspaper to pay damages for publishing an accurate report about the conduct of politicians in an electoral campaign.

Challenging media misconduct on the basis of contract rather than tort law was innovative, to say the least. Few, if any, took it seriously, however.

The change in Cohen's attorneys was the pretext for another round of ridicule, this time by the local alternative press and others looking to curry favor with the big newspapers. To these detractors, the notion that an Elliot Rothenberg could succeed against the press, where some of the nation's most powerful lawyers had failed, was simply preposterous.

For example, a now defunct counterculture weekly, *Twin Cities Reader*, pronounced the case "not important. Elliot Rothenberg has distinguished himself only as a singularly Quixotic individual."

A highly publicized local lawyer, among other things retained for legal advice by the Honeywell blockaders, peddled a press release assuring the newspapers that they had nothing to worry about. "Elliot Rothenberg has no credibility with anybody."

A Ralph Naderite broadsheet calling itself *Minnesota Statewatch* chimed in by scoring Cohen's new lawyer for perpetuating a "groundless lawsuit."

The state of the law was bad enough. The dubious prospect of getting a fair jury made the case seem even more hopeless. The newspapers un-doubtedly would present themselves to a jury as protectors of the public interest by exposing the dirty political trick of a Cohen against a Johnson, and a woman Johnson at that. The fact that the case was between Cohen and the newspapers, and not Johnson, was beside the point.

The ethnic makeup of Minneapolis, like the rest of Minnesota, is pre-dominantly Scandinavian; there are scores of thousands of Johnsons, Ol-sons, Nelsons, and the like in the telephone book. A typical jury would have a natural sympathy for someone named Marlene Johnson.

More to the point, a typical Minneapolis jury could have a natural antipathy for someone named Cohen. Minnesota prides itself on its re-puted progressive political tradition. In at least one important respect the image of progressive politics is no more than a myth, a veneer covering another Minnesota tradition civic boosters don't like to brag about: re-ligious prejudice. As recently as November 1990, the Star Tribune ac-knowledged that Minnesota was "once notorious for anti-Semitism."[2]

Even with the end of World War II and revelations of the Nazi Ho-locaust, Minneapolis had the dubious distinction of being, according to sociologist Carey McWilliams, "the capitol [sic] of anti-Semitism in the United States. In almost every walk of life, an iron curtain separates Jews from non-Jews in Minneapolis." Milling, lumbering, transportation, util-ities, banking, insurance, chain store, and department store companies would not employ Jews. The Minneapolis realty board excluded Jews, and Jews could not buy homes for any price in most of Minneapolis. The Minneapolis Rotary, Kiwanis, and Lions clubs refused to accept Jews as members. Even the Minneapolis Automobile Association, unlike any other such auto club anywhere in the country, refused to accept Jews.[3]

Minneapolis residents in general did not much like Jewish politicians. Cohen himself provided the best example of their attitude toward Jews in politics. In the 1960s, the city's most upscale and highly educated district elected a twenty-something Dan Cohen as its alderman on the City Council. At age thirty-one Cohen's colleagues elected him Minne-apolis City Council president.

In 1969, with the retirement of the incumbent, Cohen ran for mayor of Minneapolis. By the time of the general election, he was endorsed by the Republican Party, leading Democrats, the most important labor unions, and the daily newspapers. His opponent, a police burglary detec-tive, had run for office only once before; he had lost in a primary for alderman. Cohen's campaign was well-organized and well-financed. His opponent's campaign was neither. Cohen was brilliant and a skilled campaigner. His opponent had a knack for malapropisms and for calling black males "colored boys." If the voters were comparing the accomplishments and abilities of the two candidates, the election should have been no contest.

But Cohen's opponent had one advantage, and it was a huge one: his quintessentially Scandinavian name, Charles Stenvig. It was all he needed. Stenvig won with 62 percent of the vote. Even hard-core Republicans rejected Cohen. Stenvig got 72 percent of the vote in precincts that had voted for Barry Goldwater in 1964 over Lyndon Johnson and Minnesota favorite Hubert Humphrey. One blue-collar ward gave 80 percent of its vote to Stenvig despite the unions' endorsement of Cohen. Cohen would never again be elected to office.

When his suit against the newspapers arose, people who should have empathized with Cohen did not. In the Jewish community, the silence regarding his case was deafening. Jewish organizations like the American Jewish Committee and the Anti-Defamation League, with their large legal staffs, usually are eager to intervene in any controversy that even arguably carries anti-Semitic overtones. At the time, in fact, these organizations were embarked on a campaign denouncing "Jewish American princess" jokes.

In comparison with this innocuous fad, the violation of Cohen's rights should have raised real concerns. In particular, the *Star Tribune*'s representation of Cohen as a garbage can was reminiscent of the caricatures that were the staple of the viciously anti-Semitic paper *Der Stürmer* in 1930s Germany. The *Star Tribune* called it a cartoon, but it was no laughing matter. According to the Simon Wiesenthal Institute, which studies contemporary anti-Semitism, humor is just the tip of the iceberg of political caricature: "It is a weapon. Because of its destructive capacity it can convert the image it depicts into a scapegoat for the reader's aggression."[4]

Cohen, however, was not beloved by the pooh-bahs in the Jewish establishment. On the contrary, he was a pariah. The Jewish leadership, both nationally and in Minnesota, was partisanly Democratic and politically active in support of liberal candidates, including Johnson. They were not interested in helping Cohen.

I had been the national law director of the Anti-Defamation League some years earlier, and Cohen was a former officer of the Minnesota chapter of the American Jewish Committee, but that meant nothing. The local director of the American Jewish Committee volunteered that the organization would give Cohen no aid whatsoever, not even moral support. "We don't support people just because they're Jewish," he exclaimed.

A rabbi who had testified for Democratic Jewish politicians in local court battles begged off any association with Cohen as a possible character witness. "I know you will understand," he said.

One big political contributor, the owner of the Minneapolis Jewish weekly, directed his staff not to give any coverage to the *Cohen* case.

It could be said that Republicans did not like Cohen because he was Jewish, and Jews did not like him because he was a Republican.

During the *Cohen* litigation, Jewish participation in politics continued to strike a raw nerve in Minnesota. In 1978, Rudy Boschwitz was the first Jew elected to the U.S. Senate from Minnesota, and the first Jew elected to anything there by a statewide electorate. Few outside the state's small Jewish population, however, knew that he was Jewish. Boschwitz himself did everything he could to hide the fact. He made a point of campaigning in a lumberjack outfit. In his commercials and public appearances he eschewed suits in favor of flannel shirts. The image conveyed was that of an affable German Lutheran from main street Minnesota. It worked great for two elections. Boschwitz became the most popular politician in the state.

In 1990, Boschwitz was opposed for reelection by another Jewish candidate, Paul Wellstone, when all the leading Democrats were afraid to challenge the incumbent. Wellstone had never been elected to public office; in 1982 he had lost to Arne Carlson for Minnesota state auditor. At first dismissed as an embarrassment to the Democrats, he turned out to be a scrappy campaigner. Wellstone ran several clever television ads that, among other things, skewered Boschwitz for refusing to debate him. Even so, Boschwitz had raised over $7 million, seven times what Wellstone could collect, and had a nine-point lead in local news media polls less than a week before the election. His lead had increased over that in previous surveys.[5] Boschwitz had the election sewn up. Then he did the inexplicable.

On the Friday before the election, Boschwitz sent out a letter on official campaign stationery to all identifiable Jewish voters in Minnesota accusing Wellstone of having "no connection whatsoever with the Jewish community or our communal life. His children were brought up as non-Jews."[6]

Wellstone quickly got a copy of the letter and wasted no time denouncing it. Television all over the state carried Wellstone's shrewd response. "I guess the senator is criticizing me for marrying a Christian."[7]

The next three days saw a firestorm of angry television interviews, editorials, columns, and letters to the editor excoriating Boschwitz for what everyone called the "Jewish letter."

Faced with the choice between a self-advertised greater Jew and an allegedly lesser Jew, Minnesota voters chose the latter. In four days, Boschwitz's popularity plummeted. Once regarded as invincible, he was the only incumbent senator in the nation to lose that year.[8]

Picking a fair and impartial jury for *Cohen* would indeed be a formidable task. The conventional wisdom was that the question was an academic one only. To raise it assumed that the case would get that far. The newspapers were about to make a move to make sure that it would not.

Notes

1. Leonard Garment, "Annals of Law: The Hill Case," *The New Yorker*, April 17, 1989, 90, 104; Garment, *Crazy Rhythm: My Journey from Brooklyn, Jazz, and Wall Street to Nixon's White House, Watergate, and Beyond* (New York: Random House, 1997), 79; Bernard Schwartz, *The Unpublished Opinions of the Warren Court* (New York: Oxford University Press, 1985), 240.

2. Editorial, "The Lowest Political Blow of Them All," *Star Tribune*, November 6, 1990, 14A.

3. Carey McWilliams, "Minneapolis: The Curious Twin," *Common Ground*, Autumn 1946, 61.

4. Abraham Cooper, *Portraits of Infamy: A Study of Soviet Antisemitic Caricatures and Their Roots in Nazi Ideology* (Los Angeles: Simon Wiesenthal Center, 1986), 10.

5. Dane Smith, "Governor Poll Close; Boschwitz Leads, Wellstone Falls a Bit," *Star Tribune*, November 4, 1990, 1A; "Poll Has Boschwitz Leading Wellstone 49 to 40 Percent," *Star Tribune*, November 3, 1990, 1B.

6. Dane Smith, "Boschwitz Says He Regrets Letter on Wellstone," *Star Tribune*, November 10, 1990, 1A.

7. Dennis J. McGrath, "Running Uphill: 8 Weeks Inside the Wellstone Campaign," *Star Tribune*, November 11, 1990, 1A.

8. Robert Whereatt and Paul Klauda, "One Rudy Out, One in Doubt: Wellstone Dramatically Upsets Boschwitz; Final Weekend Crucial to Underdog's Victory," *Star Tribune*, November 7, 1990, 1A.

No Threat to a Free Press in Requiring It to Obey the Law

AS I WAS walking out the door of my office at 5 P.M. on the day before Thanksgiving, 1986, a fellow who looked like a young attorney accosted me before I could get to the elevator.

"Elliot Rothenberg?"

"Yes."

"I have something for you."

He thrust at me a bulging package, from Pat and *Pioneer Press* attorney Paul Hannah, containing a motion for summary judgment to dismiss the case without trial. Like Cohen and me, Hannah was a Harvard Law School graduate; he handled all litigation for the *Pioneer Press* and several television and radio stations in Minneapolis and St. Paul. Hannah had left his partnership with one of St. Paul's largest law firms—Oppenheimer Wolff & Donnelly, with 198 lawyers—to open his own firm specializing in communications law. The Oppenheimer firm remained on the case to help Hannah. Pat and Hannah accompanied their motion with a thick brief replete with voluminous citation of cases and other authorities. They, the Oppenheimer firm, and other attorneys working for the news-papers must have worked for many months on the document, which pre-sented an exhaustive analysis of issues of First Amendment, contract, and tort law. The brief claimed that regardless of any evidence Cohen could produce at a trial, the newspapers had a constitutional and legal right to break their agreement with him.

Even working around the clock, it would take weeks to prepare an effective response. The newspapers' lawyers did not want to give me that much time. The motion directed me to prepare a brief in response and to appear at a hearing with my brief before Hennepin County District Judge Franklin J. Knoll the next Friday morning. Since then, the Minnesota Supreme Court has adopted rules requiring a minimum of four weeks' notice for such motions.

The most surprising thing about the summary judgment motion was its belatedness, three years after the case started. The great majority of persons injured by media wrongdoing do not get trials. Courts dismiss fully three-fourths of all suits against media organizations on summary judgment motions raising freedom-of-the-press arguments. For Cohen's case, too, the summary judgment motion could be the whole ball game. That certainly was the intent of the newspapers.

Pat told a legal newspaper that the *Cohen* case was "the first one of its kind in the universe." She said she moved for summary judgment on that basis. "We made the only and best decision we could with so many things happening."

On the Friday after Thanksgiving, I called Pat and asked her to postpone her hearing to give me more time to write my brief. If she did not agree, I would have to go to the judge, something I wanted to avoid.

"I'll have to talk to the others about this. I'll get back to you." The return call did not come. On Monday, four days before the scheduled hearing, I called her. She finally agreed to a postponement. The hearing would be in the first week of February. I spent the next two months preparing my brief.

Judge Knoll was a longtime Minnesota state senator and had been active in Democratic politics before Governor Perpich appointed him to the bench. He also had served as counsel for the Urban League. Knoll was not just a nominal Democrat but a leader of the Democratic Party. He supported the Democratic ticket in 1982. The *Star Tribune* was partial to liberal Democrats anyway, and invariably had endorsed Senator and Judge Knoll for election and reelection. On paper, he did not seem the best of all possible judges for Cohen. Nevertheless, though we were not close, I had worked with Senator Knoll when I was in the legislature. He had a reputation for fairness. We probably could have gotten another judge because of the past political activity of Cohen and Judge Knoll.

I thought that Cohen and I would be better off sticking with Judge Knoll. On the other hand, Pat and Paul Hannah thought Judge Knoll's assignment gave their side the advantage.

The newspapers' brief attempted to exploit the past political associations of Judge Knoll and Cohen. Pat and Paul Hannah pushed Ms. Johnson's rights and interests, as much as their own, in urging dismissal of Cohen's case. The brief pounded on Cohen for giving the newspapers "documents disclosing the unfortunate events of Ms. Johnson's past." The brief accused Cohen of seeking to "smear the reputation of Ms. Johnson while secreting his own role in the spoliation." For newspapers to condemn an informant for not suppressing information about crimes of an important politician was anomalous, to say the least, especially with an election approaching.

When it came to Cohen's exposure of Johnson's record, however, the newspapers' lawyers insisted they not only had a right to but were "*obligated* to print Cohen's name. The chilling effect and self-censorship that would result if the publishers could not make an editorial decision about publishing the name of a confidential source of political information would be intolerable." Moreover, declared Pat and Paul Hannah, "the Supreme Court views self-censorship as an evil that must be eradicated." Finally, if they did not disclose Cohen as the source of the court documents, the *Star Tribune* and *Pioneer Press*, according to their attorneys, "would have engaged in self-censorship and thus deprived the citizenry of accurate information about the candidates." Their brief relied upon *New York Times* v. *Sullivan* and *Time, Inc.* v. *Hill.*

By that standard, the newspapers should have rewarded rather than censured Cohen for making available to the public accurate information about an important candidate's criminal record.

In my brief I argued that with all their talk about censorship, the newspapers were demanding an unprecedented immunity for calculated misdeeds like deliberate torts and breaches of contract. They claimed a right to deliberately violate with impunity an agreement from which they had benefited by obtaining news they published at a profit.

Pat and Hannah had *New York Times* v. *Sullivan* and other Supreme Court cases. I had an important one as well. *Branzburg* v. *Hayes*, a 1972 Supreme Court decision, ruled that a newspaper publisher "has no special immunity from the application of general laws. He has no special privilege to invade the rights and privileges of others." In the *Branzburg* case, ironically enough, the press claimed a First Amendment right to refuse to disclose the names of confidential sources before a grand jury.

I also stressed that cases protecting publication limited their applicability to situations where the news organization obtained its information lawfully. Deliberately breaking agreements is not, I argued, a lawful way to obtain information.

As long as the newspapers' lawyers wanted to bring politics into their summary judgment motion, I used the case of *Galella* v. *Onassis*, a 1973 Second Circuit U.S. Court of Appeals decision, where an aggressive photographer claimed that the First Amendment gave him unlimited access to Jacqueline Kennedy Onassis. The court there ruled that the First Amendment is not a "wall of immunity protecting newsmen from any liability for their conduct while gathering news. Crimes and torts committed in news gathering are not protected. There is no threat to a free press in requiring its agents to act within the law."

It was one thing to argue with my former wife by written briefs. It was quite another to debate her in an open courtroom, sitting only a few feet from her. It was to be a new experience; we had settled our divorce without going to court. My stomach was churning as Judge Knoll entered the courtroom on a typical bitterly cold Minneapolis February morning.

In an interview with a national legal publication, Pat saw the matchup between the two of us—and my representation of the antipress side—as the big thing in the case. "Elliot considers himself to be a fighter for the underdog. What's changed is his theory of who's the underdog."[1]

At the oral argument, Pat and Hannah argued that the suit was about politics, not law, and did not belong in court. Speaking first, Hannah immediately made a big point that Cohen was a "Republican politician" and that he had "unclean hands" by attempting to smear Johnson. It was an obvious attempt to appeal to Judge Knoll's political past. I responded that any party connection was irrelevant to the legal issues and that rights should not depend upon political affiliation. On a more substantive level, Hannah argued that the newspapers should not be punished for publishing true information and for giving the public as much information as possible about the candidates and their campaigns. Allowing Cohen to proceed with his case, he said, would have a "chilling effect" on the coverage of political campaigns.

Pat told the judge that the question was one of journalistic ethics only and not of law. The court had no authority to enforce Cohen's agreement with the newspapers and no business considering Cohen's dispute. Editors, she said, have the sole discretion as to what to print in their newspapers without interference by courts.

Both Pat and Paul Hannah contended that someone like Cohen who makes an agreement with a newspaper may not rely on the newspaper's promise even though he may have fully performed his part of the bargain and has given the newspaper something from which it profited. Cohen was just out of luck. Courts must overlook injuries the press inflicts on some for the greater good of freedom of the press to publish.

It was not so much an argument as a lecture, and not a very patient one at that, about what the newspapers regarded as an obvious and un-necessary rehash of the law that the Supreme Court already had decided repeatedly in their favor.

I argued that the law imposed on all persons and businesses an obligation to abide by contracts. Newspapers did not have a preferential First Amendment right to deliberately violate agreements and cause injury to those with whom they deal.

The court, Pat said, should dismiss the case right then and leave Cohen to seek a remedy with the Minnesota News Council. It was a clever offer to the judge of a convenient way of getting rid of the case while still giving Cohen some recourse.

In reality, relegating Cohen's complaint to the News Council would have been a no-lose situation for the newspapers. The newspapers were not always as enthusiastic about the News Council as Pat was in this hearing. Some time earlier, *Pioneer Press* editor William G. Sumner wrote an editorial column headlined "Press Council Totally Worthless." Among other things, Sumner described the Council as "this self-anointed band of busyworkers." Sumner acknowledged, though, that "it can't really do anything" and "exists to get the public heat off our backs."[2] It was perfect for the *Cohen* case.

The Minnesota Newspaper Association had established the News Council in 1969 to consider complaints of unethical conduct against the press. Half of the board members are journalists. The News Council has no authority to award damages to compensate victims of media misconduct for injuries suffered, and indeed has no power to serve as anything but a sounding board for complaints. All of its decisions are advisory only, and the targets of complaints are free to ignore its advice. At best, as a *Star Tribune* columnist put it, "When the media lose, they're embarrassed—or probably should be. That can be an incentive to perform better or differently." Regardless of the existence or extent of any such embarrassment, even if a complainant prevailed before the News Council, it would be no consolation for someone who had suffered financial losses. I pointed this out to Judge Knoll and said that the News Council, even with the best of intentions, could not redress Cohen's grievances.

Interestingly, later in 1987 the News Council happened to consider a case of violation of a promise of confidentiality. A woman complained that a newspaper in Owatonna, Minnesota, had jeopardized her safety or even life by publishing her name despite a promise of confidentiality in a story about a murder suspect. In contrast to all the attacks on Cohen, no one had accused the woman of doing anything wrong. Still, only by the narrowest of margins, a vote of 8–7, the News Council said that the newspaper should have honored its promise.[3] Even with this finding, the News Council did not recommend that the offending newspaper give any compensation or other assistance to the victim. No wonder the newspapers wanted to send *Cohen* to the News Council.

Judge Knoll asked several questions during the two-hour oral argument, but he gave no indication of whether he would kill the case or send it to trial.

After the judge left the courtroom, Pat turned to Hannah, scowling. "I can't believe we'll have to try this thing."

It took almost four and a half months for Judge Knoll to issue his decision, but the wait was worth it. Judge Knoll rejected Pat's claim in the oral argument that Cohen's only recourse was to take his plea to the News Council. He slapped down the newspapers' claims that the First Amendment gave them the right to violate contracts. While acknowledging a newspaper's right to publish the truth, he rejected the argument that the First Amendment "excuses news organizations from the consequences of a decision to publish when that decision involves the breach of a valid contract or of the general tort laws."

The judge explained that the Supreme Court had never interpreted the First Amendment to protect news organizations from the consequences of unlawful conduct. In fact, he said, the case was not about free speech at all but about broken contracts and misrepresentation.

Finally, Judge Knoll gave short shrift to the newspapers' "vehement" claims that requiring them to abide by their agreements would "censor the news" and violate constitutional guarantees of a free press. "There is no threat to a free press in requiring its agents to act within the law."

Judge Knoll scheduled the trial for July 5, 1988, more than a year later.

Pat told me the newspapers likely would again attempt to block a trial by appealing Judge Knoll's decision to the Minnesota Court of Appeals. Win or lose, it would have been a smart use of unlimited legal resources. It would have diverted my time and energy from preparing for the trial to the preparation of appellate briefs. As it happened, they did not carry out the threat to appeal.

Notes

1. Michael Orey, "Minnesota Maverick Targets Liberals and the Press," *The American Lawyer*, September 1989, 123.

2. William Sumner, "Press Council Totally Worthless," *St. Paul Dispatch*, May 16, 1978, 6.

3. *In the Matter of the Complaint of the Bunkers Against the Owatonna People's Press*, Determination no. 70, Minnesota News Council (October 23, 1987).

CHAPTER 6 ────────────

A Solitary Crusade

WITH JUDGE KNOLL'S decision, Cohen's case ceased to be just another case. It became my legal career. I became totally immersed in it—more, obsessed with it. Putting all my eggs in one basket was courting catastrophe when I was supposed to have but two chances of winning, slim and none. Fortunately, my wife was working then.

When I took on Cohen's case, I had a small office. It did not make much sense to continue paying the rent when I would be spending all my time working on the one litigation. Anyway, the office was much too cramped for the huge quantity of paper I would produce and accumulate. At the end of 1986, I moved out of the office.

Throughout the rest of the case, I worked out of makeshift quarters in my basement. Not only the basement but also the rest of the house overflowed with documents and newspapers to be used in the trial as exhibits.

Not one other lawyer offered to work on the case with me as a volunteer or even for pay. To me, it was the case of a lifetime—the sort of case I had daydreams about as a law student. It raised fundamental issues of the First Amendment, the glamour area of constitutional law. There had never been a case like it. In the event, however, there was no rush of lawyers volunteering to get involved in the case, at least on Cohen's side.

I should not have been surprised at this absence of interest. No one wanted to challenge the two largest newspapers and most powerful political institutions of the state, and buck the conventional wisdom that there was no possibility of winning. Besides, supporting Cohen would be as politically incorrect as you could get in Minneapolis. As one advertising executive said, it was "socially unacceptable" to have anything to do with Cohen. Pursuing a losing cause for a pariah would be a bad career move.

Then, too, I had lost many of my connections to the legal community after my candidacy for Minnesota attorney general in 1982. I tried to get hired by some prominent law firms, thinking my major party nomination for the state's highest legal office would be a draw. It wasn't.

My public-interest legal foundation, the North Star Legal Foundation, had some interesting cases but kept afloat only by extreme parsimony in the use of money. We could never afford expensive litigation. I raised enough money for a marginal salary. It was not the sort of future I had expected twenty years earlier at Harvard Law School.

After years of glad-handing as a politician, I became more and more of a recluse. I preferred staying home and listening for the umpteenth time to my treasured recordings of Arturo Toscanini or Artur Schnabel or the Budapest String Quartet performing Beethoven to attending meetings where the compelled socializing became increasingly uncomfortable. I dropped my memberships in many organizations, staying only with the two that mattered most: Mensa and the Harvard Law School Association.

One day, my wife surprised me by bringing home an English springer spaniel puppy. She had insisted on getting a dog but I was reluctant at first, not realizing that a grown man still could be best buddies with his pooch. I had not had a dog for twenty-five years. When I was a little boy in the late 1940s and early 1950s, my old dog, Skippy, a combination Labrador retriever and cocker spaniel and who knows what else, used to walk me to school every day and walk home on his own. That was before leash laws and other regulations. We named the new dog Beechie after the great English conductor Sir Thomas Beecham. For years, early every morning, rain or shine, Beechie would go with me on long jogs. Beechie and I became inseparable, just as my old dog and I had been.

Because of the case's unpopularity and my solitude, I would do Cohen's case by myself. That wasn't so bad. I always liked to work alone on cases, no matter how complex. A committee approach dominated by conventional wisdom could not win Cohen's case. Any victory would have to come from creative, unorthodox, and even eccentric lawyering.

I did all my own research in law libraries in Minneapolis and St. Paul, as well as all word processing. Most of the time, I typed briefs and other court papers on an old IBM Selectric typewriter purchased twelve years earlier and much repaired in the interim. There was no memory feature in the machine, so every time I wanted to change more than a word or two, I had to retype at least one entire page, and often more.

Until the *Cohen* case became my full-time occupation, I had done some writing for the Claremont Institute, a think tank in Claremont, California, that distributed op-ed articles to newspapers around the country. In late 1987, the president of the Institute bequeathed to me a much-traveled early-model Tandy computer with a ten megabyte hard drive and a primitive version of the Microsoft Word word-processing program. The software and hardware never interfaced perfectly, often leaving strange configurations of type on the page. Still, it was an improvement over the typewriter.

It was not nirvana, though. The computer frequently broke down, usually at the most inopportune time. About three weeks before trial, the hard drive broke down. I nearly had a heart attack. It took about a day to get the computer repaired, and it got me through the trial with no further trouble.

I needed every day of the year between Judge Knoll's summary judgment decision and the trial. First of all, I had to learn how to try a case before a jury. I had never done a jury trial. I took several continuing legal education courses on trial practice. As valuable as they were, they were no substitute for actual experience in a trial. A mock trial would have helped. That, however, would have required other attorneys, something I did not have.

My on-the-job training would have to be the early stages of the trial itself. I would try to substitute thorough preparation, mastery of the facts, and a sound strategy for winning the trial for smooth trial technique. There would be no other way.

Not only was I lacking in trial experience, but the trial would not be a simple one. The *Cohen* case was the first one of its kind anywhere, and I was sure it would become a landmark. The trial could not just be a one- or two-day affair with Cohen and the reporters testifying that promises had been made and broken. It was my plan to put the promises in the entire context of how journalists gather information, demonstrating how pervasive promises of confidentiality are in the journalistic profession. This would show the jury how seriously the newspapers' conduct departed from standard journalistic business practices and ethics. A comprehensive trial record on how journalists gather information also would be essential to defend any favorable verdict from renewed First Amendment attacks in the inevitable appeals.

I spent the months before trial becoming an expert on the use of confidential sources. The *Star Tribune* and *Pioneer Press* themselves, through their back issues, would make my case that they had violated their own ethics and customary business practices in breaking their promises to Cohen.

The first thing every morning, I pored over the *Star Tribune*, the *Pioneer Press*, the *New York Times*, and the *Wall Street Journal* for articles that could be used at the trial. I also searched the Minneapolis public library archives for articles going back to 1982 and before. By July 1988, my basement overflowed with file folders stuffed with newspapers.

My collection grew to 462 articles using confidential sources, mainly in connection with political campaigns and controversies. Most of the articles were from the Minneapolis and St. Paul newspapers, but I also had a lot from the *New York Times* and *Wall Street Journal*, and some from the *Des Moines Register*, which was owned by the company that owned the *Star Tribune*.

I accumulated as well articles about shoplifting and editorials demanding that the names of shoplifters be publicized regardless of the amounts involved and the personal humiliation for those caught shoplifting. For good measure, I also collected numerous *Star Tribune* and *Pioneer Press* articles publicizing revelations, often from confidential sources, of crimes and other transgressions by politicians, often many years in the past. Their own articles and editorials belied the newspapers' argument that Johnson's conviction was a trivial matter and that Cohen, rather than the politician's crime, deserved exposure.

Collecting the articles was fun. What was nerve-racking was organizing the accumulation so that the articles would be instantly accessible for impromptu questioning on cross-examination. I spent weeks on end cataloging and recataloging the articles. I had to devise a system by means of which I could get to the right article instantly when an unexpected opportunity opened up in the questioning of a newspaper witness.

In the end I had them assembled in more than fifty file folders in three large file boxes with a fourteen-page, single-spaced index. Only once during the trial would I be stymied in trying to find a particular article.

As the trial date approached, I delivered scores of subpoenas to reporters and top editors of the *Star Tribune* and *Pioneer Press* to testify on these articles and their newspapers' practices on honoring promises to confidential sources.

Even all that preparation might not be enough. In contrast to me, the newspapers' legal team had a surfeit of jury trial experience. After the newspapers lost their summary judgment motion, the *Star Tribune* brought in a new lawyer and law firm. Heading the newspapers' trial team would be James Fitzmaurice, perhaps Minnesota's finest corporate trial lawyer and chief litigator for the nationally prominent Minneapolis firm of Faegre & Benson with 229 lawyers. Fitzmaurice did all the major trials for the *Star Tribune* and for many other large corporate clients. He was renowned for his ability to persuade juries. Along with everything else, Fitzmaurice was a communications law expert. It ran in the family. His father had been *Newsweek's* chief White House correspondent in the Truman years.

Pat still would be representing the *Star Tribune*, but now as an assistant to Fitzmaurice along with many attorneys in Faegre & Benson. Faegre & Benson would not be the only megafirm in the trial, either. Oppenheimer Wolff & Donnelly, with 198 lawyers in Minneapolis and St. Paul, would be working with Hannah in representing the *Pioneer Press*.

I would handle the trial alone.

One lawyer against 430 did not offer the prospect of a fair fight. *The American Lawyer* magazine wrote that it was not only my client but "Rothenberg himself who seemed to be the underdog."[1]

Jim Fitzmaurice was a superstar in the Minneapolis legal community, but I had never met or spoken with him. In fact, for nearly a year after Judge Knoll's summary judgment decision, I heard nothing from anyone working for the newspapers. They were about to break their silence.

Three weeks before the trial, the *Washington Post* published an article on the case. I had shunned interviews in order to avoid tipping my hand about my plans for the trial. The opposition was not so reticent. Quoting *Pioneer Press* attorney Paul Hannah, the *Post* reported that the newspapers' lawyers would argue that Cohen was trying "to manipulate the news. The information was designed to maximize damage to the lieutenant governor but distance the act from the Republican candidate so he could not be blamed for a dirty trick."[2] The article was a godsend, confirming what I had suspected all along would be the trial strategy for the newspapers.

A week before the trial, the phone rang.

"This is Jim Fitzmaurice."

"Hello, Mr. Fitzmaurice."

"You are aware that I am representing the *Star Tribune* in the *Cohen* case. I am calling to offer your client a settlement of $50,000. We are offering that much because that would be our costs for a trial."

"I will tell Cohen about your offer. With everything that has happened to him, I don't think that he would settle for anything less than $200,000."

Pause.

"200,000?!?" Fitzmaurice gasped. "No one would settle for anything like that. You should know that if we go to trial, one of us is going to be a big winner and the other a big loser. It's all or nothing."

From the tone of his voice, Fitzmaurice did not have a lot of fear that he was going to be the one to wind up as the big loser.

After that, Fitzmaurice made one last motion to block a trial, using the U.S. Supreme Court decision in *Hustler Magazine* v. *Falwell*, issued only four months earlier.

Fitzmaurice claimed that Cohen's legal position was even shakier than Falwell's. He reiterated past arguments that the newspapers had published the truth in identifying Cohen. He also argued that Cohen, like Falwell, was claiming emotional distress injuries. Judge Knoll refused to dismiss the case. The trial would go forward. The issues of Falwell's case raised by Fitzmaurice, however, would not go away.

The newspapers' resources were not limited to the best legal talent in Minnesota. The *Star Tribune* and *Pioneer Press* had unlimited quantities of ink and newsprint to influence judge and jury. The *Star Tribune* fired these weapons on the eve of the trial. It would not be the last time.

One of the most popular sections of the *Star Tribune*—along with the comic strips and "Dear Abby" and the like—is its "Fixit" column, which dispenses all sorts of practical, home-handyman-type advice. To add to readership, the newspaper positions the column near the daily television schedule. If the typical prospective juror were to read anything in the *Star Tribune*, it would likely be the "Fixit" column. Just before the trial, the *Star Tribune* departed from Fixit's ordinary fare. Only an extremely trusting soul would have regarded the timing and subject matter as merely a coincidence. Under the headline "Fairness Complaints Should Be Made to News Council," the "Fixit" column, in question-and-answer form, went like this:

Q. Are there any principles and rights that journalists are obliged to follow in order to provide fair and ethical treatment of their stories and subjects? What are they, how are they enforced and can the public or a private citizen help to insist on their implementation?

A. There are no principles and rights journalists are obliged to follow; therefore, there is nothing to enforce. General fairness and balance, however, can be discussed through the complaint process of the Minnesota News Council.[3]

The column did not mention the upcoming *Cohen* trial. It also did not inform readers that a year earlier Judge Knoll, in addressing the *Star*

Tribune's own motion, had explicitly and forcefully ruled that courts—not just the News Council—indeed could "oblige" journalists to "follow" principles of the law and rights of citizens.

The "Fixit" column was, not to put too fine a point on it, just plain dishonest. It was a harbinger of the trial to come. It would be bare knuckles the rest of the way.

The newspapers simply did not like to take no for an answer, even in a court order from a judge. The judge and the jury now would have another opportunity to demonstrate their authority to enforce the law.

Notes

1. Michael Orey, "Minnesota Maverick Targets Liberals and the Press," *The American Lawyer*, September 1989, 123, 124.

2. Eleanor Randolph, "Editors, Reporters at Odds over Confidential Sources," *Washington Post*, June 13, 1988, A4.

3. "Fixit: Fairness Complaints Should Be Made to News Council," *Star Tribune*, June 27, 1988, 3E.

Journalistic Malpractice on Trial

AT 9 A.M. ON July 5, 1988, all the newspapers' lawyers—Jim Fitzmaurice, Paul Hannah, Pat, and the others helping them—and I gathered in Judge Knoll's courtroom. Everyone knew that we were in for a long and hard-fought trial.

Why should that have been necessary? After all, no one denied that the newspapers had made promises to Cohen in exchange for his documents and that they had broken their promises. The only conflict, one would have thought, would have been over the amount of damages Cohen suffered as a result.

The trial, however, would not be so simple. From at least the time of their summary judgment motion, the newspapers made no bones about their refusal to limit the trial to the legal issue of whether they had made and broken contracts with Cohen.

They would try to divert the jury from their own conduct by demonizing Cohen. It would not, if they had their way, be a trial about the violation of an individual's rights by two huge, impersonal corporations. Instead, they would convert Cohen from the wronged to the wrongdoer. The putative victim—not of the newspapers' broken agreements but of Cohen's "dirty tricks"—now would be Marlene Johnson, who was not even a party to the agreements between Cohen and the newspapers. They would change the subject of the trial from a breach of contract to a gender offense by a male Cohen against a female Johnson—a much better match-up for them in Minneapolis, especially in front of a female jury.

Just showing that the newspapers broke promises to Cohen, then, would not work. I would have to go much further—I would have to indict the newspapers for what amounted to journalistic malpractice.

I would call witness after witness and introduce into evidence newspaper article after newspaper article to show that countless times each day, these newspapers and other media organizations make and honor promises of confidentiality as a common business practice to obtain information.

These promises especially pervade political reporting, where journalists invariably dig up damaging information about politicians, not from the politicians themselves but from their opponents, who demand anonymity. Many of these disclosures, like those from Cohen, come late in campaigns, when they will have the greatest impact. All of these promises of confidentiality in exchange for information are commercial transactions from which newspapers benefit. They obtain news to be published at their profit. The *Star Tribune* and *Pioneer Press* had never before deliberately violated a promise of confidentiality because they did not approve of a source's motive or for any other reason.

By dishonoring their promises, the *Star Tribune* and *Pioneer Press* not only violated the law of contracts but also committed a cardinal sin against the ethical code of the journalistic profession. It was not just journalistic ethics, either. They violated the simple but basic ethical and legal imperative of honoring your promises.

That was my overarching theme.

As for the notion that the public did not deserve to know about such a supposedly trivial matter as a favorite politician's theft conviction, I would counter with veritable column miles of articles and outraged editorials in the *Star Tribune* and *Pioneer Press* exposing shoplifting offenders to public ridicule.

In the end, I would show that the newspapers' contempt for solemn promises was without excuse or justification either in law or in ethics. The newspapers would have their forum on ethics, but it would be their own ethics on trial.

The first order of business was selecting a jury. It can be decisive to the outcome of a trial. Regardless of the preparation for the trial and the justice of the cause, getting the wrong jurors can sink a case as soon as they take their seats in the jury box.

The myth is that twelve or six good and true men and women will fairly weigh the evidence and inevitably produce the most just result. The reality isn't always so good. Juries may secede from their civic responsibility. In what some euphemists call "jury nullification," they may abdicate the rule of law through a verdict embodying their collective prej-udice.

The ostensible objective in selecting jurors is to get an impartial jury; the real purpose is to seat a jury who will more likely favor your side of the case. A whole industry of highly paid jury "consultants" exists to help attorneys achieve that result.

The newspapers' strategy called for a female-dominated jury. A jury of women presumably would be more vulnerable to emotional charges of a male using "dirty tricks" to victimize a female candidate.

When the judge and lawyers started to question prospective jurors, it looked at first as if the jury would be too good to be true. That quickly changed. One potential juror had studied the case in his journalism class and said that he supported Cohen. Fitzmaurice moved to exclude him for bias. Judge Knoll excused him. Two others also had heard of the case and said that businesses should abide by their agreements. Fitzmaurice moved to exclude them, too. Judge Knoll agreed. My heart sank. Others with professional or business positions asked to be excused because they could not afford to take several weeks off from their work. The judge excused them. They were all very intelligent.

Something is wrong with a process that systematically excludes or dis-courages intelligent and knowledgeable persons from serving as jurors on an important and complicated case. I kept the thought to myself.

The others in the jury pool were less forthcoming than those removed. None responded to my questions in a way that would have allowed re-moval for cause. They all seemed eager to ingratiate themselves with the lawyers and judge so that they would get on the jury. Most of the pro-spective jurors who were left told us that they were unaware of the case and hardly ever read the newspapers.

Even in the questioning of prospective jurors, Fitzmaurice was subtly arguing his case, trying to build sympathy for Marlene Johnson for the indignity of having had exposed "some petty shoplifting event [sic] that occurred a long time ago." He was a real master of the craft of persuading jurors.

It took less than four hours to select the jury. Minnesota law in a civil case allows each side only two peremptory challenges to oust potential jurors without court order. In the end, the jury had four women and two retired men. It was not the jury I had hoped for.

There was one note of nostalgia. One of the two alternate jurors was the daughter of a high school classmate of mine. We had played the bass violin in the junior high and high school orchestras. She never mentioned that during the questioning of jurors, and I did not make the connection until her father told me at our thirtieth high school reunion, a week after the verdict. As it happened, she did not participate in the verdict because none of the six regular jurors left the case.

Trusting one's fate to a jury can be as chancy as leaving it to a roulette wheel. That is a big reason why the vast majority of cases are settled before trial. A six-member jury in general is even more unpredictable than the more traditional twelve. A single juror with a strong personality can dominate the proceedings. The question is which side will be hurt more.

If either side started out with an advantage, it was the newspapers. They had gotten rid of some potentially unsupportive jurors, and they had achieved their goal of a female majority.

Even more important was simple arithmetic. A verdict required the votes of at least five of the six jurors. The newspapers needed to convince only two of them that they should give Cohen no compensation because he was such a despicable character. If neither side got five votes, the jury would be hung, compelling the ordeal of a new trial.

A split jury in theory would be a draw. The "right" to a second trial in practice would be illusory. Could anyone go through the agony of weeks of character assassination a second time? The newspapers did not think so. They could then, they thought, force a settlement lower than Fitzmaurice's original offer.

As it happened, two of the jurors were problems right from the start. One, a librarian who said that she belonged to a Catholic church, turned and sneered at Cohen every time a lawyer or witness attacked him for a "dirty trick." Another juror, who became the forewoman, took a liking to Hannah, frequently directing little winks and smiles his way. Hannah was a charming guy, but it would be a real travesty to determine the case on who was the best matinee idol.

The trial was held in the middle of one of the steamiest summers in Minneapolis history, the temperature rising into the hundreds on many of the trial days. The local taxpayers, at horrendous cost, only a few years earlier had constructed the venue of the trial, the Hennepin County Government Center. Unfortunately, the building more successfully accommodated the egos of the Hennepin County commissioners than the public comfort. The Government Center was notorious for the expensive oriental carpets and other furnishings worth tens of thousands of dollars in each commissioner's office. The voters sacked several of the miscreant commissioners. The problems with the bad design remained, however.

No amount of air-conditioning could bring the courtroom temperature below the 80s. Judge Knoll frequently invited the attorneys to doff their suit jackets. Fitzmaurice, who was very formal, declined the invitation. I did not dare do so alone, fearing the effect on the jury—who, for all I knew, expected lawyers to wear their suits to sleep. So all the lawyers sweated it out, strangling in suits and ties. The jurors dressed casually.

Fitzmaurice and Hannah both had extensive jury trial experience. I could not match their trial victories, but I had something else. My political years, which up to now had been less than helpful in my legal career, would come in handy at the trial.

The trial would not be about a cerebral disquisition on constitutional law. It would be more like a hardball political brawl with appeals to the constituency, here the women of the jury, most often bearing little resemblance to a highbrow Harvard Law School moot court competition.

After my three campaigns, I had some idea of what worked and what didn't in politics. My two successful campaigns were at the retail level of the state legislative district. The big mode of campaigning for the legislature in Minnesota is block work—going door-to-door and ingratiating yourself with voters by engaging each individually in conversation about anything he or she wants to talk about. Much of the time, it has very little to do with high public policy. Relating to the jurors should be akin to building rapport with voters on a one-on-one basis. Or so I hoped.

Fitzmaurice and Hannah planned to divide all examination and cross-examination between themselves. Pat's role would be limited to negotiating with me the scheduling of witness testimony and coaching or assisting the lead attorneys. She did not conceal her consternation over this assignment. That only made her more zealous to beat me in the trial. She wore a scowl whenever she had to come over and talk to me about who would be on the witness stand that day.

Pat sat at the newspapers' counsel table a few feet from me the whole time, dour and silently censorious throughout the trial. It was just plain unnerving. Whether or not the other side had planned it that way, it was skilled psychological warfare.

The jurors took their places, and we started the trial with the attorneys' opening statements. Going first, I began by emphasizing to the jurors their obligation to make a decision on the basis of the law of contracts. "You are about to hear a case unique in the United States, which adds to the interest and to your own responsibility to render justice. This case involves a broken promise by the two largest newspapers in Minnesota and the punishment of someone for revealing facts about a powerful political candidate. All he did was turn over authentic copies of court records to reporters after receiving promises of confidentiality."

I described Cohen's discussions and agreements with each of the four reporters, and the *Star Tribune* and *Pioneer Press* articles identifying Cohen, in violation of their promises. "The whole story became not the conviction of shoplifting of a prominent political candidate but the fact that someone had brought these materials to the newspapers."

Then I told the jury about each of the articles, columns, and cartoons attacking Cohen. "Another kick in the face for Mr. Cohen by the newspapers, for the crime of revealing factual information about a candidate and for trusting the promises of reporters."

I then read to the jurors the October 29, 1982, *Pioneer Press* editorial "Relevant Disclosures," and told them, "It's very important to how we should look at this case."

It was time to introduce the jurors to my collection of articles from the *Star Tribune*, *Pioneer Press*, and other newspapers.

Confidential sources are "part and parcel of the journalistic profession. We're going to have a lot of testimony, we're going to show you many, many articles, about how common the use of confidential sources is. You could pick up a newspaper any day and you will notice many articles where they refer to information that was provided on a confidential basis, where the person did not want to be identified. He may have feared for his job, he may have feared for his life—he or she may have had several reasons. But whatever the reasons were, the newspapers gave promises of confidentiality and honored promises of confidentiality in order to obtain information they would not otherwise have. We're going to show you many examples.

"We're going to show you revelations late in political campaigns where there are anonymous sources. It happens all the time. We're going to show you many, many examples of late revelations about political candidates, about things that happened many years earlier.

"In all of these the newspapers defended their action as merely providing relevant information to the public."

I pointed out that the *Star Tribune* and *Pioneer Press* had quoted unidentified sources in stories about plagiarism, while a law student, by former presidential candidate Joseph Biden, marijuana smoking decades earlier by Reagan Supreme Court nominee Douglas Ginsburg, mental health problems of vice presidential candidate Thomas Eagleton, and mob connections to vice presidential candidate Geraldine Ferraro's family.

"Even astrologers have been allowed to remain anonymous." Articles before the trial reported Nancy Reagan's reliance upon astrologers to plan President Reagan's schedule.

I referred to a spate of *Star Tribune* and *Pioneer Press* articles and derogatory cartoons earlier in 1988 about shoplifting by Miss Minnesota candidates. "But perhaps the most interesting article appeared in the *Pioneer Press*, and that had to do with Bess Myerson. Remember, she was a former Miss America and former consumer affairs official in New York City. In early May of this year this article said that Ms. Myerson had been arrested for shoplifting eighteen years earlier in London. That was interesting in itself. But also interesting was that the article was based on information provided by undisclosed sources.

"So we're going to show you the differences of treatment between a political figure who is convicted of shoplifting and Miss Americas who are also convicted of shoplifting."

The climax came when I told the jury that they would hear tape recordings of a conference a few days earlier of investigative reporters and editors. "We're going to play for you comments by the chief editors of both newspapers. Joel Kramer was asked if he had told his reporters that their promises of confidentiality can be revoked by editors. Mr. Kramer made a very interesting response which is highly relevant to this case. What he said was this—he hopes he would have the courage when faced with such a situation simply to not run the story."

Fitzmaurice sprang to interrupt. "The tape that counsel is discussing is an item that I did not realize was going to be part of this. We're going to be objecting strenuously to it."

I went on, "Just to conclude regarding the conference, the editor of the *Pioneer Press* said that this was the first time something like this has happened in her twenty-seven years of experience in journalism."

My peroration addressed "the substantial damages that Mr. Cohen has suffered as a result of the broken promises. We are going to be presenting evidence by leaders of the advertising profession that it became socially unacceptable to deal with Mr. Cohen because of the attacks by the newspapers, attacks which continue to this very day. The June 13, 1988, issue of the *Washington Post*, a newspaper with national circulation, contains a personal attack by Mr. Hannah, one of the attorneys for the defendants. We are going to show you the losses in business that Mr. Cohen suffered. We're going to show you the suffering of him and his wife and daughters as a result of the embarrassment and humiliation. We are going to ask you for punitive damages because of the willful indifference to his rights.

"We hope that you will give him the justice that he deserves."

The *Star Tribune* and *Pioneer Press* were the defendants, but there was nothing defensive in their approach to the trial. On the contrary, they struck a pose of moral superiority in a trial as much about ethics as about law. Fitzmaurice and Hannah did not deny that the newspapers had broken their reporters' promises of confidentiality. That, they would have the jury believe, didn't matter. Their clients' treatment of Cohen warranted not so much as an apology. Cohen, not the *Star Tribune* and *Pioneer Press*, was the villain of the piece. From the first, they proclaimed the issue of the trial to be Cohen's character and not the newspapers' broken agreements.

Their opening statements pummeled Cohen for the "dirty trick" of supplying accurate copies of public court records. Fitzmaurice charged that Cohen was part of a conspiracy of "political operatives" to crush Marlene Johnson. Playing to the gender of the jury majority, Fitzmaurice thundered that "this group of men" got together in a deliberate effort to destroy the political career of Marlene Johnson.

Fitzmaurice portrayed Cohen as a man of privilege who had graduated from the most expensive prep school in Minneapolis, then Stanford, then Harvard Law School. After Harvard, Cohen became a litigation attorney "for the largest law firm in this town," and "he started his career in politics on a national level."

Marlene Johnson, on the other hand, "was a woman from humble background who had pulled herself up by her own bootstraps" and was "about to become lieutenant governor" until Cohen "suddenly dumps this out as news."

Fitzmaurice became more agitated. The newspapers were right in deciding to publish Cohen's name, he said, because he had perpetrated "a real dirty trick." That "dirty trick," said Fitzmaurice, was the news, and not Marlene Johnson's conviction twelve years before for shoplifting "only" $6 worth of sewing equipment "at a point in time in her late twenties where she had a great deal of turmoil because it was about one year after the death of her father." Cohen's employer "was distressed," he "was disturbed," he "was stunned by it because this was just a real dirty trick," he "was stunned because his company had stood for integrity and Cohen committed an act that had no integrity." Fitzmaurice raged, "Anybody who heard about this event was stunned by it because this was just a real dirty trick."

And Johnson was not the only victim of Cohen. Cohen, Fitzmaurice proclaimed, also had showed no integrity in manipulating *Star Tribune* reporter Lori Sturdevant. Far removed from all the advantages enjoyed by Cohen at a tony prep school and Stanford University and Harvard Law School and the big law firm, Sturdevant "had come from South Dakota, had gone to Coe College, and had worked on small-town newspapers in South Dakota" before getting her big chance with the *Star Tribune*.

Fitzmaurice gave short shrift to the matter of whether the newspaper had broken contracts with Cohen. Other, more important obligations, he said, took precedence over the promises to Cohen. Fitzmaurice claimed a *Star Tribune* "promise" to the readership that "we're not going to lead you astray. We're not going to supply you with a bunch of information that will confuse you." An amazing comment for an institution that is supposed to inform the public. Fitzmaurice also claimed an overriding *Star Tribune* "promise" to its endorsed candidate, Marlene Johnson: "If you run for public office you can count on this newspaper not coming out and dumping this six days before the election and saying to the readership, here, read this."

Pioneer Press attorney Paul Hannah told the jury in his opening statement that nothing the newspapers did had caused Cohen any harm. Cohen's problems were his own fault, and he deserved no compensation or even sympathy. "If he suffered a loss, he suffered it because of his own actions. When he participated in this act, he knew the chance he was taking."

The critical thing in preparing Cohen as the first witness was to humanize him from the sinister caricature drawn by Fitzmaurice and Hannah. To begin, I wanted to get rid of any religious question fast. No one said explicitly that Cohen was Jewish, but the archetypal Jewish name, together with the harping on Cohen's elite educational and professional background, was enough to convey the message. If there was any prejudice among the jurors—and it would be struthious to ignore that danger in a Minneapolis jury—the cries that a male Cohen had perpetrated a dirty trick on a female Johnson, and had conned a main street South Dakota girl (Sturdevant) besides, would strike a fortissimo chord.

I deliberately avoided questions that would suggest anything Jewish. The mere hint would do more harm than good. Instead, I concentrated on things that at least would confuse the religious issue. For one thing, I made a point that Cohen sent his oldest daughter to Texas Christian University. I showed the jury brochures Cohen had prepared for the Billy Graham Evangelistic Association as part of his advertising and public relations work. I had Cohen explain in detail for the jury his volunteer work for an inner-city Methodist church in Minneapolis. He was on what was called the council of ministries of the church. We were careful not to state that Cohen actually belonged to the church.

By the time I was through, Cohen could have passed for a born-again Christian. In fact, in its next day's summary of the testimony, the *Pioneer Press* reported that Cohen was a church member.[1] It should, I hoped, have neutralized any religious issue.

To show the women jurors that Cohen had empathy for the interests of women, I presented brochures he had prepared for a health center urging women to get mammograms. To add to his kinder and gentler image, I also put into evidence two children's books Cohen had written with characters modeled after his daughters.

To show that Cohen was a good Minnesotan, and not just a political partisan, I introduced into evidence an adulatory biography he had written about Hubert Humphrey. Cohen had written the children's and Humphrey books in the 1970s, while in the employ of a Minneapolis publisher.

None of this, of course, had anything to do with the only legitimate legal issue—whether the newspapers had made and broken contracts with Cohen.

Fitzmaurice and Hannah jumped up with one objection after another, trying to bar all this testimony as not "relevant" to the issues of the case. I countered that they themselves, not we, were trying to make Cohen's character the central issue of the case. All we were doing were responding to their charges.

Cohen had to submit to cross-examination from Fitzmaurice that introduced what would become a recurring theme of the trial, the Watergate scandal and the fall of President Nixon in 1974.

A legendary confidential source had supplied *Washington Post* reporters Bob Woodward and Carl Bernstein with massive quantities of inside information that eventually helped force Nixon's resignation. Some wag dubbed the anonymous individual "Deep Throat" after a popular pornographic movie of the same title. The name stuck.

More than two decades later, neither the reporters nor the editors nor anyone else connected with the *Washington Post* has even hinted at the identity of Deep Throat. Interestingly, the *Washington Post*, unlike a great many other major media organizations, never inserted itself into the *Cohen* case in support of the Minnesota newspapers.

The historical record of the honoring of promises of confidentiality to Deep Throat was very pertinent to the legal and ethical issues in this case. More dubious were attempts by the newspapers to have the jury connect Cohen with Nixon and Watergate.

Nixon was less beloved in Minnesota than just about any other place, more than partly because he defeated Hubert Humphrey in 1968. In the guise of asking questions about Cohen's background, Fitzmaurice tried to associate Cohen personally with Nixon.

"You have been involved in the political arena for years, have you not?"

"Yes, sir."

"You had been involved on behalf of Mr. Nixon and his campaign nationally."

"Yes, sir, in 1960."

Carrying on the Nixon theme, Fitzmaurice charged that Cohen's disclosure of Johnson's criminal record somehow was "comparable" to Watergate.

"Your employer took the position that what you had done was comparable to certain of the things that had been done in Watergate."

"Yes. And I indicated to him that Watergate was a place where some petty crimes were committed and exposed corruption of the government, and fortunately there was someone called Deep Throat who was an unidentified source and saved the government for us."

"He took the position that your conduct reflected, in his view, a flaw in character, and that the activity was comparable to things that had gone on in Watergate."

"Yes, sir. And I responded to him with my belief as to what Watergate represented."

"And the reason that he advanced this proposition is because he believed that what you had done was a dirty trick."

I objected to that, and Judge Knoll struck it from the record.

"Do you know what a dirty trick is in the political sense?" said Fitzmaurice to Cohen.

"Yes. It's when someone doesn't tell you the truth after they've made an agreement with you."

"I meant more in the political sense."

"I do, too, sir."

"Did you consider Watergate dirty tricks?"

"Yes, sir."

"Watergate didn't involve any promises. It involved a break-in, did it not?"

"It involved an awful lot of things. It involved criminal offenses, yes."

Cohen parried well. But Fitzmaurice was unrelenting in pursuit of his theme that what he called Cohen's "flaw in character" trumped any rights he had under the law of contracts.

At the end of his cross-examination, Fitzmaurice read from a three-year-old deposition where Hannah had asked Cohen why he wanted to be anonymous. Cohen responded in 1995, "I think that were my identity revealed because I was the messenger of ill tidings, the public, my employer, the press, the world at large would heap opprobrium on my head." No one paid much attention then, but it turned out to be a less than felicitous choice of words.

Fitzmaurice had prepared meticulously for this moment.

"The word that you selected to use as to what would befall you was opprobrium, right?"

"Yes, sir," said Cohen.

"O-p-p-r-o-b-r-i-u-m. That was the word that you selected, correct?"

"That's correct, sir."

"Now, I would like to hand you a copy of the *Webster's New Collegiate Dictionary* and ask you if you would look up the word opprobrium," Fitzmaurice continued.

"Got it."

"Would you be kind enough to read it."

Cohen did. "Opprobrium [from the Latin to reproach] 1. something that brings disgrace 2. public disgrace or ill fame that follows from conduct considered grossly wrong or vicious; infamy, contempt, reproach, disgrace."

"Thank you. That's all I have."

Next on the stand were the *Star Tribune* and *Pioneer Press* reporters who made the promises of confidentiality. Fitzmaurice in his opening statement had heightened anticipation for Lori Sturdevant's testimony in particular by declaring that Cohen had victimized not only Marlene Johnson but Sturdevant, too. The newspapers seemed to be trying to persuade the female-dominated jury that Cohen had a penchant for treating women badly.

Sturdevant, however, did not agree with Fitzmaurice that she was a victim, at least of any conduct by Cohen. Instead, right from the time the *Star Tribune* published its first article identifying Cohen, she opposed her newspaper's decision to dishonor her promise.

Neither was Sturdevant the wet-behind-the-ears neophyte right off a South Dakota farm, as Fitzmaurice would have had the jury believe. On the contrary, she testified that she had been a political reporter for several years and in 1982 was the chief gubernatorial campaign reporter for the *Star Tribune*. By the time of the trial, the *Star Tribune* had promoted her to assistant editor. I had known Sturdevant and Bill Salisbury since they covered the Minnesota legislature in the late 1970s, so it was like talking to old friends again.

"Promises of confidentiality in exchange for information is a common practice, isn't it, Ms. Sturdevant?"

"Yes."

"Before October 27, 1982, you personally had made these promises at least once a week."

"That sounds about right," she said.

Sturdevant testified that she believed she could bind her newspaper by her promises of confidentiality.

"You did not tell Mr. Cohen that your promise of confidentiality would be subject to being overruled by your editors, did you, Ms. Sturdevant?"

"I did not tell him that."

"You felt that you had the authority to grant sources promises of confidentiality by yourself."

"Yes, I did feel that way."

Sturdevant said that the violation of her promise to Cohen was unique in her journalistic career.

"Your promises of confidentiality had never before been dishonored by your editors, had they?"

"No."

"And they've never since been dishonored by your editors either," I continued.

"Not that I recall."

"So this was the only time in your entire history in the journalistic profession that you've had a promise of confidentiality dishonored by your editors."

"Yes," said Sturdevant.

"You objected to the decision to dishonor your promise."

"I disagreed with it, yes."

"You refused to allow your name to even be used on the article, didn't you?"

"That is correct."

"That's a rather drastic step, isn't it, to take your name off an article?"

"It's seldom done."

"And it's done only for the most extreme reasons?"

"In my experience, yes."

"So the editors then would honor a request made by a reporter for anonymity, but they did not honor the promise made to a source to be anonymous," I said.

"That's a fair observation."

"Ms. Sturdevant, you take promises very seriously, don't you?"

"I try to, yes."

"And you think it's something of great importance when an editor tries to dishonor your promise, don't you?"

"Yes, I do."

"Could you give us your one basic reason for telling your editors that you wanted your name off that article?"

"I did not want to have my name associated with the breaking of a promise to a source," Sturdevant replied.

Next, I retrieved from my collection of articles a long *Star Tribune* front-page exposé written by Sturdevant in 1984 about financial troubles in Florida five years earlier of Minnesota State Treasurer Robert Mattson, who was seeking the 1984 Democratic nomination for the U.S. Senate. Unlike Johnson, Mattson was not the subject of any criminal charges or convictions. The newspaper was supporting his opponent, Minnesota Secretary of State Joan Growe. The *Star Tribune* published the article on Mattson only nine days before the primary. The newspaper obtained the financial documents from sources it promised confidentiality.

Mattson screamed foul. He accused the *Star Tribune* of a "malicious smear" for running its article so close to the primary. Editor Joel Kramer denied perpetrating any dirty trick. The article about Mattson carried this statement by Kramer: "Our only motive is to supply valuable information to our readers." The *Star Tribune* did not then or ever identify the source of the documents about Mattson.

Fitzmaurice attempted to exclude the article. "We object on the grounds of relevancy."

"This is an article," I responded, "nine days before a primary referring to the many problems of Robert Mattson. The issue was raised by Mattson . . . that these were late charges, they were an attempt to play a dirty trick on him, and this is information possessed by the *Star Tribune* earlier. Here is another situation where there are late revelations against a political candidate. In this situation, the *Star Tribune* denies that there's any sort of dirty trick."

"That just isn't relevant," repeated Fitzmaurice.

"It is," I said. "The whole case of defendants is that there was somehow a dirty trick played by the release of this information by Mr. Cohen, and that therefore he should be identified as the source. Here is a comparable situation. These Mattson things came from undisclosed sources, too."

Fitzmaurice withdrew his objection with the shot, "We are going to be here for a year, we really are, with this case, because every time one of these articles comes in, we have to deal with it."

With that done, I questioned Sturdevant about the Mattson article.

"Is it not true that there was at least one and possibly more undisclosed sources or tipsters tipping you off to the existence of this information in Florida?"

"There may have been a tipster at the outset."

"So at least there is no source of the information identified."

"The source would be the court documents obtained by our staff in Florida," Sturdevant pointed out.

"So in this case the source is considered the court documents themselves."

"That is correct."

"Whereas in the article involving Mr. Cohen, the source was considered to be Mr. Cohen rather than the court documents."

"That is correct."

When I asked her to explain Kramer's statement that it was not a "smear" to supply last-minute revelations about years-old financial problems of candidate Mattson, but it was a "dirty trick" to disclose more serious court records about a criminal conviction of candidate Johnson, Sturdevant said, "You'll have to ask him."

I concluded the questioning of Sturdevant by returning to the *Star Tribune*'s violation of her promise to Cohen.

"In the process of making the decision by the editors, were you allowed to participate in the process at all? After all, it was your promise that was broken. Were you allowed to take part in any meetings that took place?"

"I took part in no meetings."

"Were you ever invited to take part in any meetings?"

"No, I was not," she said.

"Who was the person who made the decision to break your promise?"

"I'm not entirely positive."

Even with all this, *Star Tribune* editors directed Sturdevant to call Cohen "to ask that he relieve me from the promise." There were as many as three such calls that afternoon and evening.

"In all of these conversations, Mr. Cohen refused to allow you or the *Star Tribune* to withdraw from the promise."

"That is correct."

"Again, do you regard a promise as being something very important, something involving a person's integrity, something you don't want to be broken?"

"That is correct."

"And in all your years of journalism and all the promises you have made, not one has been dishonored except for the promise to Mr. Cohen, is that right?"

"That is right."

"And you still object to the breaking of your promise."

"I still dislike the situation, yes," Sturdevant declared.

That ended the first full day of testimony. Neither Fitzmaurice nor Hannah asked Sturdevant any questions. The jury could sleep on Lori Sturdevant's last words of anger over her newspaper's flouting of her integrity.

Sturdevant's supervisor, Assistant Editor Roger Buoen, supported her. He testified that the *Star Tribune* should not have named Cohen. He also testified that he did not know of any other violation of a promise of confidentiality.

The newspapers' lawyers did not ask Buoen any questions.

Salisbury, who like Sturdevant had frequently given promises of confidentiality, also opposed his newspaper's violation of his promise to Cohen and repeatedly expressed his anger to *Pioneer Press* editors. Like Sturdevant, Salisbury was not hostile to my questions.

"Were you approached with regularity by persons with unsolicited information which would only be given to you in exchange for a promise of anonymity?"

"Yes," said Salisbury.

"So Mr. Cohen's proposal to exchange the information for a promise of confidentiality was not uncommon."

"No, it was not."

"And you thought that the public had the right to know that a candidate for a high public office had been convicted of a crime, didn't you?"

"Yes, I did."

"In fact, you expressed your discontent, your anger, your objection to the naming of Mr. Cohen over your promise at a meeting of editors and senior reporters even a month after the original article?"

"Yes, I did," Salisbury agreed.

"Before this happened with Mr. Cohen, had a promise of confidentiality by you ever been dishonored by your editors?"

"No."

"And has it ever happened since?"

"No."

I introduced a *Pioneer Press* article by Salisbury published four months before the trial, "Legislative Shakedowns Under Attack." Hannah objected that it was not relevant to the case. Judge Knoll asked me why it was relevant.

"Your honor, this article quotes unidentified lobbyists accusing legislators of extortion and blackmail. One of the issues here, apparently, is in the political context a person is not supposed to make charges; it's somehow considered a dirty trick. It shows the continued practice, the common practice. It shows the use of undisclosed sources. The real issue being raised by defendants is not the contractual issue. It's an attack on Mr. Cohen for somehow perpetrating a dirty trick by the anonymous release of information about a political figure. We're showing that the newspaper, in an article written by the same reporter, contains anonymous, very serious charges against legislators."

Judge Knoll allowed the article into evidence.

The article reported about legislators twisting lobbyists' arms for campaign contributions. The unidentified lobbyists "used terms such as extortion and blackmail to describe legislators' practice of soliciting campaign contributions from lobbyists who have legislation pending. While lobbyists grumble about the practice, they go along with it. Their business is winning friendly ears for their causes and buying fund-raising tickets is a cost of doing business."

"The article," I asked Salisbury, "does not identify the names of the persons who are accusing legislators of extortion and blackmail, does it?"

"No it does not," Salisbury said.

"And then it says, 'A legislator can raise between $4,000 and $40,000 at a fundraiser, a legislator said.' It does not identify the name of that legislator either, does it?"

"No, it does not."

"Are there any examples in that article of a source who asked to be confidential where that person was identified?"

"No."

The newspapers' lawyers did not ask Salisbury any questions.

Salisbury's supervisor in 1982, *Pioneer Press* City Editor Douglas Hennes, also testified that he did not know of any other case where a newspaper published the name of a source it had promised confidentiality.

Pioneer Press Editor Deborah Howell, testified Hennes, "was at the time and continues to be a good friend" of Marlene Johnson.

At a *Pioneer Press* meeting after the 1982 election, Hennes said, many reporters objected to the violation of Salisbury's promise of confidentiality. "People were upset," he testified.

I asked Hennes, "Do you recall whether anyone expressed the opinion that Cohen should have been identified?"

"Ms. Howell. Beyond that, I don't know anyone."

"So, Mr. Hennes, the only person supporting the decision to violate the promise of Mr. Salisbury was the same Ms. Howell who happened to be a personal friend of Marlene Johnson."

"Yes."

Fitzmaurice and Hannah did not cross-examine Hennes.

Gerry Nelson was the Associated Press reporter in 1982 who also promised Cohen confidentiality. The AP had honored his promise to Cohen. At the time of the trial, however, Nelson no longer was with AP but was working for the Perpich-Johnson administration. In fact, he had been Governor Rudy Perpich's press secretary for five years. Even so, he was steadfast about the sanctity of promises of confidentiality.

"As an experienced journalist," I asked Nelson, "how do you feel about the obligation of promises you give to sources? Do you take it very seriously?"

"Yes."

"And do you feel that those promises are something that should not be broken?"

"Yes, indeed. My own creed was when you promise somebody anonymity, you keep that promise."

"And did any editor overrule the promise that you made to Mr. Cohen?"

"They did not."

Later, Nelson wrote in a letter to the Star Tribune editor, "There's only one real issue, and that is when someone gives their word, that word ought to be good. Don't blame the courts; don't blame Dan Cohen. Blame the arrogant, second-guessing editors of the Star Tribune and Pioneer Press who promised anonymity in the Cohen case."

David Nimmer of WCCO-TV was the fourth reporter who had promised confidentiality. I had spoken with Nimmer frequently about the case and met him for lunch shortly before the trial. All this time he was fired up in anger over the newspapers' treatment of Cohen. Nimmer, in fact, had been an outspoken critic of the newspapers' conduct in public forums like a March 1985 seminar at St. Thomas University in St. Paul, "Media Ethics: Reality or Myth?" I had a tape recording of that seminar. Nimmer was just plain outraged. Among other things, Nimmer said there, "Cohen got skewered, pure and simple. He got thrown to the wolves."

Nimmer was a gifted public speaker and had several years' experience as a television and newspaper journalist. He would be, I thought, a powerful witness. When the time came for his testimony, though, Nimmer, unlike the other reporters, was unusually nervous and circumspect in his answers. I didn't know whether the newspapers' lawyers had talked to him before the trial, but Nimmer was rather more ambivalent about Cohen than he had been earlier.

"Mr. Nimmer, have you ever had any of your promises of confidentiality dishonored by your employers either at the *Minneapolis Star* or on WCCO-TV?"

"No, sir."

"Mr. Nimmer, didn't you appear on a panel at St. Thomas a while back, discussing this case?"

"Yes, I did."

"How do you feel about the decisions of the *Star Tribune* and *Pioneer Press* to dishonor their promises to Mr. Cohen?"

"I try not to have opinions. What I said at the forum is what I'll repeat here. I thought they hung Mr. Cohen out to dry because they didn't regard him very highly as a source."

"As a question of journalistic ethics, what do you think about the decision of the *Star Tribune* and *Pioneer Press* to dishonor their reporters' promises to Mr. Cohen?"

"I would have done differently than they did."

I had hoped for a stronger response from Nimmer.

Fitzmaurice, who did not ask any questions of either newspaper's reporter, singled out Nimmer for cross-examination.

"You said that when you got the information, you made a recommendation that it not be used at all," Fitzmaurice said to Nimmer.

"Yes, sir."

"Was the reason that you made the recommendation a judgment you made that the information about Marlene Johnson was basically old information, dealing with an insignificant and petty thing that had happened a long, long time ago?"

"The word I remember I used was 'chicken shit,' sir." No one in the courtroom laughed.

"In making that recommendation, did you think that publishing the information raw, Marlene Johnson convicted of shoplifting twelve years ago, or something to that effect, without identifying the source at all, would have been unfair to her?"

"I didn't believe it was fair to the campaign. I thought it was silly."

"Would it fall within the general category of political dirty trick at the eleventh hour in the campaign?"

"The answer would be yes, except that I've seen it happen in every campaign I can ever recall, and it was no worse than most." This time Nimmer surprised Fitzmaurice.

"But nevertheless in the same category, correct?"

"Yes, sir. There were other rumors about her." Nimmer did not elaborate on these "other rumors."

I followed up with some additional questions of Nimmer.

"When you have information that a candidate might not want the public to know about, you would generally get it not from the candidate herself or her supporters, you would generally get it from persons who oppose that candidate, wouldn't you?"

"Yes, sir."

"And that's the way you get information to inform the public about the merits or demerits of candidates, isn't it?"

"Many times, sir."

"And in all those times when you've gotten this information, the promises of confidentiality were upheld, weren't they?"

"Yes, sir."

"Mr. Fitzmaurice referred to the phrase 'dirty trick,' as he has throughout this trial. Now, Mr. Nimmer, isn't the exposure of a source, a violation of a promise without the source's consent, does not that fall within the category of 'dirty trick'?"

"In journalistic terms?"

"Yes, sir."

"Yes, sir, in my opinion."

In the end, Nimmer came through with some valuable testimony.

Columnists Jim Klobuchar and Doug Grow, who had savaged Cohen in October and November 1982, went on the witness stand after the reporters. Klobuchar again chastised Cohen as "shabby" and "unsavory" for revealing "a small indiscretion out of a person's past which wouldn't constitute an important news story" while "attempting to avoid identification as the source."

Klobuchar, however, was attempting to avoid some identification of his own. He did not mention that the revelations about Johnson got published in his newspaper only because of a broken promise by it. Nor did he disclose then or later his own speechwriting for Johnson's running mate, Rudy Perpich.

The Klobuchar column ridiculed the public's right to know about Johnson's "arrest on a charge" (Klobuchar persisted in refusing to acknowledge the conviction) of shoplifting: "Alongside other cases of human fallibility on the ballot, Marlene Johnson's is mild.

"This means that all candidates must come forward with every marital indiscretion or act of adultery, every instance when they dragged on a joint of pot at a private party, or got blasted out of their skulls on booze and howled racial epithets. When they all have come forward with their revelations, then we can damn Marlene Johnson for not making hers."

Judge Knoll interrupted the testimony. "Doug Grow and the other reporters are sitting back there and they're giggling at each other and nudging each other like a bunch of schoolkids. I feel kind of old." Fitzmaurice had to quiet them down.

From the collection of Klobuchar columns in my file boxes, I then presented into evidence a 1987 piece, "Candidate's Good Sense or Lack of It Does Matter." There, Klobuchar said that it was proper to expose presidential candidate Gary Hart's "marital indiscretions" with Donna Rice. That time, Klobuchar upbraided the candidate and not the source of the information.

Public figures in a jam often blame their blunders on the people who bring those blunders to the public's attention. Gary Hart's morality does matter. It matters more than yours or mine. He cannot reasonably come before the public with a complaint that nobody should face that kind of scrutiny. He's wrong. They spend years and millions of dollars clamoring for attention and reaching for the power. They can't cry if that attention arouses doubts about their personal discipline and therefore their discipline at the controls of power. The candidate and, above all, his good sense are what elections are all about in this country, or should be. They are held to levels of prudent behavior that the rest of the sinners aren't. There is a connection between the judgment a man or woman uses in private life and the judgment that same person exercises publicly.

It was a perfect explanation of why the public deserved to know about Johnson's criminal court record.

Regarding Klobuchar's point about no need to disclose politicians' pot smoking, I asked him, "Your newspaper gave extensive publicity to revelations that Judge Douglas Ginsburg, who was a candidate for the U.S. Supreme Court in November 1987, had smoked pot long before, in the 1960s and 1970s."

"Yes," Klobuchar said.

"Do you think the *Star Tribune* was in error in giving this extensive publicity?"

"No, I don't believe it was in error."

"And the *Star Tribune* gave an enormous amount of publicity to information from confidential sources that Senator Joseph Biden had copied from papers or tests or something or other twenty years earlier, or even more, in college or law school."

"Yes."

"And you don't find anything inappropriate in that?"

"No, I do not."

Grow was next. His column had censured the University of Minnesota for giving Cohen some work several weeks after he had been fired and after Marlene Johnson had been elected. Grow's testimony pointed up the double standard and vindictiveness prevailing at his newspaper.

Grow confirmed my suspicion that he was protecting a confidential source who had told him about Cohen's new job.

"Mr. Grow, who tipped you off to Mr. Cohen's employment at the University of Minnesota?"

"A source," Grow answered.

"In other words, this is a source to whom you promised confidentiality?"

"Yes."

"And you have kept that promise of confidentiality until this very day?"

"And I still will," Grow proclaimed.

"Did your editors approve your promise of confidentiality?"

"We didn't discuss it."

"Do you feel that there is anything wrong with an individual giving information to a reporter and asking for confidentiality?"

"It depends on motivation," Grow answered.

"But you have refused to name a confidential source even though the motivation of the source may have been to harm Mr. Cohen. Is that not correct?"

"I didn't know what the motivation of the source was."

"You didn't really care what the motivation was as long as he gave you the information. Is that not correct?"

"Yes, sir," Grow conceded.

In answering friendly questions from Fitzmaurice, Grow asserted that it would be "very unwise" and "inexpedient" not only for the University of Minnesota but also for any Minnesota state agency to employ Cohen, because his release of the court documents had offended the now lieutenant governor. This was six years after the fact.

I asked Grow if that would be the case "even though Mr. Cohen is doing good work?"

"That's part of the spoils system, yes, sir." It was a strange comment from a writer who adopts an aggressive "good government" posture in his columns.

One reason the trial dragged on for weeks was the constant objections by Fitzmaurice and Hannah to every effort to introduce as an exhibit or to ask a question about any of the hundreds of articles I had brought to court in my three file boxes. They even objected to providing to jurors the articles, the Klobuchar and Grow columns, and the cartoon the newspapers had published about Cohen after they identified him in violation of their promise to him. Every objection involved a several-minute battle before Judge Knoll.

Some rules of trial practice, such as the proper form of questions for direct examination and for impeaching the testimony of adverse witnesses, seem elementary on their face but can be devilishly tricky to execute in the heat of a trial. All the law school courses, continuing legal education seminars, and textbooks are no substitute for doing a real jury trial.

I had to get this experience during a complicated trial against extremely skilled opponents. Fitzmaurice's formidability was nationally recognized. *The National Law Journal*, for example, admired his "easy way of informing the jury."[2]

It was much more ragged for me at the beginning, learning as I went along not at an ivory tower Harvard but at the hard knocks school of a real trial. Sometimes I had to ask a witness the same question two or three times, in the face of objections by Fitzmaurice and Hannah, before I got the correct form down. A couple of days into the trial, Judge Knoll got exasperated. "Did you hear what I said? I said if you were to form this question right, I think it's appropriate to show me an inconsistency in his opinion. You're not doing it right. I'm going to make you go up to the library after this is over and read books on it."

I didn't want to tell the judge that I already had read the books there.

Whatever happened at the beginning, I did not make the same mistakes twice as the trial went along.

So the trial proceeded in its measured way.

One witness I thought would help show the importance of making and keeping promises of confidentiality was a legendary but cantankerous sportswriter named Sid Hartman, who had been the area's most prominent sports columnist since I was in grade school. Everybody in town knew him.

Hartman never spared the feelings of athletes, coaches, and executives. Anonymous sources peppered Hartman's columns with attacks on the sports personalities who happened to be out of favor with the columnist at the time. Hartman was a law unto himself who did not take orders from any other journalists, including editors.

I had a sheaf of his columns in my file boxes. I thought that his testimony about sports would be a good change of pace from all the talk about politicians and might have special appeal to the two men on the jury.

Sid, however, was not happy about being subpoenaed to testify in this case. He stormed into the room, sans tie, muttered "Hello, Elliot," and strutted uncomfortably around until he started the day's proceedings. Judge Knoll tried to banter with Hartman.

"I should point out, I can't resist this, I swept under the seats in Nicollet Park [the wonderful old Minneapolis minor league baseball park demolished in the 1950s], and I think I met you when I was sweeping under the seats at the park. Because once in a while we were allowed to enter the press box."

"I see," harrumphed Hartman.

"That was about seventy years ago," quipped the judge.

"Long time."

"That's the comic relief for the day. Go ahead."

I questioned Hartman.

"You could pick up virtually any one of your columns at random and you will see references to sources who don't want to be named—insiders or confidential sources—wouldn't you?"

"I would say that statement's correct."

"And how important do you view confidential sources in your ability to write your column and to write your stories?"

"I think in my case I would consider it very important."

"And I would assume, Mr. Hartman, that you feel it's important, also, to keep promises of confidentiality to these sources, don't you?"

"In most cases, yes. There are exceptions. I would say an exception would be if I went to the university this afternoon and the football coach told me confidentially he was going to resign tomorrow. I think I'd have to consult with Mr. Finney or Mr. McGuire [both editors] or one of the people at the newspaper and tell them I knew that."

"And then, of course, you would certainly not be happy if any of these individuals broke your promise, would you?"

"I wouldn't be happy, but I think you'd be in this position, Mr. Rothenberg, that you wouldn't want to pick up the St. Paul paper the next morning and see that they had the story that you knew about."

Hartman probably had not asked any editor's permission to do anything for decades. The notion that he would ask two of them for instructions about using a confidential source was preposterous, but there was no point in getting into an argument with him. I got him off the stand quickly, before things got worse.

Other *Star Tribune* and *Pioneer Press* reporters more categorically embraced the sanctity of promises of confidentiality. One of the best was Dean Rebuffoni, a longtime environmental reporter for the *Star Tribune*. I had known Dean since 1974, when I was litigating environmental cases for the Minnesota Public Interest Research Group. On several occasions as a lawyer and as a legislator I had given him information after he promised confidentiality. He always kept his promises to me, and I was sure to his other sources as well. He never would dissemble. I knew that he would be strong on the stand.

"How long have you been a reporter with the *Star Tribune*?"

"Since 1972," answered Rebuffoni.

"And during that period, you've had many occasions to use confidential sources."

"Yes."

"Are you in the habit of breaking promises of confidentiality when they are granted?"

"Never."

"You've never done so?"

"No," Rebuffoni reiterated.

"Not in fifteen years of reporting?"

"Only if the source should say it's okay."

"You would consult with the source first and ask to be released of the promise?"

"Certainly," Rebuffoni said.

"If the source did not agree, you would not break that promise of confidentiality."

"Certainly not."

"And your editors have never done that to you either, have they?"

"No, they have not."

Pioneer Press reporter Linda Kohl was another good witness. She told the jurors, "The golden rule of investigative reporting is that if you make a promise of confidentiality to a source, you must not break that promise. Be totally honest in dealing with your confidential sources. Don't mislead or double-cross them. They're the ones who keep you in business."

Getting this testimony from Kohl was not accidental. One month earlier, Kohl had been a panelist at a conference of investigative reporters and editors, and had expressed similar sentiments. I learned of the conference and purchased tapes of the proceedings. These tapes would be even more helpful in dealing with a witness not as cooperative as Kohl.

Sturdevant, Salisbury, Rebuffoni, and Kohl were eloquent and courageous to testify against their employer. None, however, had been a top editor. By sheer luck, I found one who shared their views.

Six months before the trial on a bitter winter night, a friend dragged me to a fund-raising dinner for Senator David Durenberger. I had avoided all these since 1982. But this one had some interest because Durenberger's opponent that year was my old adversary, Hubert Humphrey III. I happened to sit at a table next to a big, friendly guy named Robert King. I had no idea who King was, but after a couple of minutes he told me that he was the editor in chief of the *Minneapolis Star* in the 1970s, when it was a separate afternoon newspaper. That woke me up. We got to talking about the case. King criticized his former newspaper's behavior. To call this encounter serendipitous would be an understatement.

King agreed to be a witness. He did want me to make it clear on the record, though, that he came there because of a subpoena.

"At any time when you were editor of the *Star*, did you ever overrule a promise of confidentiality given by a reporter to a source?"

"No, we didn't. I would remember," King answered.

"When you have information which comes from a court document, would it be the case that the source of the information would be the document itself rather than the person who happened to deliver it to you?"

"The source for the story in the newspaper would be the document."

"In your entire career in the journalistic profession, do you know of any other situation where a promise given by a reporter to a source was violated by editors?"

"I can't think of another case," answered King.

"Would you express your opinion regarding the editors' handling of the Dan Cohen situation?"

Hannah objected. "The question of journalistic ethics is just not relevant to the legal issues of the case."

I responded, "Journalistic ethics are not relevant? It's an interesting admission, I would think."

Fitzmaurice objected, too, claiming that King was not an expert on journalistic ethics. Judge Knoll allowed King to answer the question. King gave a pithy response.

"I thought he was treated badly by the *Star Tribune* and *Pioneer Press*. They didn't do the right thing by him."

Fitzmaurice tried to get King to admit that editors had authority over reporters and therefore would prevail in any disagreements between them over honoring promises of confidentiality. King did not give the answer the *Star Tribune* lawyer wanted.

"We dealt with some pretty serious issues, but we never dealt with whether or not to break a promise of confidentiality. We dealt with whether or not to publish the information."

Fitzmaurice inadvertently helped reinforce my argument that if the *Star Tribune* did not like Cohen's court documents, it had the option to refuse to publish them but not the right to violate an agreement with their source.

There would be a lot more twists and turns as the trial proceeded.

Notes

1. David Shaffer, "Newspapers Say Cohen Didn't Deserve Anonymity," *St. Paul Pioneer Press*, July 7, 1988, 1C.

2. Dan Oberdorfer, "Is 'Burning a Source' a Breach of Contract?" *The National Law Journal*, August 1, 1988, 8.

The Ghost of Deep Throat

THE CASE THAT had started with a complaint over the breaking of a promise had become one involving fundamental issues of ethics in the journalistic profession.

Arnold Ismach, a nationally prominent expert on journalism and dean of the University of Oregon School of Journalism, had volunteered his services. No other recognized expert was anxious to testify against the newspapers. Ismach was generous in coming forward as a matter of principle, but I was worried that his having been a consultant for candidate Wheelock Whitney in 1982 would compromise his effectiveness.

Ismach testified that promises of confidentiality in return for information on political candidates like that Cohen supplied "is a very common practice with most news organizations."

"Would that information tend to come from a person who might not be supporting the candidate about whom the information is provided?" I asked.

"Usually," Ismach said. "That would be the normal case. Political campaigns are competitive arenas, and the campaigns are seeking advantage, and reporters are seeking information. So this sort of transaction, and that's what it is, goes on quite frequently."

"Can you tell us about the importance that journalism attaches to promises of confidentiality?"

"Newspapers are in the business of acquiring information. That is their trade. Sometimes that information is difficult to acquire. With some frequency, part of the transaction between reporter and source is the agreement to be given information in exchange for not identifying the source."

I emphasized the commercial nature of these agreements for newspapers. "In this transaction, then, there is payment by the reporter in the promise of confidentiality. There is benefit to the reporter also."

Ismach agreed. "Confidentiality is one form of currency that journalists use to get something they want and need, which is information."

Ismach discussed shield laws, legislation that media organizations pushed in Minnesota—under the name Minnesota Free Flow of Information Act—and many other states to deny courts the power to order journalists to disclose the names of their confidential sources. Many do not consider even these laws enough, Ismach testified. "Journalists tend to carry even beyond what the courts interpret as the limits of disclosure. There have been several who have gone to jail for contempt because they refuse, even upon court order, to disclose the name of a confidential informant."

"Would exposing the names of those sources," I asked, "cut off the free flow of information needed by the public?"

"Very definitely. That is the fear of many journalists and one of the major incentives for the movement for protection of confidentiality through shield laws.

"If sources who provide information on the basis of anonymity found that they could not trust those agreements, journalists feel that those sources would dry up. We would be cut off from information that is valid to the public."

"So the public would ultimately be hurt?" I asked, expecting only one sort of answer. Ismach gave it.

"The public is the ultimate loser, that's correct."

"This means," I said, "that promises of confidentiality, then, are regarded as being very important to the journalistic profession, promises that should not be broken."

Ismach agreed. "If journalists consider anything sacred, it's that trust. When you give your word, you give your word. They will do anything, very often, to keep that word, even to the point of going to jail. The journalist lives on reliability, on credibility, and keeping an agreement speaks to the credibility, reliability, and responsibility of the journalist. That's why journalists almost universally consider this a bottom-line question. When you make a deal, you make a deal.

"It is a universal ethic that reporters and editors believe that there is no circumstance under which you violate the agreement."

After several minutes of objections by Fitzmaurice that it was not "relevant" to the case, Ismach read from a *Boston Globe* account of editors supporting promises of confidentiality made by sportswriters in return for information about drug abuse among members of the New England Patriots football team. The *Globe* took the position that "commitments must be honored. To have done less would subject the media, which continues to suffer a credibility gap with the public, to further damage. A newsman is only as good as his word."

Ismach then quoted Bob Woodward, the *Washington Post* reporter who promised confidentiality to Deep Throat, that promises of confidentiality remain binding until the source dies or releases the reporter from the promise.

As a final illustration of how reputable journalists regard their promises, Ismach cited this remark by television correspondent Marvin Kalb. "You can't eat off a source's plate and then later say you don't like the food." Ismach commented, "This captures the essence of the professional's view of the sacredness of a promise of confidentiality."

Ismach testified about options the *Star Tribune* and *Pioneer Press* had consistent with their agreement with Cohen. If the editors felt Cohen's information was "inappropriate," they could decide not to publish the story.

Another option, said Ismach, would be to "describe the informant by type, such as 'a Republican activist,' or 'a Whitney campaign supporter,' or some generic term like that, as long as the person cannot be identified."

"If an editor disapproves of the information brought by a confidential source," I asked Ismach, "is it consistent with journalistic ethics for the editor to break that promise?"

"I have not encountered editors who feel that they have that prerogative. I would honor the pledge but chastise the reporter."

"In terms of journalistic ethics, do you feel that editors should have the power to punish confidential sources who provide information they do not approve?" I asked.

"I don't believe that editors have the right to punish anybody. Their obligation is to report on the news, and responsible journalists don't attempt to abuse their occupation by inflicting punishment.

"Editors may refuse the information and not publish it, but not abrogate the agreement," Ismach continued. "It is the traditional and widespread ethical practice in journalism that once an agreement is made by a reporter, that reporter speaks for the news organization."

Concluding, I asked Ismach's opinion of the two newspapers' actions toward Cohen. Ismach replied succinctly.

"The Cohen incident is one of the more serious breaches of journalistic ethics that I've seen in the Twin Cities. It was a mistake in judgment that resulted in an unethical act that was unnecessary."

Ismach had taken with him to the witness stand a file folder of what he had told me were articles and papers to support his testimony. I did not go through the file. That was a mistake. Fitzmaurice sprinted to the attorney's podium for his cross-examination of Ismach. Before he even got there, and without so much as a good morning or other pleasantry, Fitzmaurice pounced.

"Can I see your file?" Fitzmaurice demanded.

"Do you want to see everything in this folder?" asked Ismach, in a rather worried tone of voice.

"You bet."

"Okay. There's a lot of paper in here."

Indeed there was. Fitzmaurice read from Ismach's file a set of notes that appeared to be directions for me on how to try the case. "Why are you emphasizing or even mentioning that Cohen had any role in the campaign or contact with Whitney? Your best bet is to show that Dan did this on his own and that the campaign didn't have anything to do with it. Nothing this trivial could have much impact on the campaign."

This was not the sort of thing I wanted to be surprised with before the jury. I couldn't believe that this was Ismach's idea. It was déjà vu back to October 1982 when the Whitney campaign and Republican leadership in general were telling everyone in the media that Cohen was on a frolic of his own and they had nothing to do with the release of the documents about Marlene Johnson. They never were happy about Cohen's suit in the first place, and now were embarrassed at the exposure in the trial of their role in the disclosure of the Johnson court records.

In assaulting Ismach for taking part in the Whitney campaign meeting that released the court records, Fitzmaurice repeatedly insisted that the court had "expunged" the records and that a "reporter would not be able to find them." That was just plain false. Neither the attorneys nor anyone else ever produced a plausible explanation of how all the full-time political and courthouse reporters from two large city newspapers had managed to avoid discovering these documents that anyone else could come off the street and examine.

Fitzmaurice tried to use Johnson's very act of theft to transform her into a victim. "Shoplifting is associated with difficulties that people were having in their life, and by visiting a doctor they might get to the bottom of it and solve the problem."

Ismach answered, "I'm aware of the reasons that people have problems and break the law and recover from problems and so forth."

"You had no concern that releasing that information six days before the election would not lead to charges that this was a dirty trick late in the political campaign?" Fitzmaurice had found another opportunity to hit the jury with another repetition of the newspapers' mantra.

"Well," answered Ismach, "that didn't enter my mind because it wasn't a dirty trick, no matter who released the information. It was legitimate information and factual. A little piece of the puzzle that makes up individuals."

Fitzmaurice intoned the epithet "dirty trick" no less than ten times. He tried to set Cohen's alleged "dirty trick" and Ismach's complicity in it against the supposed innocence of "what had happened to Marlene Johnson twelve years before when she was down on her luck."

This was too much. I jumped up to object because there was nothing whatsoever in the evidence to show that Johnson was "down on her luck" when she committed her theft. Judge Knoll agreed.

Ismach showed that the *Star Tribune* and *Pioneer Press* not only violated Cohen's rights but also were outlaws from general standards of journalistic practices and ethics. The question was whether Fitzmaurice's ferocity on cross-examination would distract the jury from Ismach's message. There was no doubt that Ismach's testimony would be very effective in supporting legal arguments on appeal. The trick was getting to appellate courts in the first place. It would not make any difference how good his or anyone else's testimony would look on appeal if we did not win the trial.

For the matter at hand with the jury, I needed to reinforce Ismach with an expert witness relief pitcher who had no connection to the Whitney campaign. Fortunately, I had one. My second expert witness, Bernard Casserly, was not a national figure like Ismach. He was, however, a long-time and highly respected journalist in Minnesota with numerous awards to this credit.

I had gotten to know Bernie Casserly ten years earlier—ironically, through my former wife. Casserly was on the same side of the suit Pat was doing for the Minnesota Newspaper Association to require the Minnesota state government to reveal the identities of abortion providers receiving state funds. Now he would be testifying against her client.

Casserly had been the editor of the *Catholic Bulletin* in St. Paul for twenty-five years. That could help with the librarian who did not seem to like Cohen.

I asked Casserly about the importance of confidential sources to journalism. He was more lengthy in his answers than Ismach.

"No one who reads a newspaper or watches television today can be unaware of how society relies on confidential sources. It's bread and butter for media people. We couldn't live without it. It is a way of doing business, a common practice.

"Hasty and hurried news conferences are often called by legislators who have something to divulge that would be considered unfriendly if their names were known by others.

"I've attended meetings in Washington where editors were invited to spend the day and learn about what was going on. Jimmy Carter was the president then. A whole day was a confidential extravaganza, from morning till night. We listened to Zbigniew—I can't remember his last name—to top people in the government tell us, for nonattribution, all kinds of things that were happening. We were not to divulge the source. It was a given."

"Then you have situations where legislators and government officials themselves want to remain anonymous?" I emphasized.

"Absolutely," Casserly said. "In fact, I brought with me something that I think might be helpful. It's a classic description. This source is *Law and Media in the Midwest*."

"Who wrote that?"

"This was written by John R. Finnegan and Patricia A. Hirl. It's a chapter called 'Protecting Sources.' "

Fitzmaurice stood up to complain on the ground that using her book could force Pat to become a witness and compromise her status as a lawyer in the trial. It was much ado about nothing. I was not planning to call Pat as a witness and neither was Fitzmaurice. What was important was not Pat's authorship but Finnegan's. Finnegan was vice president and assistant publisher of the *Pioneer Press*. Finnegan would testify later in the trial. After much brow-scratching, everyone agreed that Casserly would summarize the chapter and would refer solely to Finnegan as the author.

"In essence," answered Casserly, "it says that anonymous sources are a way of doing business and the protection of these sources is important. It says the reason for protecting confidential sources is that many of these people are at risk. They're afraid of loss of jobs, they're afraid of public reprobation, public disdain if their names are used."

Finnegan and Pat were 100 percent accurate as applied to Cohen.

"Mr. Casserly, from your experience and knowledge of journalism, do you feel that editors should be aware of the consequences which would result when promises of confidentiality were violated?"

"Yes, obviously they must be aware of them. That's what they're paid for. They know the risk involved. They would not have risen to their ranking without knowledge of the problems and dangers that can arise from such exposure. It would be a sign of incompetence if they didn't know this."

I asked Casserly about Deep Throat.

"We don't know to this day who Deep Throat is. As a result of Deep Throat, a confidential source, a government was toppled. That changed the course of American history. If the people at the *Washington Post* had said that it was a political issue and divulged the source, sources would have dried up. Deep Throat is only one, but probably the most dramatic, example of the importance of confidential sources to journalism and to society. We're talking about knowledge that you and I and all of us need. Once these sources are burned, they will not speak.

"Employees of big firms will stop blowing the whistle. Much of the news comes from these anonymous sources who know that if they're revealed, they're going to lose their jobs."

No one picked up the piquancy of the reverence of the devoutly religious editor of the *Catholic Bulletin* for someone with the nom de plume of a pornographic movie.

"Based on your knowledge and experience," I asked Casserly, "how important do journalists view a promise to a source? Is that something that's to be taken seriously in the ethical sense?"

"Keeping your word is not something of concern only to journalists. All of us believe in it. It's a concept that a man's word or a woman's word is as good as his bond. It's a matter of truth, it's a matter of reliability, of people's trustworthiness in dealing with each other. A promise is a promise. It's a way of life. It's simply the basic ethical consideration of fair play."

Casserly hit just the right note about the morality of the newspapers' conduct.

"What is your opinion, Mr. Casserly, on the basis of journalistic ethics, of the two newspapers' dishonoring of their promises to Mr. Cohen?"

Casserly nailed it again. "To me, it explains why newspapers have a bad image. Trust is what is involved here, and a trust has been violated. This is a case where honor was violated, where trust was ignored, and where questions will forever be raised about the danger of giving information to newspapers. There will be feelings that, in the future who can trust newspapers."

Bernie Casserly was seventy years old. Despite his myriad accomplishments, he put on no pretensions of status or expertise. He was the furthest thing from a slick professional expert witness. In fact, he never had testified in court before. He just answered questions like a regular guy. He rambled at times. But he was the genuine article, and the jury knew it. Casserly was a real star witness. No other witness had anything like his gentle charisma. His sincerity and goodwill had the jurors riveted for an hour and a half.

The newspapers' attorneys did not risk cross-examination of Casserly.

The *Star Tribune*'s and *Pioneer Press*'s handling of the revelations about Marlene Johnson evinced an attitude about shoplifting that was, at the least, cavalier. I couldn't believe that most people would share it. In combing through the public library's microfilm files, I discovered two October 1977 essays by a longtime *Star Tribune* columnist named Robert Smith. In the first, he ridiculed a suburban prosecutor for bringing charges for the theft of "only" a seventy-eight-cent toy by "a woman I refuse to name in such a silly case."

A week later, Smith wrote another column detailing the torrent of criticism he received from the first one. I went through the column in loving detail with Smith, who now was a witness eleven years later.

"I notice you have several comments. One says, 'It is my opinion that K-Mart should be applauded for the apprehension of thieves. Thus, they help to protect the public against the high prices we pay to subsidize those who steal and are not brought to justice.' Am I reading correctly?"

"Right," said Smith.

"And then, 'I'm sure smaller shop owners cannot afford the security system K-Mart has and are appreciative of the example that is set each time someone is prosecuted.' "

"Right," Smith responded again.

"And then you have the executive president of the Minnesota Motel Association who was 'very upset with the column. I had the opportunity to discover that we do have a very serious problem with shoplifting nationally and in this state.' "

"Right."

"Then you have the executive director of the Minnesota-Dakotas Retail Hardware Association saying, 'It is estimated that $500,000 a day is shoplifted out of Minnesota stores.' "

"Right."

"And then he says, 'It all starts with a nickel candy bar or the small toy, then to radios, tape recorders, jewelry, watches, and bigger ticket items.' "

"Right."

"Then he says, 'The shoplifter feels invulnerable. They won't prosecute, many believe. I'll get out of it by returning the merchandise. Apologies, ad infinitum.' Right?"

"Right."

"The article refers to several other comments regarding the evils of shoplifting, even small shoplifting. Isn't that true?"

"Right," concluded Smith.

Going after shoplifters, then, was not so silly after all.

Lou Gelfand wrote the November 7, 1982, *Star Tribune* editorial column that was the authorized apologia for the newspaper's identification of Cohen. He was an editor of the *Star Tribune* with the title of "readers' representative." There was considerable grist for the mill in his writings.

Gelfand also was a neighbor of mine. We would sometimes see one another while jogging. I wanted to call Gelfand before the process server hit him with his subpoena. "Say, Lou, you know that I am Dan Cohen's attorney. I will have to get testimony from you. I hope that you won't take it personally."

"That's all right, counsel. It's what you have to do."

Gelfand turned out to be a key witness. His column said that Johnson's conviction was inconsequential and not worthy of public disclosure. "The substance of Cohen's tip was beneath the threshold of acceptable, unattributable information." Cohen's identity "was the news, more than the facts of Johnson's arrest and conviction."

"What you're saying, Mr. Gelfand," I asked him on the witness stand, "is that the substance of the shoplifting arrest and conviction was minor?"

"Correct," Gelfand answered.

That gave me the opportunity to expose the *Star Tribune*'s double standard. On the one hand, the newspaper displays exaggerated solicitude for a favored politician by maintaining that it is positively evil for anyone to disclose her theft conviction. Where ordinary people are concerned, however, the same newspaper aggressively publicizes their shoplifting arrests and convictions, notwithstanding the attendant embarrassment. Gelfand opened the door to bring into the case a stack of *Star Tribune* and *Pioneer Press* headlines about the tribulations of Miss Minnesota candidates. The articles, published earlier in 1988, reported that the original Miss Minnesota USA winner was arrested and charged with shoplifting. She resigned her title. The newspapers reported a few days later that the re-placement Miss Minnesota USA had been arrested some years earlier for shoplifting, when she was eighteen years old. The second Miss Minnesota also resigned. The newspapers did not identify, much less criticize, the sources for the stories.

The newspapers then published editorial page cartoons. The *Star Tribune* published a caricature depicting a Miss Iowa, a Miss Wisconsin, and a "Mis Demeanor" in striped prison garb with a ball and chain. The *Pioneer Press* published a cartoon showing the various Miss Minnesotas in a police lineup.

The disparate treatment of an elite politician and middle- or working-class candidates in a beauty contest reeked of class bias. I wanted to show the jurors that whatever the newspapers were doing to advance the interests of women was only for selected beneficiaries, which did not include people like them.

"When Miss Minnesota USA candidates were arrested and convicted of shoplifting, do you feel that's a serious offense?"

"It was serious enough to warrant the organization to ask her to resign, because a person in that position has to be a role model," Gelfand granted.

"Do you feel that a high political officeholder, like the lieutenant governor, also should be a role model?"

"Yes, I do."

"Therefore, the shoplifting of Ms. Johnson was not a minor offense," I said.

Gelfand insisted it was. "It happened twelve years prior to the campaign, and I believe under the circumstances with some kind of forgiveness I would not have thought it was serious at that time."

"Along that line of reasoning, Mr. Gelfand, would it be a serious offense for a Miss Minnesota USA candidate to have been convicted of shoplifting when she was sixteen years old, years before she was selected as a Miss USA candidate?"

"That's a borderline case. It would depend on the circumstances at the time. I wouldn't make a blanket statement dealing with human beings."

"Do you feel that such an offense by a sixteen-year-old girl, a few years before running for Miss Minnesota USA, would warrant extensive coverage in the *Star Tribune* and her eventual withdrawal as a result of that coverage?"

Gelfand would not budge in defending his newspaper. "I think it was appropriate under the circumstances. It was a well-known story that had been generously covered in all of the media. In view of reader interest, the coverage was very appropriate."

"May I ask your opinion of this cartoon which has a picture of Miss Indiana, Miss North Dakota, Miss Wisconsin, Miss Iowa, and 'Mis Demeanor' with a jail ball attached to her, all dressed as Miss America candidates?"

"The cartoon meets the requirements of what a good, if not excellent, cartoon should have. It uses exaggeration to catch the reader's eye and to make the point. It makes no pretense at being fair or balanced. It is highly opinionated, and it meets all those tests. In terms of the purposes, it was very good."

With the jury makeup in mind, I asked, "Is it very good making fun of a young lady who had been convicted of shoplifting when she was sixteen years old?"

"Right. It did, and that's what it was intended to do."

"Mr. Gelfand, you're saying that it's appropriate to give extensive coverage to a candidate for a beauty contest for something which happened to her earlier, when she was a teenager, that's information the public should know about, but that a similar situation should not apply for a candidate for the second highest office in Minnesota. That's trivial, is it?"

"They are two totally different situations. To try to make a comparison is not fair."

"As a matter of fact, shoplifting is a very serious offense, is it not?"

"Serious in what context, counsel?"

I pulled out an editorial from his newspaper of November 30, 1972 and read excerpts to him.

One of the larger "selling" jobs merchants face is getting across to the public the simple but stern fact that shoplifting is stealing. And stealing it is, in merchandise of several hundred thousand dollars daily in Minnesota alone.

The average value of a stolen item is about $13. A major problem representatives of the Minneapolis Downtown Council and the Minnesota Retail Federation note is making would-be shoplifters realize that such theft is not a game or taking something the store won't miss anyway. Adults, particularly housewives under 40, are the biggest offenders.

More stores plan to prosecute. Conviction might mean only a small fine or probation, but stores hope the prospect of embarrassment and the blot on a person's record, if convicted, will act as deterrents.

So often forgotten or ignored by shoplifters and any who sympathize with them is that customers ultimately pay the shoplifting bill because stores add shoplifting losses to their overhead and pass this cost on to the customers. Shoplifting is not a lark. It is serious business for everyone.

Gelfand wouldn't budge as far as Johnson was concerned.

"I believe that when a judicial system forgives someone, vacates the order, indicated that the person has learned a lesson, I think that's good for all of us."

"It wasn't enough for the second Miss Minnesota candidate, was it, sir?"

"It sure wasn't," Gelfand retorted. "Twelve years hadn't expired between the time of her charge and the time that she was named queen."

That led to another and much more famous beauty queen.

"Mr. Gelfand, what would you say about a situation where another beauty contest winner had an article on the subject eighteen years after the event took place?"

"Tell me a little bit more about it," Gelfand answered helpfully.

"I will do that, sir. Are you aware that the *Pioneer Press* ran an article in May 1988 saying that Bess Myerson, former Miss America, former official of New York, was convicted of shoplifting eighteen years earlier? Do you think that's appropriate?"

Gelfand thought Myerson's conviction was different from Johnson's. "In light of her other problems, charges in federal court of a felony, I don't think it's that serious, particularly since it happened so long ago. Would I have published it? Yes, because she is a public figure."

"And certainly the lieutenant governor of Minnesota also is a public figure, isn't she?"

"She is a public figure, correct."

"And are you aware, Mr. Gelfand, that the information in this story on Ms. Myerson also came from confidential sources?"

"Well, I don't think that counsel has the story of the *New York Daily News*, do you, counsel?"

"Yes, I do."

I had sent away for the original article in the *New York Daily News*.

"I'll take counsel's word for it that it was a confidential source."

Needless to say, neither the *Pioneer Press* nor the *New York Daily News* nor the *Star Tribune* identified or criticized the source of the information on Myerson's shoplifting conviction.

Fitzmaurice and Hannah tried to get the judge to squelch questioning on these articles. Hannah charged that I was "inflaming the jury" with the ball and chain cartoon. I responded that "there is a distinction between the treatment they gave to these Miss Minnesota USA candidates from the treatment they gave to Ms. Johnson. They're attempting to say that there was something wrong in revealing Ms. Johnson's shoplifting conviction, where we can do it for these Miss Minnesota candidates. It's not only the right thing to do, but there's good reason for it." Judge Knoll permitted the questions.

The Miss Minnesota articles and cartoons resonated in at least two ways. First, they discredited the *Star Tribune*'s argument that shoplifting is trivial. Second, they showed the jury that the newspaper, contrary to its pose as a gallant defender of women like Johnson from attack, could be brutal in assaulting women not so favored. I thought the women on the jury would identify more with the Miss Minnesota candidates than with a politician.

The *Star Tribune*'s disparate treatment of a preferred politician and less favored, ordinary middle-class people was not limited to beauty contest winners. The newspapers had repeatedly claimed that the disclosure of Johnson's court records had "smeared" her. I confronted Gelfand with one of his columns from February 1988. Gelfand was responding to the complaint of a scrap iron dealer, another occupation not of the wine-and-brie sort, that the paper had harmed him by publicizing a conviction of some long past offense. Gelfand said, "I detect no smear in recalling one's criminal record."

In questioning by Fitzmaurice, Gelfand raised the issue of exclusivity. "When you give the same information to more than one reporter," said Gelfand rhetorically, "is it still confidential?" The newspapers had argued that promises of confidentiality are not binding unless the particular newspaper is given the information exclusively, so that it will have a scoop. Neither Sturdevant nor Salisbury, though, had asked Cohen to agree to exclusivity before he or she would give him the promise of confidentiality.

Moreover, I had several articles where the *Star Tribune* and *Pioneer Press* had honored promises of confidentiality to sources who had given the same information to other news organizations. I started to ask Gelfand questions about stories published a few weeks before the trial, on the same day, in the *Star Tribune* and *Pioneer Press* about a former Minnesota congressman named Gerry Sikorski. Both articles contained anonymous attacks on Sikorski by the same former staff members of his office. Despite the fact that the sources gave their information to both newspapers, the *Star Tribune* and *Pioneer Press* honored their promises to these sources.

Gelfand demanded to see the Sikorski articles. To my chagrin, I could not instantly find the articles in my file boxes.

"Your honor," I pleaded, "may I have just a moment?"

"Well I'll tell you," said Judge Knoll, "you can't. You can look for those exhibits at a break. We can't take five minutes between each question."

There would be no break for quite some time. I had to improvise. I took another approach with the next question to Gelfand.

"Let's hold that in abeyance for the time being. Are you saying that if your newspaper had the story about Marlene Johnson's shoplifting conviction on an exclusive basis—that the *Pioneer Press* did not have the story, WCCO did not have the story, the Associated Press did not have the story—are you saying that then the newspaper should have honored its promise to Mr. Cohen?"

"I would have been inclined to have done so."

Gelfand's answer was almost too good to be true.

"So then the real issue we're talking about here is the issue of commercial advantage, competitive advantage to a newspaper, having a scoop, not the issue of a campaign dirty trick, as has been charged by your counsel. The only reason justifying your newspaper's identification of Mr. Cohen was not any moral reason, not any ethical reason, but merely the fact that you did not have that information on an exclusive basis and that you did not have a scoop on your opposing newspapers."

"The other issues remained, but as I said, I would have been inclined to have gone ahead and used the story without the source if I had it exclusively."

This was one of the key exchanges in the trial.

Gelfand's testimony stripped the *Star Tribune* of its robes as moral guardian for the electorate. It exposed the newspaper's true motive in breaking its promise—to punish the source not for a political "dirty trick" but for thwarting the newspaper's pursuit, for commercial advantage, of a scoop over rival media organizations. The newspapers' witnesses and lawyers would continue to accuse Cohen of dirty tricks, but the attacks would ring hollow.

Not everything in the trial was so dramatic. Three witnesses testified about Cohen's financial losses resulting from being fired. The testimony about all the numbers could glaze over the eyes of anyone who did not love accounting. We prepared a series of charts and graphs to sort out all the figures for the jury.

Patrick Fallon, whose Minneapolis advertising agency had won numerous national awards, testified that neither he nor any other agency could have hired Cohen because of the *Star Tribune* and *Pioneer Press* articles identifying and attacking him. "He was just too hot. It would not have been socially acceptable to do that. I didn't feel I could put him with our clients who were aware of that episode. It would have been the exception of someone who would want to hire or be able to hire him at that time."

I asked, "You found that it would be unacceptable to deal with Mr. Cohen?"

"That was my opinion."

Were it not for his firing and "the cloud placed over him" by these articles, Fallon said, by 1988 Cohen with his abilities would have been earning more than $100,000 a year at Martin-Williams or a similar advertising agency. Cohen was making much less than that from his one-man advertising and public relations office.

David Printy, the president of a financial planning company and former Minnesota commissioner of economic development, used Fallon's figure to calculate Cohen's financial damages. Printy testified that Cohen's lost income from October 1982 to time of the trial was $187,000 plus $36,000 in interest. Printy projected another $500,000 in future income and pension losses.

Star Tribune managing editor Tim McGuire was the lead witness for the newspapers. McGuire testified that before Cohen came along, "I had never considered" breaking a promise of confidentiality.

McGuire said it was appropriate here because this was what he called a "double-barreled" story with "two points that have to be made simultaneously to the reader." The "newsworthiness" of the Wheelock Whitney campaign's "eleventh hour campaign maneuver just before the election" was "at least as important" as Johnson's conviction. Naming Cohen was more newsworthy because, he said, "there was no current context for unveiling the twelve-year-old information."

Then why not just make a veiled reference to the source as a person having some connection with the Whitney campaign, without naming Cohen? That would not do, said McGuire, because Whitney and his campaign officials denied having anything to do with the disclosures. "The Whitney campaign is denying it, and the reader is left scratching her [sic] head wondering what in the heck is going on. It seriously leaves the reader hanging."

What about not running the story at all, like WCCO-TV? That could not have been done either, said McGuire. The *Star Tribune* "inevitably would have been accused of covering up for the Perpich campaign."

According to McGuire, the newspaper simply had to identify Cohen to "level with its readers."

Of course, by far the most "newsworthy" aspect of the whole affair was the *Star Tribune*'s violation of its reporter's promise to a source. The *Star Tribune* article, however, made no mention of the making or the dishonoring of the promise.

In cross-examination I asked, "Mr. McGuire, you said that you had to 'level with the reader,' and that's why you had to identify Mr. Cohen."

"Yeah, that's what I said."

"What we have here is not only a double-barreled story," I replied, "but a triple-barreled story. Indeed, the triple barrel is more important than the other two, and that is the dishonoring of the promise of your reporter. In that very long article there is no mention of the promise to Cohen, is there, Mr. McGuire?"

"No, there's not."

"And this is the first situation where you or the editors of the newspaper had dishonored the promise of a reporter?"

"Yes, it was my first time, that's right."

"So you weren't really leveling with the reader on that issue, were you, Mr. McGuire?"

"Not on that disclosure, and I regret that," McGuire answered.

There was nothing especially "newsworthy" about anonymous revelations late in political campaigns, either. I asked McGuire, "It is true, is it not, that while you were managing editor there have been several *Star Tribune* articles with revelations late in political campaigns?"

"Not in campaigns of this magnitude, but perhaps there have been."

I reminded him of the Lori Sturdevant article from confidential sources that so angered Robert Mattson. "Here is an example of a revelation very late in a campaign involving troubles going back over a period of several years where your editor confronts an accusation and says that this is valuable information for the readers."

"Yeah, in this case."

"In that case."

"In this particular case, that's right."

"We're talking about particular cases here. Let's take some more particular cases here, too, Mr. McGuire."

I then brought up a *Star Tribune* article published less than two months before the trial. The article, about a 1988 suburban school board candidate, which the newspaper printed only three days before the election, carried the headline "Candidate Was Accused of Sex Harassment." The charges had been made five years earlier and then dropped. The *Star Tribune* did not identify any person who provided the information but merely referred to the source as "court records." The candidate lost the election.

"So there your newspaper is providing information which is valuable to readers even though it appeared only three days before an election?"

"I can't speak to that."

David Hall, the *Pioneer Press* executive editor in 1982, was that newspaper's lead witness. He took responsibility for the *Pioneer Press* decision to identify Cohen. He did so immediately after learning from Hennes of Salisbury's promise. "Honestly, I don't think that we ever considered doing it another way other than using his name."

"You didn't consult at all with Mr. Salisbury?"

"That's right."

"And the decision was made rather quickly, wasn't it, sir?"

"The decision was made in a small amount of time. Yes, it was made quickly."

The reason, Hall said, was that "the readers needed to know the total circumstances under which that information was being made available. I felt very strongly about that then; I do now." As with the *Star Tribune*, the "total circumstances" did not include reporting that the *Pioneer Press* had made and violated a promise of confidentiality to Cohen.

I continued the cross-examination of Hall. "We're going to be talking about your obligation to your readers for completeness and accuracy under your criterion. Should your article not have mentioned that Cohen was promised confidentiality by your reporter and that he did not provide the material to you until he received that promise?"

"I don't think it should have been in the article, no."

"So the readers and the public don't have the right to know that the newspaper broke its promise to Mr. Cohen?"

"I don't think that it was particularly relevant in the article."

I reread to Hall, and more importantly the jury, the *Pioneer Press* editorial "Relevant Disclosures."

"You are aware of this editorial, you approved of this editorial?"

"I did not have anything to do with that editorial. The editorial page editor reported to Mr. Finnegan, not to me. I ran the news operation."

"Mr. Finnegan was above you, then, sir."

"That's right."

Mr. Finnegan would testify later.

More than McGuire or Hall, the newspapers' lawyers had planned that

David Floren, Cohen's 1982 supervisor at Martin-Williams and in 1988 the president of the company, would be their star witness. It was not something they wanted me to know about.

A few weeks before the trial, I phoned Floren to try to get some indication of his feelings about the case. I was worried that he was on the newspapers' witness list. Martin-Williams had booted Cohen out the day the newspapers identified him and the company. I did not expect to hear much in the way of good wishes for my client. The passage of six years, though, seemed to have healed the wounds with Martin-Williams. In fact, to my surprise, Floren was quite friendly. "Please give regards to Dan. I wish Dan well. I don't want to do anything to hurt him. He did good work for us. But please don't involve me in the trial. The company wouldn't want the publicity." Floren said that none of the newspapers' lawyers had contacted him. Of course, they still could drag him in with a subpoena. Whatever, Floren assured me, there was nothing to worry about.

Floren was scheduled to testify on the afternoon of July 15, after the usual hour and a half lunch break. I never could afford the time to have lunch. This day, especially, it was good that I stayed at work. Going through my briefcase after everyone else had left the courtroom, I discovered to my horror that I did not have Floren's pretrial deposition. My God, had I lost it? I hurried home in the 100-plus degree heat to look for the document. It was too hot even for my dog to bestir himself to greet me. Fortunately, the deposition was on top of a stack of *Cohen* papers. Drenched in perspiration, I staggered back to the courthouse.

Floren arrived in the courtroom just after my return. Waiting for him were three newspaper lawyers—Pat, Fitzmaurice, and Hannah. The four were laughing and joking like old pals. Pat had a wicked grin. Floren averted his eyes from me. It was all too obvious that Floren would be anything but a recalcitrant witness for the newspapers. From what I was able to overhear, Pat and the others, through stealth, had painstakingly prepared Floren's testimony to do maximum damage to Cohen. It was to be, they hoped, an ambush.

After some banter, the three lawyers and Floren left the courtroom to find somewhere else to go over his presentation out of my earshot. At least the cat was out of the bag. I had some warning of what was to come minutes later.

Over the phone, Floren expressed concern for Cohen's welfare. On the stand, however, Floren turned nasty.

Again, Fitzmaurice rather than Pat asked the questions in court. Floren, responding to Fitzmaurice's guidance, began with an unflattering assessment of Cohen's work for Martin-Williams in 1982. His "productivity level," averred Floren, "was on the wane."

Proceeding to the revelations about Marlene Johnson, Floren declared that he was "stunned" when Cohen reported to him, right after providing the court documents to the four news organizations.

"Would you explain to the jury what your concerns were?"

Floren took the cue and turned to the jury as he intoned the mantra of the newspapers. "It was just plain distasteful. It was a campaign dirty trick." Worse, Cohen was "proud of what he had done."

"How about the concerns you had relative to the firm?"

"All of a sudden, one of our members had done something that could be characterized as not a very neat thing to do. This was an employee of ours, and we obviously became concerned about whether that would reflect on our own reputation."

The next day, when the newspapers published their articles naming Cohen and also his employer, said Floren, the president of the company summoned Cohen to a "hot, very heated meeting" in the course of which he shouted, "How could you have done this?"

After all this, Floren claimed that the firm did not fire Cohen that day; he resigned. According to him, Cohen said at the end of the meeting, "Well, if you feel that way about it, I have no choice but to resign." Whereupon, continued Floren, Cohen and the firm agreed to a $12,000 severance payment.

Finally, Floren disputed my experts' analysis of Cohen's financial losses. Using figures in a salary survey by an advertising industry group, he declared that it was "not likely at all" that Cohen would have been earning $100,000 annually at Martin-Williams if he had remained there. "If he were still there and performing adequately, it would be between sixty and seventy."

Floren's testimony was the most destructive of any witness for the newspapers. One could argue that the editors of the *Star Tribune* and *Pioneer Press* were trying to save their own hides. Cohen's former employer did not have such an obviously selfish motive. But Floren was just too enthusiastic in beating up his former employee. There was a mean-spirited edge to his testimony suggesting that the support of the state's biggest newspapers by the head of a major advertising agency was far from disinterested.

Floren was not through, however. It was time for cross-examination. I began with each adverse witness by offering a "good morning" or "good afternoon." How the witness responded to that simple greeting gave me a pretty good gauge of how he or she would perform on the stand.

"Good afternoon, Mr. Floren."

Floren did not answer and just looked down at the floor.

"Mr. Floren, do you recall a telephone conversation we had a few weeks ago?"

"Yes, I do."

"Do you recall saying that Mr. Cohen had indeed performed well at Martin-Williams?"

"I don't recall saying that."

"Would you recall what you said in your deposition taken earlier in this case?"

"I don't know. It's been a long time."

"Let me show you, sir. The question was, 'Was his performance satisfactory as far as Martin-Williams was concerned?' And what did you say, sir?"

"I said, 'On the whole, yes.' "

"You were aware, were you not, Mr. Floren, that the work that Mr. Cohen was doing for the Whitney campaign was being billed to Martin-Williams?"

"It seemed to me there was a two-way deal going on there, part of it attributable to Martin-Williams and part of it to Mr. Cohen."

"It is true, is it not, that during the last couple of months of the Whitney campaign of 1982, $3,438 were billed from Martin-Williams to the Whitney campaign for the work that Mr. Cohen had done for the campaign?"

"I don't know," Floren said.

I then introduced into evidence a copy of a report of the Whitney campaign to the state of Minnesota that detailed the billings of Martin-Williams for Cohen's work. Fitzmaurice interjected, "We don't dispute this. Mr. Floren does not dispute this."

"Mr. Floren," I asked, "You've had several meetings with counsel for defendants in this case, have you not?"

"Yes."

"And they counseled you, did they not, to use the word 'dirty trick?' "

"No."

"Well, Mr. Floren, despite the fact that you have alleged this was the case in relation to the activities of the Whitney campaign, you still accepted the money from the Whitney campaign, did you not, sir?"

"I guess that is true," Floren admitted.

All the sanctimony, then, over the so-called dirty trick did not stop Martin-Williams, like the *Star Tribune* and *Pioneer Press*, from profiting by it.

Then I turned to the issue of Cohen's potential income had he remained with Martin-Williams. The report that Floren had used to claim that Cohen would have been earning much less than $100,000 had he remained at Martin-Williams in fact showed that Cohen could have had a salary of as much as $150,000. Patrick Fallon was conservative in his projections.

Floren was a not very friendly competitor of Fallon, who had been an executive at Martin-Williams until he formed his own agency. I wanted to get Floren himself to verify Fallon's qualifications.

"Mr. Fallon is a highly respected, highly honored member of the advertising community in Minneapolis, is he not, sir?"

"Yes," Floren said.

"And his firm has won more advertising awards in recent years than any other firm in the entire country, has it not, sir?"

"I believe that's true."

"And Mr. Fallon's firm has advanced at a faster rate than any other advertising firm in the country, is that not true, sir?"

"I think it's true."

"And therefore, would you agree that Mr. Fallon is indeed qualified to address the jury on this subject?"

"I suspect he is."

I then turned to Floren's claim that Martin-Williams did not fire Cohen.

"Is it the habit of Martin-Williams to make severance payments of $12,000 to people who resign from the company?"

"No."

"And it has never been done, has it?"

"I don't think it has."

"And it isn't the practice of Martin-Williams to tell people who resign that they have to vacate the office the next day, is it?"

"It wouldn't be the usual case, no."

"And it also is not the usual case for persons who resign from Martin-Williams to find themselves subjected, a couple of days later, to newspaper articles containing criticism from their former employer. You don't generally do that to people who resign, do you, sir?"

"No."

I showed Floren a letter from Martin-Williams to Cohen stating, "As a matter of record, you were terminated October 29, 1982."

"You don't generally use the words 'you were terminated' to describe a person who resigned voluntarily, do you?"

"I suppose not."

Finally, I wanted to deflate Floren's pretensions of shock at Cohen's conduct rather than at having his firm named in the *Star Tribune*.

"It is true that after Mr. Cohen had supplied these materials to the newspapers, he did tell you about this?"

"Yes."

"And you did not make any objection to Mr. Cohen at the time?"

"Right."

"And indeed, that entire day and that entire evening, you did not contact Mr. Cohen, seek him out in any way to express any displeasure whatsoever?"

"That's right."

"And the only time that displeasure was expressed to Mr. Cohen was after the *Star Tribune* came out with its article identifying not only Mr. Cohen but also identifying Martin-Williams. Is that not correct?"

"Correct."

Floren had been buoyant, even insouciant, as he entered the court-room, but he was not smiling when he left the witness stand. His eyes were fixed on the floor, and he would not look at Cohen or me as he walked out of the courtroom. Floren would have been better off following his original advice of avoiding the trial. Still, the specter of Cohen's former employer coming into court to condemn him could not be helpful.

Meeting Megan Carter

SOME OF THE most important testimony came from the top editors of the *Star Tribune* and *Pioneer Press*. That was to be expected. What was less anticipated was that much of it turned out to be helpful to the newspapers' opponent in the case.

One of the editors had his own disagreement with the way the newspapers reacted to Cohen's disclosures. I had met Ron Clark, the *Pioneer Press* editorial page editor, when I was running for Minnesota attorney general in 1982. His newspaper did not endorse me, but Clark impressed me as a straight shooter.

"Good morning, Mr. Clark."

"Good morning, Mr. Rothenberg," Clark answered with a smile. I could tell then that he would be an honest and cooperative witness.

Clark testified that he was responsible for everything that went into the *Pioneer Press* editorial pages, although assistant publisher John Finnegan had the authority to overrule him.

I then recited again the text of the October 29, 1982, editorial, "Relevant Disclosures." It was the best antidote to the "dirty tricks" charges. I took every opportunity in the trial to pound it in and impress upon the jurors that something repeated so many times must be very important.

"Did you approve that editorial, and Mr. Finnegan approved that editorial as well?"

"Yes," Clark answered.

"And that editorial, then, became the position of the *Pioneer Press*?"

"That's the editorial opinion of the paper, yes."

The newspapers' expert witness, David Lawrence, was the publisher of the *Detroit Free Press*, owned by Knight Ridder Publications, which also owned the *Pioneer Press*.

"Just so the jury understands, what is Knight Ridder?" Fitzmaurice asked.

"Knight Ridder," Lawrence replied, "is a very big communications company with annual revenues somewhere in the territory of 2.2 billion dollars."

Fitzmaurice blanched. Lawrence gave the jury a little too much understanding about Knight Ridder.

In response to Fitzmaurice's question about his opinion of the newspapers' actions, Lawrence said, "My personal definition of good journalism suggests that the stories that ran were reasonable and with honor."

"How about, as another option, a veiled source? By that I mean," said Fitzmaurice, "phrases like 'individuals close to the campaign,' 'a party partisan,' or something of that sort?"

As Ismach had testified, that would enable the newspapers to inform readers of a source's motivations without breaking an agreement of confidentiality. Even that was not good enough for Lawrence.

"I would be disinclined to take that route. A full and fair and complete story would tell readers who the source is."

Fitzmaurice asked Lawrence, "In your professional opinion, would it be a viable option to disclosing the name of the source to kill the story?"

"There could well be a number of acceptable right answers, depending on the person, and one of those options could be simply not run the story."

That was another answer by Lawrence more helpful to me than to Fitzmaurice.

In my cross-examination of Lawrence, the $2 billion figure was too good to let pass. "Your newspaper and the *Pioneer Press* are part of a newspaper empire with an income of 2.2 billion dollars a year," I reminded the jury.

"I don't think I'd use the term 'newspaper empire.' I think I used the words 'a big communications company with annual revenue of about 2.2 billion dollars.' " Lawrence helpfully repeated the figure.

"An income of about 2.2 billion is or is not an empire. The salient point is this, Mr. Lawrence. You're not here appearing as a disinterested expert witness on this case, but you're appearing on behalf of your employer, which is also the employer of the *Pioneer Press*."

It was comeuppance, and mild at that, for the aspersions on Ismach. Lawrence turned beet red.

"You're exactly wrong. The most important thing I own is my integrity, and it's not for sale to anyone."

"The fact here," I replied, "is that the newspapers do not deny that promises of confidentiality were made and not kept. You never faced a situation like that, sir, in your newspaper."

"I can't recall of one, no, sir."

"Do you feel that the article in the *Star Tribune* gave a full, fair, and complete story?"

"It was a reasonable attempt under the exigencies of the moment."

"And a full, fair, and complete story should tell all the facts."

"Not exactly," said Lawrence. "All the pertinent and relevant facts."

"Don't you think that it was a pertinent and relevant fact that a reporter had made a promise of confidentiality to obtain certain information which was the subject of the story and that promise was dishonored by the editors?"

"It is arguably relevant, yes, sir."

"Was there any mention in the story of the breach of the promise?"

"No, sir."

"So if you were the editor," I said, "you would not have done it in the same way as the *Star Tribune*."

"No, sir."

"Surely there is a general principle within the journalistic profession about the necessity of keeping one's word?"

"I certainly think that one of the guiding principles of a good society is integrity, yes, sir."

"And that principle was not followed by the newspapers, is that not correct?"

"That particular guiding principle, yes, sir."

After Lawrence got off the stand, Hannah sighed. "Why can't these guys just answer the questions and shut up?"

The next local editor was not nearly as friendly as Ron Clark. As the executive editor of the lead defendant in the case, Joel Kramer, more than anyone else, called the shots on the newspapers' strategy and tactics.

Despite all the intensity of the dispute over the right of newspapers to break contracts, the trial had been free of personal rancor directed against the attorneys for each side. At times it sounded like a Harvard Law School seminar debate over the components and limits of freedom of the press.

Because Kramer had nothing to do with the events that started the litigation, not having started work at the *Star Tribune* until March 1983, one might have expected him to be even more dispassionate about the matter.

Indeed, not having the need to save his own face, Kramer was in a perfect position to engineer a settlement of the case before it reached trial. It would have been the rational thing to do.

Yet, more than anyone else at the newspapers, Kramer brought a truculence and, worse, a personal animus to the case. He manifested that as early as the time I began representing Cohen, with his 1986 letter to the *Columbia Journalism Review*.

I had told the jury in the opening statement that I possessed a tape recording of Mr. Kramer talking about confidential sources a month earlier to a meeting of investigative reporters and editors. Fitzmaurice protested. On the day scheduled for Kramer's testimony, I placed a tape recorder on my table so that everyone in the courtroom could see it. Kramer and Fitzmaurice knew that I would hit Kramer with his comments at the seminar. No one in the courtroom could have been surprised.

The confrontation with Joel Kramer would be a dramatic peak of the trial. There was a palpable tension when he approached the witness chair and took his oath to tell the truth. If anyone was an unwilling and hostile witness, it was Kramer. The formality of language in questions and answers did little to conceal our less than warm feelings for each other. I began the questions.

"You are aware that one of the options for editors, if their reporters obtain information after a promise of confidentiality and the editors don't like that information, is to simply not run the story."

"That is true," Kramer agreed.

"And, in fact, if you were faced with such a situation as editor, you would regard the best option—indeed, the only option for an editor to take rather than violate a promise of confidentiality—would be simply not to run the story."

"No, that's not true."

"It's true, is it not, Mr. Kramer, that you said in response to a question at a public meeting, 'I hope that my solution would be not to run the story. I hope that I would have the courage not to run the story' "?

"I said at that meeting that a promise of confidentiality was not an absolute in my mind and that the only absolute in our business was not to mislead the readers. I did, in answer to a hypothetical, say that in that hypothetical case that was presented to me, I would hope not to run it.

There are some cases in which I would hope not to run it, and other cases in which I would."

"Your honor, may we approach to run a tape, please?"

Fitzmaurice objected. For the next fifteen minutes, Fitzmaurice and I argued about whether I should be allowed to play the tape. All the while, the jurors were wondering what was on the tape and what Mr. Kramer was afraid of. Kramer had helped dramatize and magnify the importance of something they otherwise might have ignored.

Judge Knoll ruled that I should ask the question again and give Kramer another opportunity to answer.

"Mr. Kramer, if I may ask the question again, in answer to a question from a reporter which went as follows: Do you inform . . ."?

Fitzmaurice objected again. "I object to the form of the question. If he is going to give a verbatim quote to the question, I think that ought to be the way it's phrased."

That was exactly what I was trying to do.

"The question is as follows: 'Do you inform reporters that you can unilaterally revoke promises of confidentiality?' Answer: 'I have never done that. I hope that I would have the courage not to run the story.' "

Before I could continue, Kramer retorted, "What are you asking me?"

"Did you say that at the meeting, sir?"

"I could have said it. I recall saying that in answer to a question, yes."

"And interestingly enough," I asked, "the name of the panel where you gave this presentation was 'The Sins of Investigative Reporting,' wasn't that right?"

"Yes."

Next I introduced, over the objections of Fitzmaurice, *Star Tribune* editorials and articles from July 1972 regarding disclosures of mental illness of Thomas Eagleton, the original Democratic vice presidential nominee for 1972. One of the editorials was titled "Let the People Have the Facts."

"Mr. Kramer, there were disclosures that Senator Eagleton had had treatments for some nervous disorders several years earlier, and as a result of those disclosures Senator Eagleton was forced out as a vice presidential candidate, correct?"

"Yes."

"And there were no crimes charged to Senator Eagleton, it was merely having some treatment for nervous disorders, an illness is what it was, wasn't it?"

"Yes."

I then read excerpts from two *Star Tribune* editorials.

We disagree with suggestions that Eagleton's mental and emotional problems be soft-pedaled or glossed over, whether the suggestions come from Democrats or Republicans and regardless of the motivation. In short, we would welcome disclosure of all the medical records and background concerning Eagleton. . . .

Voters have every right to know the physical and mental qualifications of their candidates for president and vice president. Rumors about Eagleton's problems have been heard in the Senate for some time. These rumors persisted even at the convention, but no thorough check was made.

I resumed questioning of Kramer. "It is true, is it not, that the original revelation of Senator Eagleton's treatments came from rumors from undisclosed sources?"

"I don't know. I don't remember."

I then read from a July 26, 1972, *Star Tribune* article.

The officials who invariably asked that their comments not be attributed to them by name said two rumors about Eagleton had been spreading across Capitol Hill since George McGovern chose Eagleton as his runningmate. The first was that Eagleton had been hospitalized for a nervous condition, and the second was that he had a drinking problem.

"Your newspaper took the position that the people have the right to have the facts, and in these editorials there was no criticism of the persons who provided the information on Senator Eagleton's illness several years earlier."

"I heard what you read."

"Well, do you see any criticism in the editorial, Mr. Kramer?"

"I'm not saying there is any. You asked me if I knew there wasn't, and I didn't read the whole editorial."

"Now, Mr. Kramer, the *Star Tribune* has many articles on a daily basis in which there are anonymous and confidential sources, is that not correct?"

"Yes."

"And in fact, it's really a way of life of the newspaper to make use of confidential sources."

"Yes, we try to reduce the amount and discourage it, but it is part of the business and it occurs every day."

"You continue to use confidential sources?"

"Yes."

"And you do get a lot of stories from confidential sources that you would otherwise not have. That's correct, isn't it?"

"Yes," Kramer agreed.

"And in the newspaper you can find politicians attacking other politicians with their names anonymous."

"Our policy is not to have anonymous attacks on other individuals. I'm not telling you it's never happened, but that's the policy."

"If I were to represent to you that I have several examples here which I could show to you which contain examples of politicians remaining anonymous and criticizing other politicians, would you accept that this is in fact done in the *Star Tribune?*"

"Yeah, but I would distinguish between criticizing and attacking," Kramer answered. "I know it happens, but we do have a policy against people defaming other people anonymously."

"Would you please define 'defame'? Doesn't defame mean when somebody tells a lie about someone else?"

"No. Not in the sense in which I would use it, because we don't always know that it's a lie at the time we're printing it. If someone says something that will have a negative impact on another person's reputation, we don't like that to be an anonymous statement."

"Was it defaming Senator Biden, Mr. Kramer, to quote unidentified sources to the effect that twenty years earlier, when he was going to college or law school, he committed plagiarism?"

"Well, it certainly didn't do his reputation any good."

"But you ran those stories, did you not, Mr. Kramer?"

Kramer nodded his head.

"And was it defaming Judge Douglas Ginsburg to print stories, again from anonymous sources, to the effect that many years earlier, he had smoked marijuana while teaching law school without ever being convicted of a crime?"

"It certainly was damaging to his reputation."

"And you ran those stories, did you not, sir?"

"Uh-huh."

"And was it defaming the two Miss Minnesota USA candidates to run stories referring to the shoplifting arrests and a conviction of the second Miss Minnesota candidate when she was a teenager?"

"Obviously stories like this story were damaging to her reputation."

"As a matter of fact, Mr. Kramer, you do have the option in any story involving a confidential source criticizing another person, you have the option simply to excise that, do you not?"

"Of course."

"But still you ran these stories."

"We run some and we don't run others."

I then got out two articles about the 1988 presidential campaign, one from the New York Times and the other from the Star Tribune that ostensibly reprinted it but selectively omitted two paragraphs about other newspapers' treatment of promises of confidentiality. The New York Times article concerned an anonymous attack video in Iowa regarding documented plagiarism by Senator Joseph Biden, who at the time was seeking the Democratic presidential nomination. A flap ensued. Biden charged that the Michael Dukakis campaign produced the video. The New York Times and the Des Moines Register had promised confidentiality to the source and did not reveal his name. After first denying the Biden charge, Dukakis admitted that his campaign chairman, John Sasso, was responsible for it.

My questioning of Kramer continued.

"When you get national stories from the New York Times or wire services, occasionally you delete portions which the Star Tribune would not like to run. Is that correct?"

"We edit stories from other sources, yes, for whatever reason."

"In a story run a few months ago regarding a famous flap between Michael Dukakis and the Biden campaign over an alleged attack video, did you not delete from the New York Times story that you ran in the Star Tribune two quotations, one from the editor of the Des Moines Register and one from an editor of the New York Times, quotations saying that these editors would not violate promises of confidentiality and would not disclose their confidential sources. You did delete that, did you not, sir?"

"I have no idea."

Fitzmaurice objected to these questions. Judge Knoll overruled the objection.

"Mr. Kramer, if I were to represent to you that an October 1, 1987, article in the Star Tribune, 'Two Top Aides Quit Dukakis Campaign in Flap over Biden Tape,' which was identified as coming from the New York Times, did not include a couple of paragraphs in that article of the New York Times of the same date, as follows:

Asked about Gov. Dukakis's announcement, Jim Gannon, editor of the Des Moines Register, said: "My position is I do not comment on our sources to whom we have granted any degree of anonymity. And regardless of what anyone else might say, we hold to promises of confidentiality."

Craig R. Whitney, Washington bureau chief for the *New York Times*, said: "We don't discuss our sources."

Fitzmaurice interrupted and objected again. Judge Knoll again overruled the objection. Objecting to testimony can be very dangerous if the judge does not go along. Unsuccessful objections just succeed in highlighting for the jury what is important and potentially damaging to your case.

At the end, Kramer admitted, "We always edit the stories. I'll take his word for it."

The *Des Moines Register*'s refusal to deviate from the principle of honoring promises—and the *Star Tribune*'s deletion of its statement from the *New York Times* article—was particularly pertinent. The *Register* used to be owned by the same corporation, Cowles Media Company, that owned the *Star Tribune*. Editor McGuire called the *Register* the *Star Tribune*'s "ex-sister newspaper."

As it happened, at the time of the trial the *Star Tribune* was running full-page advertisements promoting a new international news section of the newspaper, called "World Nation Extra." Much of the ad consisted of a reprint of an article by a senior reporter about Panamanian dictator Manuel Noriega. The reprinted article was filled with numerous references to anonymous sources. Not only was the *Star Tribune* not discouraging confidential sources, it was touting articles relying upon them. I had both the advertisement and the original article.

Fitzmaurice objected. After a several-minute exchange before Judge Knoll, I resumed questioning Kramer.

"Mr. Kramer, you regard it as important, do you not, for the newspaper to have confidential sources and to rely upon confidential sources for much of its news stories?"

"No, not for much, but we do use confidential sources. We attempt to discourage them wherever possible."

"You recall that one-third to one-half of that full-page ad contained the first page of an article by William Beecher?"

"Uh-huh."

"It is true that the article which comprises about one-third of the page of the ad, that that article contains several confidential sources, does it not?"

"Yeah. Well, they're unnamed in the part of the article that I saw."

"So they're unnamed sources."

"Uh-huh."

"It is true, is it not, that Mr. Beecher in his many articles for the *Star Tribune* makes liberal use of confidential sources?"

"Yes, he does."

Other than this case, the *Star Tribune* gave high priority and devoted considerable resources to protecting confidential sources from disclosure.

I asked, "You're a strong supporter of shield laws, aren't you, Mr. Kramer?"

"Yes."

"And is it considered that journalists have to have the right to avoid compelled disclosure of their sources to ensure the public has a free flow of information?"

"Yes."

"It is true that you told the panel, 'The Sins of Investigative Reporting,' that lawyers for your company spend more time in court about protecting sources than about anything else."

"I don't remember saying that."

"Do you deny saying that?"

"No."

At the end, Kramer got in the "dirty trick" theme again. "The issue of exclusivity relates to the issue of whether what Cohen was doing constituted a so-called dirty trick by the campaign, or last-minute effort to release damaging information about an opponent, and the degree to which that was shared with a large number of people was a factor in making the judgment."

"You are aware that the mere fact of not having information on an exclusive basis is not a justification for breaking a promise?"

"By itself, that is correct."

"And you're aware also of Mr. Gelfand's comment that the reason for breaking the promise was not any dirty trick but the fact that you did not have it on an exclusive basis."

Fitzmaurice objected, "That's a misstatement of the evidence."

Judge Knoll ruled, "The jury will determine what Mr. Gelfand said or didn't say."

So Kramer's testimony finished by allowing me to reiterate Gelfand's admission.

Kramer left the stand with a visage of disgust.

Kramer's counterpart at the *Pioneer Press* was Deborah Howell. Howell was the managing editor of the St. Paul paper in 1982 and had previously been an editor and reporter with the *Star Tribune*. I had to be more gentle in the manner of asking questions than with Kramer and other male witnesses. The prospect of Fitzmaurice and Hannah telling the jury that both Cohen and his attorney were beating up on women called for caution.

Howell admitted that Marlene Johnson was a personal friend but claimed that Hall, and not she, made the decision to break Salisbury's promise to Cohen.

In the trial, as in 1982, the newspapers were disparaging the disclosure of Johnson's supposedly inconsequential conviction for shoplifting. Yet, apart from that special case, the *Pioneer Press*, like the *Star Tribune*, had no qualms about exposing the perpetrators of crimes, no matter how unknown and obscure. For Howell's testimony, I had collected many examples of a weekly *Pioneer Press* column that published the names and addresses of every county resident convicted of ordinary or petty misdemeanors, including shoplifting.

Howell could not deny that her newspaper routinely gave more coverage to the petty misdemeanors of ordinary people than to the offenses of the future lieutenant governor of Minnesota.

I then turned to the *Pioneer Press*'s treatment of confidential sources. "Ms. Howell, you've taken the position that you would go to great lengths to protect your confidential sources, is that not correct?"

"Yes."

"Ms. Howell, the *Pioneer Press* from time to time has run stories with revelations late in political campaigns involving confidential sources, is that not correct?"

"Right offhand I can't recall one, but we may have."

I introduced into evidence a *Pioneer Press* article and editorial published a week before the 1978 election that exposed derogatory financial data concerning former Governor Wendell Anderson, who was running for the Senate. Someone promised anonymity gave documents about Anderson to a *Pioneer Press* reporter. The newspaper did not break its promise to the source and referred to him or her only as "a source who does not wish to be identified." The *Pioneer Press* editorial, titled "Mountain or Volcano in Audit Papers," congratulated itself for getting the "leaks" and what it called "a remarkable job in sketching out the story through tough reporting." Anderson lost the election.

Paul Hannah objected to allowing the jury to see the articles. Judge Knoll overruled the objection.

I also had a tape of Howell speaking at the same meeting of investigative reporters as Kramer. Howell had said that the broken promises to Cohen were unique in her journalistic experience. Howell, though, was less recalcitrant to acknowledge what she had said there.

"Ms. Howell, you said about the Cohen case that you know of no other comparable case in your twenty-seven years of journalism, is that not correct?"

"Yes."

Editors Hall and Clark had called John Finnegan the final authority over what went into the Pioneer Press. Finnegan had been the executive editor of the Pioneer Press for twelve years before becoming its vice president. He also was a prolific columnist.

I had read all of Finnegan's essays going back more than fifteen years, mostly on microfilm in the public library, and had amassed a big collection of his writings. It was time well spent. In particular, Finnegan had written many columns about the need to preserve confidentiality of sources. He excoriated judges who had ordered disclosure of confidential sources. He was an outspoken writer and did not mince words.

Finnegan did not equivocate on the witness stand, either.

I began, "Mr. Finnegan, in many of your columns, you've dealt with issues concerning confidential sources, haven't you, sir?"

"Yes."

"And you've dealt with issues regarding protection for reporters, like shield laws or First Amendment protections, for not forcibly revealing sources."

"Yes, that's right."

"You regard the protection of confidential sources as very important, don't you, sir?"

"Yes, I do."

"In one of your columns written a few months before the Dan Cohen case, you referred to the violation of a confidential source as a 'dirty trick,' isn't that correct, sir?"

"I can't remember the exact column, but I may have."

I then introduced as an exhibit for the jury a Finnegan column, titled "Have You Met Megan Carter?," published one year before the Pioneer Press broke its reporter's promise to Cohen. Megan Carter was a fictional reporter in a movie called Absence of Malice. The newspapers' lawyers attempted to block the use of the article. Judge Knoll denied their objection.

This is what Finnegan said in his column.

Carter is a reporter who has no ethics. She is not concerned about accuracy or fairness or integrity. She uses dirty tricks—carries a concealed tape recorder; she violates confidential sources; she allows herself to be used by a politician to attack an innocent man.

She is a tough, unscrupulous woman. I would not hire her.

My questions to Finnegan continued. "You've written several columns on court decisions requiring reporters to disclose their sources and even sending reporters to jail who don't want to reveal their confidential sources, haven't you, sir?"

"Yes."

"And you've always been very opposed to sending a reporter to jail who refuses to disclose his or her sources."

"Yes, in most cases that's true."

"And you've been a strong advocate for the Minnesota shield law, called the Minnesota Free Flow of Information Act."

"Yes."

I then introduced into evidence an August 13, 1978, column by Finnegan that he titled "The Judge Ignored the Law." The newspapers' lawyers objected again. Judge Knoll denied their objection. The article concerned a New Jersey judge's citation of New York Times reporter Myron Farber for contempt for refusing to comply with a court order to disclose to the defendant in the case his confidential sources regarding a murder investigation. Finnegan wrote:

I have heard some criticism of Myron Farber and the New York Times for putting themselves "above the law" in the Dr. X case.

Hogwash.

If anyone has put himself above the law it is the New Jersey judge. He has ignored the New Jersey shield law which provides strong protection for a newsperson to protect his or her confidential sources or notes.

There are some serious First Amendment questions at stake in this case.

Twenty-six states have reporter protection laws (we call it the Free Flow of Information Act in Minnesota). They are especially important in the field of investigative reporting where sources may fear for their lives, their jobs or the safety of their families if their identities were revealed, particularly in highly sensitive cases.

It is clear that unless there is some protection of the right to gather news and protect sources, the quality and flow of news will be seriously impaired.

I then introduced a third Finnegan column, this one published December 24, 1972. The newspapers' lawyers objected again. Judge Knoll denied their objection. Finnegan denounced a court order directing a reporter to divulge a confidential source in the early stages of the Watergate scandal.

This week, a Washington, D.C. federal judge threw a *Los Angeles Times* newsman in jail for several hours because he refused to turn over tapes and notes he took while interviewing a witness in the Watergate bugging case. He argued that the notes were confidential, that they were protected under the First Amendment and that the defense attorney seeking the notes was on a fishing trip.

The judge dismissed the First Amendment argument and made it clear that he didn't believe that forcing newsmen to reveal sources or produce notes and tapes would hamper their ability to gather news.

HIS POSITION IS RIDICULOUS. Of course, the inability of newsmen to protect their confidential sources and unpublished information will affect newsgathering operations. Sources will tend to disappear. Newsmen will be suspect, seen as government informers and investigators.

The actions of many judges border on harassment and intimidation of the media. Their attitudes will stifle the free flow of information to the public. Our democracy depends upon maintaining that flow.

If the courts are going to use their immense powers as irresponsibly as this, then all our freedoms in this nation are in jeopardy. It is not just a newsman's problem. It is YOUR problem. Make no mistake about that.

The First Amendment now seems to be judged by the courts as the lesser of those in the Bill of Rights. And I can't help but point out that whenever a country has lost its freedoms to a dictator of left or right, the first freedom to go has been freedom of the press. And the jails begin filling up with reporters, editors and publishers.

Regarding Finnegan's statement that our democracy depends upon maintaining the flow of information, I asked, "And that would require protecting the rights of reporters not to reveal their confidential sources?"

"That's correct."

I then asked Finnegan if he agreed with the following:

No one who reads a newspaper, watches a television newscast or listens to a radio news program can be unaware of the extent to which today's journalist depends on confidential sources. On any given day, some of what is reported as news would not have come to light were it not for people who talked to reporters on condition that reporters not disclose where they got their information. Because these sources are insiders, they often have something to fear if they talk openly— the loss of their jobs, threats to their safety, or disclosure of their own involvement.

"In fact you wrote those words, didn't you, sir?" I asked Finnegan.

"Well, it was a collaborative effort with. . . ."

Paul Hannah cut him off. Pat still could not get credit for being a coauthor of *Law and Media in the Midwest.*

"Turning to another area," I asked Finnegan, "you have been a strong advocate of open police records, records of arrests, records of convictions, court records. You've been an advocate of maintaining the maximum openness of these records to reporters, haven't you, sir?"

"Yes, I have. You make me sound like a gadfly," Finnegan quipped.

I then introduced a *Pioneer Press* news article of March 13, 1979, with the headline "Bill Would Muzzle Police News." The article concerned a bill introduced by a state senator that Finnegan called the "Mattson amendment." Finnegan referred to the cover-up by local police of the arrest of state auditor Robert Mattson for drunken driving. The bill would have allowed police to restrict the release of arrest information about politicians involved in embarrassing incidents.

Finnegan called the bill "dangerous, a secret police and closed government bill."

"You opposed this, didn't you, sir?"

"Yes, I did."

"You felt that the public ought to have the right to accurate information about their public officials?"

"Yes."

"And you have written or approved many editorials in the *Pioneer Press* with titles like 'Public Records, Not Private Documents,' 'A Law Gone Wild,' 'Encouraging Move Towards Openness.' This has been a major effort of yours, sir, to ensure maximum access of the public and the press to arrest records, to police records, to court records generally."

"Yes, that's correct," Finnegan said.

"And the newspaper, under your direction, has actually gone to court to obtain access to police records, arrest records, court records which various authorities did not want to provide."

"That's correct."

"And you did this because you felt that the public had the right to know what was in these records."

"Yes," Finnegan concurred.

I had to wait until the final day of testimony to get Finnegan on the stand. He had just returned from vacation. The timing turned out to be perfect.

Everything came together in Finnegan's testimony. Nowhere did the duplicity of the newspapers' excuses for breaking their promises to Cohen expose itself more vividly. On the one hand, the newspapers claimed that compelled disclosure of confidential sources will have apocalyptic consequences for freedom of the press and their ability to obtain information. On the other, they demanded, under the same rubric of freedom of the press, a right to voluntarily dishonor promises of confidentiality. On the one hand, they threatened to go to court, if necessary, in the public interest to gain access to arrest records of public officials, no matter how acute the personal embarrassment. On the other hand, they condemned as a "dirty trick" the release of public criminal conviction records implicating a favored politician.

The *Star Tribune* called a former reporter named David Anderson to claim that another participant in the Whitney campaign meeting, former legislator and Hennepin County attorney Gary Flakne, had fingered Cohen as the source of the Johnson revelations on the same day that reporter Sturdevant had promised confidentiality. Because of this independent exposure of Cohen, the claim went, the newspapers no longer were bound by their promises.

Flakne denied the charge of betrayal.

The last witness was Michael Finney, a *Star Tribune* assistant editor who took responsibility for the decision to name Cohen. In response to Fitzmaurice's questions, Finney said the most important factor in his decision was that "the information about who was releasing this information was very newsworthy. From a news point of view, it was very much worthwhile to do."

That gave me one last opportunity to use my file boxes.

"Mr. Finney, do you believe that your readers, under your analysis, should have the right to know who disclosed information in late October 1984 that vice presidential candidate Geraldine Ferraro's parents had been convicted in 1944 of gaming charges in New York?"

"It would depend on the newsworthiness of who let that out."

"Those sources were not revealed. Is that not correct?"

"I have no specific recollection."

An article published in the *Star Tribune* three days before a Minneapolis School Board election in 1987 reported anonymous rumors against a candidate opposed by the newspaper and identified his religion as Catholic. The newspaper did not publicize the religion of any other aspirant for the office. The candidate lost the election and blamed the *Star Tribune* for his defeat.

"And do you feel that your readers ought to have the right to know

the source when charges are made, three days before an election, identifying the religion of a candidate for the Minneapolis School Board as
Catholic?" I asked.

"Again, it would depend on the specific circumstances," said Finney.

Focusing on the issue of religious bigotry against a local Catholic candidate could help with at least one juror. And the Geraldine Ferraro
article showed that the *Star Tribune*, in contrast to its solicitude for Johnson, was not averse to protecting confidential sources who tar other
women politicians with the much more ancient offenses not of themselves
but of their relatives. It didn't hurt that Ferraro was Catholic.

It was a good end to the testimony.

Later, Finney said in a televised panel on confidential sources for the
Society of Professional Journalists that he would not have identified Cohen if he had to do it all over again. By that time he was managing editor
of the *Rocky Mountain News* in Denver.

The testimony went on for almost three weeks. I had no help at the
counsel table. I never had time for lunch because I always spent the lunch
break preparing for the afternoon testimony. Every night I spent several
hours on the phone with the next day's witnesses. Important things were
going on in the world and in the nation outside of the courtroom, but I
was oblivious to all of them.

I got very little sleep. By the end of the trial, I had lost twenty pounds.
My daily runs with my dog, Beechie, helped me retain my sanity.

More than forty witnesses had testified. But perhaps the one most ea-
gerly awaited was conspicuous by her absence. The newspapers had attempted throughout to make the trial a contest between Cohen and their
designated victim, Marlene Johnson. Right to the end, they threatened
to call Johnson as a witness. She never appeared in the courtroom.

At the conclusion of the testimony, the newspapers moved for a directed verdict to dismiss the case before it went to the jury. Fitzmaurice
and Hannah made the same First Amendment and other arguments they
raised in their motion for summary judgment. After a complicated question on First Amendment interpretation from Judge Knoll, Fitzmaurice
asked the judge if Pat could answer.

"Why? Who's speaking for the newspaper?"

"On the issue that you raised, I think she might provide you with a
better insight than I did, and I thought that might be helpful," Fitzmaurice said.

"I'm not going to have double barrels here."

Judge Knoll did not allow her to speak. Pat looked crestfallen. She had not questioned any witnesses. It was her last opportunity to get on the record of the trial, and it was gone.

To no one's surprise, Judge Knoll denied the newspapers' motion. The jury would decide the issues of the trial.

Both sides had prosecuted the case with fervor.

More than two weeks of testimony established without question that the newspapers had made and broken promises to Cohen. That should have been enough to make the newspapers liable for breach of contract. But how would the jurors react to the relentless moral assault on Cohen? Would they, could they, abjure the law of contracts and punish Cohen yet again for a "dirty trick"?

The closing arguments would be decisive for the jurors.

Casting the Attacks into Oblivion

JUDGE KNOLL SET closing arguments for 2 P.M. on Tuesday, July 19. He gave the newspapers' attorneys one hour each for their argument. I would conclude with an hour for my own. Fitzmaurice and Hannah would not have the opportunity for rebuttal.

All the work over so many years—and the potential of a landmark defining the rights and obligations of media organizations—would come down to three hours of speeches in a steamy courtroom.

As the time approached, the little courtroom filled with family members of the lawyers and Cohen, reporters, and any others who could squeeze in. There were not enough seats for everyone. The standing-room-only crowd only heightened the drama.

Judge Knoll entered the courtroom and told the newspapers to begin their argument.

Fitzmaurice went first. The thrust of his argument—that Cohen deserved nothing because he had committed a "dirty trick"—was no surprise by now. Fitzmaurice cleverly wrapped the moral argument in the language of contract law.

"Let's start with the contract proposition," he said. "What is the meeting of the minds? On the one hand we have Lori Sturdevant. She had been a religious reporter and then went on to state politics. She came to the meeting with Cohen with no agenda; she was straightforward, open, honest, nondeceptive.

"Mr. Cohen, on the other hand, brought a different agenda."

Fitzmaurice called the revelations about Johnson "disgraceful, "very sneaky stuff," and "trash."

Even though Lori Sturdevant made a promise of confidentiality to Cohen, there was no contract, proclaimed Fitzmaurice. Why? "Did she know there had been a secret meeting between five very powerful political figures that took place at the Whitney headquarters? All of this trash came to this meeting. This group of individuals sat around and planned and plotted and used it to manipulate the reporter who came to the meeting with a fair, open mind. Is that the sort of thing that you expect to do when you're bargaining for something? On this performance you wouldn't buy anything, and you wouldn't consider that you had entered a contract if that's the circumstance under which it occurred, because there was no legitimate offer, and because there was no consideration, and because there was no meeting of the minds, and because somebody came with a secret agenda and somebody came with an open agenda."

Cohen "extracted the promise" from Sturdevant, who knew nothing of his plot to defeat Marlene Johnson. Had Cohen disclosed his scheme, said Fitzmaurice, Sturdevant would have said, "Wait a minute, hold up before I make a commitment."

Star Tribune editors, according to Fitzmaurice, "did the right thing" in identifying Cohen. "Every single solitary editor that appeared in this trial stood as one on a basic proposition: their aim in life is to present news to the public that is fair and accurate. These people have not committed fraud and misrepresentation.

"Compare that to the meeting where lawyers, the head of the Republican party, and a professor of journalism are sitting around saying 'How can we use this strategically and is it politically expedient?' Did anybody in this whole mess ask, 'What's the right thing to do?' They never asked.

"Mr. Rothenberg is going to get up here and tell you that this was misrepresentation because they granted confidentiality in other cases. The failure to do it in this case was the first time that it had ever been done. It's rare. It's rare that individuals who have integrity of the type that has been demonstrated here do this. But if there was ever a case that screamed out for it, it was this one."

Doing "the right thing," continued Fitzmaurice, meant protecting the political interests of Marlene Johnson, who never did appear at the trial. "They gave Marlene an ample opportunity to explain who she was, what the circumstances were, and you will see that she had come a long way. She was a woman who, at twenty-four, when all of this had happened, had lots of problems. Now she's sitting there on the threshold of the greatest thing in her life, and Cohen and those individuals get together and come up with a great idea—ruin her."

Of all the other participants in the meeting at the Whitney headquarters that decided to distribute the court documents regarding Johnson, Fitzmaurice singled out Arnold Ismach to heap ridicule on. (That Ismach was the only one there besides Cohen who had a Jewish surname may or may not have been a coincidence.) "I am astounded, absolutely astounded, by Mr. Ismach. This is a man who is the dean of a school of journalism. Did it ever occur to him to sit down and ask the basic question, 'What is the right thing to do? Do I need to be a professor to answer that question about any human being? How do I treat anybody, let alone somebody who has come from where Marlene Johnson came from and got to?'

"The answer is obvious. Do not engage in this kind of activity. Doesn't the political arena have enough dirt and mud and filth and slime so that people don't want to enter it?

"The public has a disdain for politicians and lawyers. That goes back to Watergate. And the professor comes in here and tells you that the treatment of Mr. Cohen by the editors was immoral."

Fitzmaurice told the jurors that they should not be sympathetic to Cohen for his financial troubles.

"What Mr. Cohen did, he did to himself.

"The question really is this: Was Mr. Cohen fired because his name was in the paper? Or was Mr. Cohen fired because of what he did? Those are two different things. It's like if you commit a crime and get caught, you say the only reason I'm in jail is because the police caught me. That isn't why you're in jail. You're in jail because you did something. What happened to Mr. Cohen's job was not because Mr. Cohen's name was in the paper, but because of what he did. His employer was furious at what Cohen had done. What was in issue was an issue of character. It wasn't a matter of your name is in the paper. It went to character.

"In that regard, I'd like to take you back to the deposition. His sworn testimony was this: 'I felt that were my identity revealed, the public, my employer, the press, the world at large would heap opprobrium on my head.' Those are the words of the writer.

"Opprobrium is a disgraceful reproach incurred by conduct considered outrageously shameful. Infamy. The reason Mr. Cohen was in his dilemma wasn't because his name was in the paper but because he had committed an act of infamy. And Marlene Johnson felt that this was an act of infamy."

The editors and columnists of the two newspapers, insisted Fitzmaurice again, "are people of integrity. If you compare the conduct of them with that of Mr. Cohen, it's a vivid contrast. Mr. Cohen did not come into this courtroom with one single shred of compassion or feelings or sorrow or regret or any human emotion as far as Marlene Johnson is concerned.

"I think it's sad. I find it extremely sad that an individual with his talents, with his education—Stanford, Harvard—a lawyer, one of the great law firms in this city, risen to high political office, held important positions in Washington—I find it sad that someone with all this talent has not shown one single ounce of regret for this terrible act that's the subject of this lawsuit. Thank you."

Fitzmaurice's slams on Cohen's character and motivations reached new levels of excess with the comparison to Pearl Harbor. Cohen's character— whether good, bad, or indifferent—had nothing to do with the legal issues of whether the newspapers had made and broken contracts with him. Still, Fitzmaurice delivered a real stem-winder that, regardless of the law, could have swayed the jury.

And there was more to come. Fitzmaurice not only used up his assigned hour but took up most of Hannah's as well. Nevertheless, Hannah had enough time to land some punches of his own.

Following Fitzmaurice's line of attack, Hannah argued that Cohen did not have a contract with *Pioneer Press* reporter Bill Salisbury, because he did not tell Salisbury that he was an "active participant in a last-minute political act to attack Marlene Johnson. There was no agreement on Mr. Salisbury's part or the newspaper's part to keep Mr. Cohen's part in a dirty trick, in a political act, confidential.

"Mr. Hall had to make a difficult decision. Mr. Salisbury did not commit fraud or misrepresentation because he wasn't telling a lie. What he said was innocent and at the time true. Mr. Hall is dealing with facts that Mr. Cohen knew about and Mr. Salisbury didn't. He made the best decision he could. Neither person defrauded Mr. Cohen.

"An innocent act by Mr. Salisbury. A difficult but straightforward and honest decision by Mr. Hall. Innocence and honesty does not equal fraud and misrepresentation."

Hannah reiterated Fitzmaurice's theme that Cohen's continuing economic misfortunes were his own doing and not the responsibility of either newspaper.

Hannah told the jurors that Cohen's own employer in October 1982 regarded Cohen as "lacking in character and lacking in judgment. Mr. Floren felt that the entire matter was distasteful, and that he was stunned by his employee's actions. Ask yourself what would any prospective employer think after hearing those statements from Mr. Cohen's prior employer, having nothing to do with the newspaper articles.

"Any loss Mr. Cohen suffered came from his own voluntary participation in an attempt to hurt Marlene Johnson's campaign. That harm did not come from an article that is true.

"This is a fair article. Given the obvious fairness of this article, to seek punitive damages from the defendants who worked as hard as they did, trying to bring the facts to light, is preposterous.

"Thank you."

Both Fitzmaurice and Hannah gave powerful closing arguments.

I was up against the wall. My speech had better be good—a lot more than good.

After Hannah's presentation, Judge Knoll called a recess of a few minutes before my summation.

I looked at some of Cohen's supporters in the courtroom. They were ashen. I recalled Fitzmaurice's warning before the trial that there would be a big winner and a big loser in the trial. The message to others with grievances against the newspapers would be clear from a Cohen defeat: Don't dare sue us, or we will destroy you in a trial.

I ran to the bathroom.

I brought an outline of the final argument to the podium, but after the first couple of minutes I was speaking extemporaneously. My eyes were riveted on the jurors and not the notes. And the jurors were responding. There had not been such rapt attention since Casserly's presentation.

"Thank you, members of the jury, for your consideration during the trial. We're going to conclude by telling you what the real facts of this case are."

I told the jury who the real underdog was here. Contrary to what Fitzmaurice and Hannah would have had jurors believe, the case was not about some dispute between a privileged-Harvard-political bigshot and a couple of helpless rural Minnesota Scandinavian women, Lori Sturdevant and Marlene Johnson. Instead, the protagonist was a little guy seeking redress for the violation of his rights by corporations representing overwhelming media power.

"This is a case of a broken promise, of a violation of a contract, and of the punishment and the destruction of a career of a man and his family by two wealthy and powerful media giants.

"Who are the parties in this case? Dan Cohen is an individual who, until the stories in the *Star Tribune* and *Pioneer Press*, had been a respected and honored member of the advertising-public relations community in Minneapolis.

"He has written books; a book about Hubert Humphrey in many respects tells more about Dan Cohen than it does about Hubert Humphrey. And he has written children's books based upon characters modeled after his two teenage daughters.

"Dan has done volunteer work for the Park Avenue Methodist Church, he has done work for Billy Graham, he has won awards for work he has done as a volunteer for correctional facilities, he has done work for foster care programs for this county.

"Who are the parties here? The parties are Dan Cohen, a self-employed advertising and public relations man trying to make enough money to support his wife and two teenage daughters, and on the other side we have two media giants.

"We have the *St. Paul Pioneer Press*, which itself has assets of between fifty and a hundred million dollars. But the *Pioneer Press* is only one newspaper in a giant conglomerate. David Lawrence came from the *Detroit Free Press* to testify on behalf of the two newspapers, and the *Detroit Free Press* is also part of this same conglomerate. It's called Knight Ridder Publications, which has newspapers and media organizations all over the country.

"Mr. Lawrence said that the annual earnings of Knight Ridder is in excess of two billion dollars a year. [I drew out and suspended in mid-sentence the word "billion."]

"Cowles Media Company owns the *Star Tribune* and other newspapers, radio, and television stations around the country with assets of over 250 million dollars.

"We're talking about colossal organizations with enormous resources which are the parties in this case against Mr. Cohen. There in fact has been malice in this case warranting the award of punitive damages. And you don't have to believe me. Just recall the address given a few minutes ago by Mr. Fitzmaurice. Did Mr. Fitzmaurice talk about the legal issues involved in the case? Most of his case was a diatribe, a personal attack, talking about infamy and words of that sort.

"But what was this so-called infamy? All Mr. Cohen had done was provide copies of authentic court records to reporters. Those records had to do with a previous conviction of a candidate for a very powerful political office.

"In the official position of the *Pioneer Press*, stated long before there was any thought of a lawsuit, there's no mention of infamy, there's no mention of evil acts on the part of Mr. Cohen.

"What was this official position?

I then displayed a blowup of the October 29, 1982, editorial of the *Pioneer Press*.

"You have it in evidence. I hope you will look at it when you get to the jury room, because it probably is the single most important document in this case regarding the position of the two newspapers. It says:

Too much is being made by supporters of Rudy Perpich about Republican fingerprints on documents leaked to the press showing his runningmate was convicted for shoplifting 12 years ago. An aide said Wheelock Whitney had nothing to do with the disclosure. Whether he did or didn't is irrelevant. To focus on how the information got to the public's attention is to overlook a larger issue; that is, the information about Marlene Johnson is something the voting public deserves to know. It is legitimate to examine her past as part of an assessment of her fitness for public office. The last-minute disclosures could have been avoided if Perpich and Johnson had informed the public themselves earlier and confronted the issue squarely.

"So that's the official position of one of the two parties in this case. No criticism of Mr. Cohen for providing the information to the reporters. In fact, the editorial says that this is relevant information that the public has the right to have. The whole thing could have been avoided if the campaign had come clean and provided the information voluntarily by itself.

"We're talking about an agreement to provide information in exchange for a promise not to disclose his name. We've heard testimony from many editors and reporters and experts on all sides that this is a common practice in the journalistic profession.

"And why do people ask for promises of confidentiality? They fear retaliation if they're identified as the source of information. They fear, oftentimes, that they may lose their jobs, which is precisely what happened here, and which is precisely the reason why these promises have to be honored.

"What are we talking about when we are talking about honoring promises of confidentiality? It comes down to the basic issue of a man's or woman's word is his or her bond. That's the basis of journalistic ethics regarding promises of confidentiality.

"This case is unique, ladies and gentlemen. We've asked editors, we've asked experts, and no one has been able to point to a case in the entire country where a promise of confidentiality by a reporter has been voluntarily broken and dishonored by the editors of a newspaper.

"Reporters and editors go to jail rather than break promises of confidentiality. Newspaper people around the country have sought to enact shield laws like the Minnesota Free Flow of Information Act. Why do they want these laws? They want to ensure that reporters and editors are not forced in any court to reveal the names of their confidential sources.

"Why do they fear that? First is the journalist's honor; a promise has been made, a promise has to be kept. There's another reason. The public's flow of information would be harmed if reporters and editors could not make promises to get information and if they could not keep those promises. That's why it's called the Free Flow of Information Act.

"So this is the first time anywhere that anybody knows about where there has been, without any compulsion whatsoever, a voluntary dishonoring of a promise of confidentiality.

"There have been many instances of promises of confidentiality for political and other types of information. This is the first time that newspapers have sought to set themselves up as some sort of moral censor on the quality of information that is provided to them.

"One thing that's very interesting, ladies and gentlemen. The two reporters, Lori Sturdevant and Bill Salisbury, who made these promises, did you hear them testify on behalf of the newspapers? The reporters would not testify on behalf of the newspapers because they were so angry that their word was broken, that their promises were being dishonored by their editors. They testified for Mr. Cohen, both Ms. Sturdevant and Mr. Salisbury. What did they say? They both said that they both have made many promises of confidentiality, and not once were their promises dishonored by editors.

"This is the only case that anyone seems to know of where this has happened. You have this pattern of promises of confidentiality being made by reporters and promises being honored by their editors up until this one case.

"This is misrepresentation—the editors holding out the reporters as having the authority to make these promises. The reporters believed they had the authority, and indeed they did, except for this one instance.

"If a promise is broken soon after it is made, that is evidence of misrepresentation as well. You remember what Ms. Sturdevant told you. Ms. Sturdevant was so angry that her promise was being dishonored, she didn't want to have anything to do with that article. It was an unethical act, an immoral act, and she said, 'Take my name off it. I don't even want to have my name on that article.' Even today, six years later, she is still bothered by the dishonoring of her promise. And Mr. Salisbury objected strongly to the breaking of his promise to Mr. Cohen.

"The newspapers came in many months ago to claim that they, because of the First Amendment, are not bound by the rules of law of tort and contract. That was rejected by the judge. So they are bound by the rules of law just like all of us are.

"They had choices. They could have run the article without identifying Mr. Cohen, they could have run the article by identifying the person as some sort of Whitney supporter without identifying Mr. Cohen's name, or they could have just not run the article at all.

"They have given various excuses. That does not alter the law of contracts. If they ran that article identifying Mr. Cohen in violation of a promise to him, then they are liable to pay damages to him.

"They said they wanted to be complete and to level with the public. That article which was purportedly complete was very incomplete. It did not disclose that the information had been obtained from Mr. Cohen in return for a promise of confidentiality. It did not disclose that the newspapers had dishonored the promise of their reporters. It did not disclose that the person who wrote that article, Lori Sturdevant, was so angry at that decision that she refused to allow her name to be used. All that would have been of some interest for readers.

"The article also disclosed the name of Mr. Cohen's employer. They've never given us any satisfactory explanation of why they had to identify not only Mr. Cohen's name but also the name of his employer. Mr. Cohen was fired that very day.

"Mr. Floren admitted that Mr. Cohen had told him the day before that he had provided copies of these court documents to the newspapers. Mr. Floren said nothing. He raised no objection. He didn't during the day, he didn't during the evening. Only the next day, after the article appeared with the name of Martin-Williams in the *Star Tribune*, did the company officials call Mr. Cohen on the carpet and fire him. They told him to vacate his office by the next afternoon.

"This isn't the final story. The next day, as Mr. Cohen was clearing out his office to an uncertain future, an article appeared by Jim Klobuchar. You will find that article contains some of the harshest attacks on a human being that you will see anywhere.

"But this article by Mr. Klobuchar which so harshly attacked Mr. Cohen again made no mention of the fact that Mr. Cohen had given this information in return for a promise of confidentiality, it made no mention of the fact that the promise had been dishonored by the editors of the newspaper.

"What Mr. Klobuchar did not mention as well was that he had ties with the Perpich candidacy, that a few weeks later he was to participate in a formal meeting with political professionals to help write the governor-elect's inaugural speech. That was not mentioned in the article about Mr. Cohen or in any other article by Mr. Klobuchar. For doing this, for failing to make full disclosure, for failing to level with the public, Mr. Klobuchar was suspended. But it didn't help Mr. Cohen.

"And that wasn't the end of the story, either. Because the next day there was another assault on Mr. Cohen in the form of a cartoon. A cartoon entitled 'Last Minute Campaign Smears," where Mr. Cohen is pictured as a garbage can. Hundreds of thousands of people in Minnesota have gotten this delivered to their doorstep. This issue is in every major library in Minnesota. This is a cross that Mr. Cohen is going to have to bear for the rest of his life. This vicious cartoon condemning him for the offense of trusting the promises of the newspapers. This is a cross that his wife and his two daughters are going to have to bear for the rest of their lives.

"Mr. Gelfand was asked, 'If the *Star Tribune* had obtained this information on an exclusive basis, should you then have kept the promise of confidentiality?' And Mr. Gelfand said 'Yes.'

"So the real issue is not some sort of phony moral issue about providing copies of valid and authentic court documents but merely the fact that the newspaper did not have a commercial advantage over its competitors. They wanted to have a scoop. Because they didn't have a scoop, they've engaged in a vendetta against Cohen.

"We've had a lot of talk, charges, and flowery prose about the harm to Ms. Johnson. But the fact is that there was no harm whatsoever to Ms. Johnson by the disclosure of these court documents, in contrast to what has happened to Mr. Cohen. Marlene Johnson was elected and reelected by a whopping majority. Ms. Johnson has not presented evidence in this case; maybe she's too busy running the state.

"The story does not end with Marlene Johnson's election by a huge margin. Dan Cohen with his wife and two daughters was humiliated. He was out of a job. He was looking for work. Dan Cohen got a job with the University of Minnesota.

"Lo and behold comes a telephone call from a *Star Tribune* columnist by the name of Doug Grow. This was after the election, after Mr. Cohen was humiliated. It wasn't enough. Doug Grow said 'Why in the world would you hire anybody like Dan Cohen?' Apparently Dan Cohen isn't supposed to be able to get a job anywhere. And then Doug Grow proceeded to write an article ridiculing the university for hiring Dan Cohen even though he had to admit that Dan Cohen was doing a good job there.

"But the capper was this. How did he find out about Cohen's work? 'I found out from a confidential source, and I've kept the name of that source secret for all these years. I'm not going to tell you the name.'

"Well, was this a dirty trick trying to sabotage the job of Dan Cohen? Nobody in the *Star Tribune* said that was a dirty trick. Nobody said, 'Mr. Grow, you've got to identify this source. He's maligning Dan Cohen; he's committing an act of infamy against Dan Cohen.' No. Where the source is assaulting Dan Cohen, there they return to the old policy honoring promises of confidentiality.

"Late revelations in political campaigns are extraordinarily common and have always been justified by the *Star Tribune*. Mr. Finney was asked if he thought it was okay in 1984 to run an article a few days before the election where confidential sources said that Geraldine Ferraro's parents, for God's sake, forty years earlier had been convicted of some gaming offense. It's okay to protect that source. That's okay.

"Mr. Finney, is it okay to run a late revelation from a confidential source identifying a school board candidate's religion as Catholic? Is it a crime to be a Catholic? Could be bigotry, couldn't it? Mr. Finney said that's okay to keep the source confidential.

"One of the best examples is an article by Lori Sturdevant nine days before a primary election. This article goes into great detail about financial problems going back many years.

"Mr. Mattson sent a telegram saying, 'You're smearing me. You've had this information. You waited until the last minute to publish this in an attempt to sabotage my campaign.'

"And how did the editor of the *Star Tribune* respond? Joel Kramer said, 'There's no smear. We're just reporting facts. All we're doing is providing valuable information to our readers.' So that's the *Star Tribune*'s position when a confidential source is talking about another candidate.

"In fact, there are many, many examples late in elections where there have been revelations of misdeeds of candidates. In every one of these circumstances the *Star Tribune* honored promises of confidentiality. They never claimed that there was infamy, they never tried to assassinate the character of the person who provided that information. Only in this particular case involving Dan Cohen.

"Let's look at testimony involving young women in Minnesota who have been the subject of assaults by the *Star Tribune*. You recall that a young lady named Jolene Stavrakis was going to represent Minnesota in the Miss USA contest. There were front page revelations that some years earlier, when she was a teenager, she was convicted of shoplifting. Then we had the cartoon entitled 'Miss Minnesota Mis Demeanor' where she was dressed as a jailbird with an iron ball tied around her leg. Ms. Stavrakis had to withdraw.

"Mr. Gelfand was asked about this. Mr. Gelfand was expressing a great deal of alarm over the mentioning of Ms. Johnson's previous record. What about Ms. Stavrakis's previous criminal record when she was only sixteen years old? Well, Mr. Gelfand said, 'That's okay. Miss Minnesota candidates are supposed to set an example for the rest of us.' Regarding the cartoon, Mr. Gelfand said, 'Well, it was humiliating, but it was okay. It was good journalism.'

"What about a candidate for high political office, a potential governor of Minnesota? What's sauce for the goose ought to be sauce for the gander. Where Miss Minnesota candidates are involved, there the newspapers are merciless in telling readers about past offenses, and ridiculing them with cartoons. It's information, they say, the public has the right to know. If the people are humiliated, it's just too bad. They're supposed to set a standard for the rest of us.

"Remember Bess Myerson, a long time ago was Miss America and many years ago was a consumer official in New York. She doesn't hold any political office now. But a few weeks ago an article said that confidential sources had disclosed that Bess Myerson eighteen years earlier, in London, had been arrested for shoplifting.

"Mr. Gelfand said there, 'Yeah, it's relevant, it's good information, the public has the right to know because Bess Myerson is a public figure. Anything she has done is useful information for the public, even though it's eighteen years ago.'

"Shouldn't that apply to a political candidate for lieutenant governor of Minnesota? Shouldn't you apply that same reasoning across the board to inform the public?

"Remember Deborah Howell testified that the *Pioneer Press* publishes lists of every person convicted in St. Paul of shoplifting or other misdemeanors. If you are convicted of shoplifting, you're going to have your name and your address in the *Pioneer Press*, no matter how famous or how obscure you are. That's a good idea, she said, because the public has a right to know who commits crimes."

"Mr. Cohen has suffered enormous damages in this case."

I summarized the testimony of Fallon and Printy and put in an aside about Floren.

"Oh, yes, they did bring in David Floren to testify against Mr. Cohen. You have to decide for yourselves, ladies and gentlemen of the jury, if Mr. Floren is an unbiased observer on Mr. Cohen. He is, after all, the guy who fired him and, you might agree, it came through that Mr. Floren does not have any warm feelings toward Mr. Cohen.

"This is the same man who said first that Mr. Cohen was not doing a good job for him and then had to admit, when confronted with his deposition, that Mr. Cohen was indeed doing a good job for him. And then he testified that he expressed anger at Mr. Cohen on the day he provided the documents. Then he had to admit that that letter was not sent until the next day, after the name of Martin-Williams appeared in the newspaper. So I think it is clear where Mr. Floren stands, and I leave it to you to assess the credibility of his testimony.

"The issue here is not an anonymous revelation of a misdeed of a politician. It's done all the time. The issue is not a so-called dirty trick of delivering an authentic copy of a court document, a public record. If they didn't like it, they didn't have to run the story. But they wanted to run the story because they were afraid of the competition.

"There was a dirty trick here, and the dirty trick was not providing copies of authentic court records to reporters to do as they will. The dirty trick was the violation of a promise of confidentiality. That's what Mr. Finnegan said. Those are the words of a former editor of the *Pioneer Press*. Those are the words of the current vice president of the *Pioneer Press*. Those are the words he repeated before you yesterday. So much for dirty tricks.

"The last gasp of the *Star Tribune* was to bring in their last witness yesterday, a gentleman named David Anderson, who now says after all this time that they didn't break a promise because the information was gotten from Gary Flakne and not from Mr. Cohen. That would be news to Lori Sturdevant and Bill Salisbury.

"There was reference to a book by Mr. Anderson called *Investigative Reporting*. Just to read you an excerpt, this is what he said:

Many fundamental techniques of investigative reporting involve actions some would label dishonest, fraudulent, immoral, and perhaps even illegal. Most reporters use deceptive methods to gather information.

"That's Mr. Anderson. You can assess the credibility of that testimony, too, ladies and gentlemen of the jury.

"The issue in this case is not the character of Mr. Cohen. The attacks are an attempt to divert you from the real issues. You can decide for yourselves where you've last heard attacks on an individual as vicious as those that have been leveled at Mr. Cohen by attorneys in this case.

"The real issue is this, ladies and gentlemen: Are the rules of morality, contract, honoring one's word, the ethics of persons, a man or woman's word being his or her bond, the legal rules of keeping one's agreements, rules which all of us as individuals want to live by and are required to live by—are those rules also going to bind the huge corporate entities representing the newspapers that are involved in this suit?

"These are the two largest newspapers in the state of Minnesota. They're part of publishing empires. To suggest that a person like Mr. Cohen, self-employed, barely able to survive these days, is on anywhere near an equal basis with these newspapers, in the real world, is almost laughable. But they are equal before you, ladies and gentlemen, today. The lowliest individual has rights before you equal to the rights of the largest corporations.

"If you allow the newspapers to get away with breaking their promises to Mr. Cohen on the basis of the scurrilous personal assaults which have been leveled at him throughout this trial, all other promises made by newspapers to you or any other individual will be at risk.

"And it doesn't only apply to newspapers. It applies to all large corporations able to afford the enormous cost of lawsuits.

"If they are able to evade their obligations by attacking the character of the individual who is suing them, all contracts will be at risk.

"If you find for the newspapers, you would encourage others more powerful to avoid their obligations under promises by doing what they've done here—to evade the law and concentrate on attacking the plaintiff.

"This is a common tactic of defendants in rape cases—to attack the character of the victim, the woman raped, rather than dealing with the issues of the case.

"We ask you to enforce the basic morality which governs all of us, of keeping one's word as your bond. That is the basis of the law; that's the basis of journalistic ethics.

"Dan Cohen has been lied to, he's been humiliated, he and his family, his wife and two daughters, have had their name blackened by the newspapers' illegal conduct in this case. We ask you, members of the jury, to give justice to Dan Cohen and to restore to him and his family his good name, so that we can throw this cartoon into oblivion where it belongs."

At that, I grabbed the blowup of the cartoon from the easel and flung it to the floor. I beat Judge Knoll's hour limit by a few seconds.

On Wednesday morning, Judge Knoll instructed jurors on the law they should apply. Before he began, however, an angry Fitzmaurice delivered a statement scoring my final argument, complaining among other things about a suggestion that "the tactics employed by the defendants somehow could be equated with what was done in rape cases."

I responded that "oftentimes the defense attempts to blacken the character of the victim in a rape case. This was precisely what was done in this case. The entire thrust of the defendants' case was to blacken Mr. Cohen's character to divert the jurors' attention from the issues of contract and tort involved here."

Judge Knoll asked Fitzmaurice if he wanted a cautionary instruction.

Fitzmaurice replied, "I gave that some thought last night and tried to draft one, but I'm not sure how to do it. That was the problem that I had."

Judge Knoll came back, "Life's full of those problems."

At the beginning of his instructions, the judge told the jury, "Obviously all of the parties feel very strongly about the case, and there were strong arguments presented to you yesterday. What is important is not what counsel urges you to believe. What matters is what you believe to be true and the amount of weight which you believe should be given to the evidence."

That afternoon, the jurors began to send written messages to Judge Knoll. The first one read, "We would like a clarification of the phrase 'intervening circumstances' under misrepresentation—burden of proof as it relates to the word 'promise.' " Later that day, they asked, "What is a material fact (under the misrepresentation claim)?"

The reasons for the jury's focus on the misrepresentation issue became apparent the following day. At 9:15 A.M., the jurors sent another message to Judge Knoll. "Why are punitive damage awards tied to fact finding in favor of misrepresentation claim? Are there any alternatives?" As the day went on, the jurors gave even more emphasis to punitive damages. A note to Judge Knoll at 3 P.M. said, "If we should decide on punitive damages, are there any other guidelines that can assist us? If we can't reach an agreement as to punitive damages, what are our alternatives?"

In his response, Judge Knoll just referred the jury to his instructions.

That the jury had given so much thought to awarding punitive damages to Cohen was a good sign. The jurors would have no point in considering punishment for the papers unless they were close to deciding in Cohen's favor on the newspapers' liability for breach of contract. At the very least, their messages to Judge Knoll were not calculated to give comfort to the newspapers. How would they react? An ordinary defendant would frantically scramble to settle the case. The newspapers, however, were not ordinary defendants. The answer did not take long.

My closing argument was supposed to have concluded the trial, but the newspapers still managed to get the last word.

On Friday, the day after the jury's messages on punitive damages, the *Star Tribune* threw a bomb. I got up at 5:00 A.M. and grabbed the newspaper from the front porch. Jumping off the front page was the headline "Confidentiality Dispute Leads Star Tribune to Pull Magazine." Under the headline, a long article told readers that the *Star Tribune* had withdrawn an entire edition of no less than 640,000 Sunday magazines because a source claimed that a story in it had identified her in violation of a promise of confidentiality.[1] The newspaper did not explain how she had obtained an advance copy of the article several days before publication. The article quoted the source's attorney in effusive praise of the *Star Tribune* for what he called "excellent judgment and a lot of integrity" in squelching the magazine. In ordinary adversarial litigation, such compliments by an attorney for the conduct of opposing parties are unusual, to say the least. For all of this just to be coincidental strained credulity.

The *Star Tribune* took one more shot at Cohen and asserted "key differences" between the *Cohen* case and the magazine article. The article claimed, as the newspapers had done in the trial, that editors had disclosed Cohen's name because their "concern was that readers not be misled" over "smear tactics" and they "had no choice but to tell all they knew."

Star Tribune executive editor Joel Kramer said in the article that the newspaper would try to remove the magazines from newspapers in storage centers around Minnesota, but that it was "an impossible task" to retrieve all the magazines. Even so, not a single copy of the magazine has ever turned up. With the admitted impossibility of keeping secret 640,000 copies of a magazine, one would have expected someone, somewhere to unearth a copy of the story in question. No one ever did. To this day, the *Star Tribune* has not identified that anonymous source. If one assumes the truth of the *Star Tribune*'s account, it may have been one of the best-kept secrets of all time.

Until the *Cohen* case, the *Star Tribune* in its entire history had never been involved in a controversy with a source over a broken promise of confidentiality. If the article was to be believed, the newspaper, at the very time the jurors were about to render their verdict on the issues of the *Cohen* trial, coincidentally and very publicly resolved a dispute with a source who, through her attorney, expressed gratitude to the *Star Tribune*.

Was the timing of all this just fortuitous? Or was the newspaper deliberately trying to influence the jury to get it to believe that the *Star Tribune* faithfully honors, at enormous cost to itself, "legitimate" agreements of confidentiality with "reputable" sources, and that therefore there is no need or justification for a verdict for Cohen? How would the article affect the jurors? Would they even read it? Was the whole thing just a hoax?

Together with the "Fixit" column published at the start of the trial, the *Star Tribune* was using its considerable ink and circulation in an attempt to influence the jurors outside of the testimony and arguments in the courtroom.

The jury was not sequestered during the trial. They had free access to the media. At least some of the jurors must have read the latest article.

I agonized over what, if anything, to do about it. Any instruction by Judge Knoll to the jurors to disregard the article as a practical matter would guarantee that they would read it. A phone call at 9:30 cut short my brooding.

It was the judge's clerk. "Get down to the court right now, Elliot." The jurors had arrived at their verdict.

During the next forty-five minutes, the lawyers, Cohen, and various officials of the newspapers gathered in the courtroom. The suspense was escalating. When Judge Knoll entered, you could hear a pin drop. At last, the jurors filed into the courtroom. The forewoman smiled at Hannah and averted her eyes from Cohen and me. It was not a good sign.

All the players had assembled in the courtroom. Still, we would have to wait to get to the bottom line. There was a ritual to go through. The jury's verdict would come to be known only gradually, as the judge's clerk read the jury's answers to twenty-three questions that were part of a special verdict form.

She began to read the several-page document. Slowly. By now the tension was unbearable. My mouth was parched. I could not control my racing heartbeat.

"Number 1.   Was there a valid oral contract between plaintiff Dan Cohen and defendant *Star Tribune*?

Answer: Yes.

"Number 2.   If your answer to question number 1 is yes, then answer this question: Did the *Star Tribune* breach that contract?

Answer: Yes.

"Number 3.   If your answer to question number 2 is yes, then answer this question: Was the breach of contract a direct cause of damage to plaintiff?

Answer: Yes.

The jury answered "yes" to the same questions about the *Pioneer Press*.

The clerk then read twelve detailed questions regarding misrepresentation by the newspapers. The jury answered "yes" to all twelve.

At the very end, after many pages of questions, the clerk got to the matter of damages for Cohen.

"Number 19.   What sum of money, if any, will fairly and adequately compensate the plaintiff for his loss?

Answer: $200,000.

"Number 20.   Do you find by clear and convincing evidence that the conduct of defendant *Star Tribune* showed a willful indifference to the rights of plaintiff?

Answer: Yes.

"Number 21.   What sum of money should be awarded the plaintiff as punitive damages against defendant *Star Tribune*?

Answer: $250,000.

The jury made the same finding regarding the *Pioneer Press* and also ordered that newspaper to pay Cohen $250,000.

I looked over at the newspapers' counsel table. Fitzmaurice and Hannah were stoic. Pat was visibly stunned.

Fitzmaurice asked to poll each juror individually on his or her vote. All four women jurors found for Cohen. One of the two men refused to sign the verdict.

The forewoman explained later, "We were not there to judge morals or practices of journalism. The question was: What is the law and what happened in this case?"

Asked in an interview why she had smiled at Hannah when she had socked his client with such a huge adverse verdict, the forewoman answered, "The others wanted to give Cohen even bigger punitive damages. I got them down to $500,000!" The holdout juror said that he had agreed that the newspapers had broken a contract with Cohen, but he didn't like Cohen. "I would have given him only $1."

He alone among the jurors bought the "dirty tricks" argument. The 5–1 vote was enough for a valid verdict, but just barely. The shift of one more juror would have thwarted the majority and forced a second trial.

After the clerk got through reading the jury's verdict, Judge Knoll said, "Congratulations, Mr. Cohen." Cohen embraced his wife and sobbed.

Shock rolled in from around the country. Prominent New York media lawyer Floyd Abrams remarked, "This is absolutely unprecedented."[2] The general counsel of the McClatchy newspaper chain in California, Gary Pruitt, said the *Cohen* verdict created "a new way to circumvent constitutional protections. It is a Pandora's box that has far-reaching legal implications." Jane Kirtley, executive director of a media-funded advocacy organization called Reporters Committee for Freedom of the Press, asserted that the *Cohen* case "is an appalling use of the courts for what is an ethical matter."[3]

Others, also appalled, expressed confidence that the verdict would not survive. For example, Michael Gartner, then president of NBC News, wrote in the *Wall Street Journal*, "That ruling is wrong—it's a slippery way around the First Amendment that should be thrown out."[4] Columbia University media scholar Everette Dennis said, "I'd be surprised if it held up on appeal."[5]

New York's *Village Voice* was positively jaunty. It told the media industry not to worry. "We don't find the decision as alarming as the business buzz suggests." First Amendment arguments "will get the decision reversed."[6]

The Minnesota public television channel invited me to appear the evening of the verdict as the leadoff guest on its *Almanac* program, a weekly pontification by sundry talking heads on politics and public policy. *Almanac* was and remains one of the state's leading arbiters of political correctitude. Though it billed itself as nonpartisan, its host, Jan ("make sure you pronounce it Yon") Smaby, was a Democratic party activist and sometime lieutenant governor candidate herself. Democratic party politics ran in her family. Her mother had been a state representative. Jan had been married to the incumbent legislator I defeated in 1978. She did not consider me a friend. I was surprised that she wanted me on her show. Smaby's objective was not to offer congratulations. She made no attempt to conceal her disgust over the *Cohen* verdict and became increasingly hostile as the discussion went on.

"You were beating up on the media pretty heavily. The jury accepted it, but will appellate courts buy this media bashing?"

"This ascribes to me far more power than I have," I smiled. "To suggest that an individual lawyer can beat up on two huge media conglomerates shows the poverty of legal arguments on the other side."

It was not the answer Jan wanted. She abruptly terminated the interview. I offered to shake her hand. With the cameras focused on her, Smaby refused.

To be sure, many had thought beforehand that the newspapers never would have to concern themselves with an appeal.

Three days after the verdict, Minnesota's political insiders found in their mailboxes a feature on the *Cohen* case in the latest issue of *Politics in Minnesota*, a periodical potpourri of political gossip and prognostications put out by D. J. Leary. Leary was the state's most prominent political consultant and the confidant of Hubert Humphrey and other Democratic powerhouses. He had observed the trial and even had a bit part in it. A *Star Tribune* article about his own 1974 jailing for shoplifting came up in the testimony of Tim McGuire. D. J. was not amused, but he intended to get the last laugh.

After disdaining what he called Cohen's and his attorney's "stormy careers in politics," Leary declared it wrong to disclose information that he would rather the public not have known. "Marlene Johnson is forced to have an insignificant fact from her youth publicly discussed as if it really mattered. Some folks are wishing the whole darn thing would just go away." Leary had no doubt that he and they would get their wish. "The public feels the papers did right in identifying Cohen as the source of the leaked material on Johnson's ancient shoplifting charge." It didn't matter, Leary wrote, that the newspapers' own reporters had testified in Cohen's favor. "Keep in mind: the jury is not made up of journalists."[7] It would be some time before D. J. Leary would venture any more predictions about the case.

Cohen was not the only winner. The verdict also was a victory for reporters' autonomy from interference by editors. A University of Minnesota journalism professor, Theodore Glasser, urged reporters to actively oppose the *Star Tribune* and *Pioneer Press* in any court appeals.

To claim to have a First Amendment right to renege on a reporter's promise not only places the press above the law but denies reporters the very freedom they need to operate in the day-to-day world of journalism. Reporters have every reason to file a friend-of-the court brief on behalf of Cohen.[8]

No one followed Glasser's advice.

Jim Fitzmaurice asked me to lunch at the venerable Minneapolis Club, the favorite haunt of the city's establishment for facilitating business deals. It was not a place that I frequented. I had not been there since I left politics. Fitzmaurice wanted to talk settlement. To my surprise, he brought along another Faegre & Benson lawyer, Scott Johnson. Scott was a friend of mine but was not involved in the case.

This was the third time the lawyers would discuss settling the case. Fitzmaurice said the newspapers would pay the full $200,000 in compensatory damages but would not pay a penny of the punitive damages. We would have to walk away from $500,000. At least one journalistic supporter of the newspapers urged them not to quibble about paying the verdict. The *Twin Cities Reader* publicly pleaded with the newspapers to pay Cohen the whole $700,000 right away, to get rid of the case and avoid escalating appeals that could establish a national precedent to haunt the entire journalistic profession. After paying off Cohen, the newspapers could pass the verdict off as just a local fluke that would be quickly forgotten.

I made the mistake of ordering walleye, a Minnesota specialty. The fish, represented on the menu as filleted and fresh, was not deboned. It may not have been fresh, either. I didn't know if I would choke first on the fish or on the settlement offer. Fitzmaurice said that he would speak to the chef about the fish. He would not do anything about the punitive damages.

It quickly became clear that Scott Johnson was not there just for idle palaver. Fitzmaurice left the table, ostensibly to make a phone call. Johnson then took charge. "Fitz wanted me to work on the case, but I turned him down because I thought Cohen was right. $200,000 is a good deal for Cohen. You know that I want to do the best for you. Take the offer while you still can." Otherwise, he said, the firm would aggressively pursue appeals. "Appellate courts always side with the press. If you don't take the $200,000 now, you are in danger of losing everything. I don't want that to happen to you."

Again, there was no settlement.

The trial, grueling as it was, would be only one battle of a protracted war. The newspapers were getting set to appeal.

Notes

1. Dan Oberdorfer, "Confidentiality Dispute Leads Star Tribune to Pull Magazine," *Star Tribune*, July 22, 1988, 1A.

2. "Two Newspapers Lose Suit for Disclosing a Source," *New York Times*, July 23, 1988, 6.

3. Mary Jane Smetanka, "Media Experts Call Decision a Minefield of Possible Effects," *Star Tribune*, July 23, 1988, 1A.

4. Michael Gartner, "Anonymous Sources Hold Hidden Dangers for Journalists," *Wall Street Journal*, August 11, 1988, 23.

5. Smetanka, "Media Experts Call Decision a Minefield."

6. Geoffrey Stokes, "Press Clips," *The Village Voice*, August 2, 1988, 8.

7. *Politics in Minnesota*, 7, no. 1 (July 1988), 1.

8. Theodore L. Glasser, "Reporters Seen as Winners in Cohen Verdict," *Minnesota Journal*, October 4, 1988, 1.

CHAPTER 11 —————————————————

Something for Everyone

AS THE FIRST step in their appeals, the newspapers moved for judgment notwithstanding the verdict or a new trial. To the arguments they made in the trial and in their motion for summary judgment, the newspapers' brief added a new invention. An agreement of confidentiality, "as in other sensitive inter-personal relationships," was "less than a contract." A promise of confidentiality, the lawyers now claimed, was the legal equivalent of a promise to marry.

The lawyers met again in Judge Knoll's courtroom a month to the day after the jury's verdict. Judge Knoll greeted us. "Good morning. So nice to see you again." He had a sardonic wit.

After some preliminaries, an exchange between Judge Knoll and Jim Fitzmaurice went to the heart of the First Amendment conundrum of the case.

"What your position boils down to," said Judge Knoll, "is that because your client is a newspaper, otherwise legally binding contracts are breachable by your client without recourse against your client for damages."

"Yes, in the context of news gathering."

"Anybody who makes an agreement with your client should be aware that they cannot count on your client's performance because your client will assert a privilege."

Fitzmaurice responded with one of the newspapers' chief arguments throughout the case. "The great irony is that if the information was entirely false as applied to Mr. Cohen, and the issue was defamation because it was not true, we would have been entitled to every one of the constitutional protections that we are talking about today. It is incongruous that if it were false we would be entitled to those protections, but since it is true we are not entitled to them."

At the end of the hearing, Judge Knoll expressed irritation about his own treatment by the two newspapers. "In support of media accuracy, it should be noted that the orders of the Court, in spite of some of the statements that have been made subsequent to the jury's verdict, cannot be interpreted in any way as some sort of prior restraint. As I stated in my ruling on the motion for summary judgment, I would not entertain a motion to order a nonpublication of anything. I can see it coming up in this case. I don't believe the law would permit a temporary restraining order or an injunction proscribing the publication of what was published. The distinction ought to be made for the benefit of the public that the ruling of the Court in no way affects the newspaper's right to publish what it wants to publish. The order of the Court merely applies to the newspaper the same law that applies to any other citizen, the law of contracts and the law of torts. If a newspaper in exercising its right to print damages someone by breaking a contract or by defrauding a person, it ought to be held to the law's judgment as should any other citizen. I think that for the company to continue stating publicly that this Court's order in some way impinges on its right to publish is erroneous."

In their articles on the hearing, neither newspaper informed their readers of Judge Knoll's comments.

Judges usually deny motions for new trials in a pro forma manner. Not so with Judge Knoll, who minced no words in disposing yet again of the newspapers' constitutional claims. He dismissed their comparison of a promise of confidentiality to a promise of marriage as a "strained metaphor" attempting to support a notion that

otherwise valid contracts should not be subject to laws governing commercial relationships. The court is not persuaded that the relationship between reporter and source is anything other than commercial. The defendants entered into a contract with the plaintiff where the hornbook elements of offer, acceptance, and consideration were unmistakably present.

The newspapers' assertion that "severe criticism from fellow professionals and skepticism, loss of credibility and trust from potential or existing sources" provides sufficient deterrent against journalistic excesses rings not only unrealistic but disingenuous.

No First Amendment interest exists in protecting news media from calculated misdeeds. Certainly, the knowing and willful breach of a legally sufficient contract after hours of thought and discussion by corporate officers can fairly be characterized as a calculated misdeed. Just as the First Amendment has never been construed to afford newsmen immunity from torts or crimes committed during the course of news gathering, it similarly should not be construed to immunize news organizations from other aspects of the civil law. To do so would trivialize the First Amendment and weaken its capacity to protect true freedom of expression.

The newspapers have argued that holding them responsible to the law of contracts will somehow chill freedom of expression guaranteed by the First Amendment. It is the Court's view that to deny an injured plaintiff recovery for demonstrated harm done to him by the breach of an otherwise valid contract would be to deprive that citizen of the protection of the law without any countervailing benefit to the legitimate interest of the public in being informed. Rather than chill legitimate freedom of expression, such a result would encourage conduct by news media that grossly offends ordinary men.

In announcing that the newspapers would continue their appeals, *Star Tribune* managing editor, Tim McGuire, took a swipe at Judge Knoll for what he called "the hostility his decision denotes. We don't find it surprising at all." McGuire further remarked that the "strong attitudes" of Judge Knoll's decision were "consistent with the attitudes displayed during trial."[1]

While the newspapers were appealing to the Minnesota Court of Appeals, Judge Knoll approved my motion to add interest to the verdict.

Fitzmaurice would not be working on the appeal. John Borger, also of the firm of Faegre & Benson, would be the *Star Tribune*'s lead attorney for the appeal. Fitzmaurice did trial work exclusively. Borger was equally formidable as a First Amendment communications law specialist. He had studied journalism as an undergraduate and was the top student in his class at Michigan State University. He also had practical journalistic experience, having been editor in chief of his college newspaper. He was a graduate of Yale Law School. Pat also would work on the appeal briefs for the *Star Tribune*. Hannah would continue as lead attorney for the *Pioneer Press*.

Borger and Hannah wrote separate briefs for their newspapers. With the page limitation rules of the Minnesota Court of Appeals, that allowed the newspapers fifty more pages in their initial briefs, double what I had, and twenty-five more in their reply briefs.

As a national legal precedent, what was most important in the case was the court's ruling that the First Amendment does not give media organizations immunity from the law of contracts even if they publish the truth. The newspapers' challenge to Judge Knoll's interpretation of the First Amendment was also the biggest issue in their briefs.

In terms of dollars for Cohen, the largest portion in the jury's verdict was its award of punitive damages. It also was the part of the jury's verdict most vulnerable to attack. To be sure, the jury had found that the newspapers, especially the *Star Tribune*, had acted maliciously toward Cohen. The evidence for malice toward Cohen was more than ample. The problem was that under Minnesota law, a jury cannot award punitive damages for a breach of contract, no matter how reprehensible the wrongdoer's behavior. There must be a tort besides a breach of contract. The only applicable tort in this case was fraud or misrepresentation.

That is why the jury's finding of misrepresentation was so critical. The jury's questions to Judge Knoll before the verdict manifested a conviction to punish the newspapers for reprehensible conduct but betrayed somewhat less certainty about a finding of misrepresentation.

The essence of misrepresentation is a deliberate misstatement of fact including, as in this case, an intention not to honor an agreement at the very time that one is entering into it.

Ironically, the newspapers—whose editors had deliberately dishonored the promises of Lori Sturdevant and Bill Salisbury and had disdained the protests of Sturdevant and Salisbury over the breaking of their word— now were trying to escape liability for misrepresentation by citing the integrity of the same reporters they had previously treated with contempt. Even though they broke their promises, the newspapers' argument went, they were not liable for misrepresentation because their reporters intended to honor the promises of confidentiality they made to Cohen.

I argued that there was a corporate responsibility for misrepresentation. The reporters and their supervising editors were part of the same corporations. If the reporters had no authority to make binding agreements for confidentiality, they should have informed Cohen. They did not.

On the contrary, I continued, the newspapers had encouraged sources to give reporters information in return for promises of confidentiality. Among other things, they got the Minnesota Legislature to adopt a law called the Minnesota Free Flow of Information Act, which gives journalists the right to refuse to disclose their confidential sources to courts and administrative agencies.

Moreover, neither newspaper through the respective editors ever intended to honor their reporters' promises. What mattered, I said, was the intent of the editors, not that of the subordinate reporters. *Pioneer Press* editor David Hall admitted that he decided to break Salisbury's promise as soon as he learned of it. *Star Tribune* editors claimed that they decided to break Sturdevant's promise after some discussion among themselves. Even so, the evidence justified a jury finding that they never intended to honor the promise.

I also brought up a new argument regarding the newspaper's lack of any First Amendment right to violate their promises of confidentiality. When the newspapers voluntarily made their agreements, they waived any claim of a First Amendment right to violate them. It would be a travesty if newspapers could make contracts, benefit from what the other party gave them, and then indiscriminately claim a constitutional right to walk away from their own obligations.

As they did so often before, the newspapers once again vilified Cohen for "dirty tricks." This time around, they similarly denounced Cohen's attorney. Borger's brief told the Court of Appeals that supposed "misconduct of plaintiff's counsel" required a new trial. In a classic example of the pot calling the kettle black, the *Star Tribune* brief accused Cohen's lawyer of having

mounted a broad-based attack on the news media. Article after article having nothing to do with this case was dissected before the jury, and then recounted in closing argument—a past conviction of a scrap iron dealer, past offenses of Geraldine Ferraro's parents, the religion of a school board candidate, charges of sexual misconduct against another school board candidate, the financial problems of a candidate for state treasurer, the shoplifting convictions of two candidates for Miss Minnesota, Bess Myerson's shoplifting arrest, and many others. He condemned the newspapers for their accurate news coverage and constitutionally protected expressions of opinion about Cohen.

In at least three respects the misconduct of counsel was so egregious as to require a new trial. First, he compared the trial tactics of defense counsel to "a common tactic in rape cases to attack the character of the victim rather than deal with the true issues." Second, counsel appealed to the bias of jurors against large corporations, suggesting that Cohen was not "anywhere near an equal basis as these corporations," but that "the lowliest individual has equal rights before you," and "if you allow the newspapers to get away with breaking their promises to Mr. Cohen in this case on the basis of the scurrilous personal assaults which have been leveled at him throughout this trial, all other promises made by newspapers to you, or any other individual, will be at risk." Finally, in his broad attacks on the media and constant side-trips through unrelated articles, counsel issued an open invitation to the jury to punish these newspapers for any perceived sins of these or any other papers. This Court now must direct a new trial.

The *Star Tribune* again argued that a promise of confidentiality was like a promise of marriage and could not be enforced by courts.

In the oral argument of June 10, 1989, Borger claimed that Cohen attempted to manipulate the press by "extracting" promises of confidentiality from the reporters. Cohen and his attorney, Borger continued, were using this case as a "crusade against big newspapers." Borger again argued that agreements for confidentiality are not legal contracts. Moreover, he declared, Judge Knoll improperly took the First Amendment out of the case and permitted a jury verdict that would "chill freedom of expression."

Hannah stressed that the newspapers should not be liable for misrepresentation because their reporters acted innocently in making promises the editors broke. He again castigated Cohen. The only fraud in the case, he asserted, was Cohen's "fraudulent inducement" of the promises from the reporters who did not know that Cohen was perpetrating a dirty trick.

I responded that the newspapers were demanding a ruling that went "far beyond any previous decision to empower newspapers to disdain the rights of others. This is not an application of the First Amendment. It is a perversion of the First Amendment. The ultimate issue is, are newspapers above the law governing every other business and individual? The jury said no. The judge said no. And we are asking you to say no."

In September 1989, the three-judge panel of the Court of Appeals upheld Cohen's contract cause of action and $200,000 compensatory damages by a 2–1 vote. It rejected the newspapers' claim of a right to violate agreements on several grounds.

First, the Court of Appeals reasoned that the First Amendment was not applicable to the case because there was no government coercion of the press. It was just a case of one private party making a voluntary agreement with another private party to suppress the publication of certain information (Cohen's name) in exchange for obtaining other information to be published.

The Court of Appeals agreed with Judge Knoll that an agreement of confidentiality is a commercial arrangement subject to the law of contracts.

We find no reason to provide less protection to the reasonable expectations of a newspaper informant than to any other party to whom the newspaper makes a promise. Surely, the newspapers would not suggest that they are immune to ordinary commercial contracts for goods and services. Yet the newspapers maintain that an agreement with a news source is exempt from the law of contracts. We disagree. The agreement to provide information, like any other service, is an appropriate subject matter for the law of contracts.

The court ruled that the First Amendment did not immunize news-papers from civil and criminal laws "simply because the acts giving rise to such liability were taken while in pursuit of newsworthy information."

Like Judge Knoll, the appellate court disdained the newspapers' argu-ment that the courts need not and should not intervene to police ethics of the press. "The specter of a huge damage award is a much more effective incentive for a publisher to honor a promise of confidentiality than the fear of criticism from other members of the press. Indeed any such fear of professional criticism in this case was apparently insufficient to convince appellants to abide by their promises."

In disposing of the newspapers' admonition that enforcing their agree-ment would impose "chilling effects" on speech, the Court of Appeals retorted, "We do not think it an undue burden to require the press to keep its promises."

For good measure, the court agreed that the newspapers had waived any First Amendment rights by their agreement with Cohen. "The two people pledging confidentiality were both seasoned reporters who had given such pledges on a regular basis for many years prior to this incident. They understood that they were waiving the right to publish a potentially newsworthy item in return for obtaining another potentially newsworthy item from Cohen. The waiver was part of a negotiated agreement between experienced reporters and an experienced political operative."

Finally, the Court of Appeals gave short shrift to the newspapers' charges of "misconduct" against the attorney opposing them. First, the court ruled that the newspaper articles I had introduced were properly admitted as evidence. Some showed that the newspapers did not reveal the identities of other sources despite the newsworthiness of their iden-tities. Others honored promises of confidentiality even though the news-paper did not have an "exclusive" on the information. Finally, the garbage can cartoon and columns by Klobuchar and Grow on Cohen showed that the *Star Tribune* "was acting with willful indifference to his rights, and was continuing to disparage him while failing to disclose its own breach of promise."

Second, the court rejected the newspapers' claim that my closing ar-gument "was so inflammatory that a new trial is required. A major focus of the newspapers' trial strategy was to portray Cohen as a scurrilous and dishonest politicker. In light of these attacks on Cohen's character, com-ments on the newspapers' ignoble motivations are not unduly prejudi-cial."

One of the three judges, Gary Crippen, dissented and would have denied any recovery. Crippen viewed the First Amendment as conferring special privileges on the press enjoyed by no one else.

The award of damages here directly and substantially implicates the First Amendment, and the vitality of the freedom of the press predominates in the face of competing considerations of contract law and waiver of rights. A judgment of damages in this case erroneously restricts a fundamental freedom we are to hold inviolate. The First Amendment guarantees that the press has special immunity from officials willing to restrict its freedom. Neither the courts nor other agencies of government can deal with the conduct of publishing in the same way they handle other conduct with similar characteristics. The award of damages here defies these principles and conflicts with the very essence of a special freedom of the press under the Constitution.

In the Court of Appeals, as in the jury, one vote made the difference between victory and defeat.

The court preserved the award of compensatory damages, but the issue of punitive damages remained. The Court of Appeals' characterization of the newspapers' misconduct indicated that it would have approved punitive damages if the requisite tort existed.

The appellate court, however, accepted the newspapers' argument that the reporters' intention to keep their promises shielded their employers at the newspapers from liability for misrepresentation. It reversed the verdict for misrepresentation. With that reversal went the $500,000 in punitive damages.

Even with the reduction in damages, no one in the media profession saw the appellate court's decision as a victory for the newspapers. Far from it. For example, *Washington Journalism Review* legal affairs columnist Lyle Denniston wrote:

The higher *Cohen* v. *Cowles Media* goes in the courts, the worse it seems to get for the press. That celebrated case has passed another level in the Minnesota courts with an even more alarming result. . . . The Minnesota Court of Appeals went even further [than the District Court] to take the First Amendment out of the case. . . . According to the Supreme Court, the press is supposed to have the greatest freedom when it covers politics and government. The Minnesota case is putting that seriously into doubt. . . . It was the first time any publication or broadcaster ever lost a case based on that [breach of contract] theory. The punitive damages award had nothing to do with the breach of contract theory, so the underlying threat to press freedom remains and grows.[2]

Columbia University's Everette Dennis, who earlier had predicted that the newspapers would win their appeal, said more succinctly, "This could have a genuine chilling effect on news gathering."[3]

A couple of days after the Court of Appeals issued its decision, Paul Hannah called me. He was cheerful. "The Court of Appeals did us all a favor. There was something for everyone. It made the case ripe for settlement. Now, we all can declare victory and leave this case with dignity."

Hannah suggested the newspapers' payment of the entire $200,000, a few thousand dollars of the interest on the compensatory damages that had accumulated to around $100,000, and not a penny of punitive damages. No one would file any more appeals. Hannah said that the newspapers were not making a formal proposal, but he thought they would accept something like it.

Hannah had a stick along with his carrot. He warned that Cohen and I could regret continuing to pursue this case. Another appeal would jeopardize all the compensatory damages, so it would be in Cohen's best interest to get the case over. He sounded a lot like Scott Johnson a year earlier.

Borger then took over the negotiations. We had many conversations and the three of us met for lunch (but not at the Minneapolis Club).

Borger said that the newspapers would be willing to pay most of the interest, but they were dead set against paying a penny of punitive damages or making any payment that could be construed as a substitute for any portion of those damages. There was another catch. Borger said that the newspapers would not make a written offer and insisted that Cohen make the first written move.

Eventually he came up to around $290,000—but not, of course, in writing. Even so, it must have been serious. It was a lot of money to turn down. It was tempting.

Still, $500,000 plus interest was too much to give up without a fight to the finish. It would haunt both Cohen and me forever if we walked away from a chance to restore the punitive damages. We had to challenge the Court of Appeals' misrepresentation ruling. It seemed a nonsensical and just plain wrong interpretation of the law that the newspapers should benefit from the integrity of their reporters in making promises that the editors dishonored so shabbily.

Anyway, I thought that we had nothing to lose by an appeal. The reasoning of the Court of Appeals was, to me, irrefutable on the First Amendment and contract issues. The newspapers and their attorneys also must have felt that the compensatory damages verdict was invulnerable.

Otherwise, why would they have continuously offered to pay the full amount of it to settle the case? We would not, so I thought, put the compensatory damages award at any big risk if we tried an appeal to restore the punitive damages. At the very worst, a ruling along the lines of Judge Crippen's dissent that the First Amendment rendered the press immune from the law of contracts would be a prime candidate for review by the U.S. Supreme Court. That would not be a bad thing.

The logic of it all seemed irresistible. Could I be missing something? Was Hannah just bluffing, or did he know something I did not?

For at least the fourth time, negotiations for a settlement failed. There was no turning back now.

We all filed petitions for review with the Minnesota Supreme Court. As everyone expected, the state high court agreed to take the case.

Notes

1. "Judge Refuses to Set Aside Verdict in News Source Suit," *Star Tribune*, November 20, 1988, 7B; Julie Anne Hoffman, "Judge Lets Cohen Award Stand," *St. Paul Pioneer Press*, November 20, 1988, 1B.

2. Lyle Denniston, "Breach of Contract Burns Press," *Washington Journalism Review*, November 1989, 48.

3. Alex S. Jones, "Ruling Could Alter Use of Newspapers' Sources," *New York Times*, September 10, 1989, sec. 1, 22.

Not for Another 200 Years

ONCE MORE INTO the briefs.

Borger and Hannah again were the lead attorneys for the newspapers. Pat's name did not appear on their new briefs. As in all their briefs from the time the case began, the newspapers' central defense was that the First Amendment barred any recovery for Cohen.

The constitutional arguments by now were so thrice-familiar that each of us could have written the other's briefs. Some of the language was more apocalyptic, however.

For example, Borger declared, "If this court endorses the use of contract theory in reporter-source relationships, plaintiffs will use contract law as the preferred cause of action to avoid constitutional scrutiny." At the time, Borger's prediction seemed wildly hyperbolic even for a legal brief. It later proved prophetic.

Both newspapers' briefs demanded that the Minnesota Supreme Court reverse the decisions of the lower courts because they allegedly violated the U.S. Constitution. Hannah went to the heart of the matter. "The precise question before the Court is whether an accommodation of First Amendment interests must be made. The majority of the Court of Appeals erred when it failed to recognize that fundamental First Amendment rights are at stake in this case."

An amicus brief filed by the Associated Press on behalf of the newspapers argued that the Minnesota Court of Appeals erred because it allowed Cohen's complaint for breach of contract to "circumvent" the newspapers' rights under the First Amendment. It was the first amicus brief to be filed in the case. There was a certain irony in this since the Associated Press, unlike the newspapers, had honored its reporter's promise to Cohen. Blue-ribbon New York media lawyer Richard Winfield, the author of the AP brief, in an article published after the trial in the spring 1989 issue of the American Bar Association's *Communications Lawyer*, rebuked Judge Knoll's "exclusion of First Amendment principles." Winfield expressed himself as "confident that an appellate court will somehow look beyond the first-year law school analysis of contract and fraud" and strike down the jury verdict and the two decisions of Judge Knoll.

There was one thing, though, upon which Cohen, the newspapers, and Winfield agreed—the *Cohen* case presented profound issues of interpretation of the First Amendment. Does the First Amendment give the press immunity from the obligations everyone else would have under the law of contracts? Before Judge Knoll, no court had addressed this question. Three judges of the Court of Appeals and Judge Knoll had struggled with it. Now it was the state Supreme Court's turn.

After everyone had filed their briefs, the newspapers managed to get in the last word again. On March 12, 1990, one day before the oral argument, the *National Law Journal*, a periodical influential with lawyers and judges, published an article by an attorney for the *Wall Street Journal* named Richard Tofel that implored the Minnesota Supreme Court to throw out Cohen's case. Tofel resurrected the newspapers' comparison of confidentiality agreements to promises of marriage. None of the four judges who had previously heard the case, not even Crippen, took this notion seriously. Court enforcement of agreements between newspapers and their sources, Tofel wrote, "would damage the delicate fabric of reporter-source relationships." Tofel did add that a contract not to publish the information was, as he put it, unenforceable because of the First Amendment. The author sought to assure readers that he was not arguing that the press was "above the law"; instead, he said, it was "*apart from the law*." Neither Tofel nor the *National Law Journal* elucidated this distinction.[1]

A particular complication for the current round of appeals was the background of the chief justice of the Minnesota Supreme Court. I had known Chief Justice Peter Popovich for thirty years. We had discussed various bills from time to time when he was a lobbyist and I was a member of the Minnesota legislature. Pat also had worked with him in lobbying on some of her clients' legislation. Before that, Popovich had been a longtime and influential legislator. He had been celebrated for decades as one of the state's most astute politicians.

I first met Popovich back in 1960, when I was an undergraduate at the University of Minnesota and, as chairman of the student government Legislative Affairs Commission, was contacting various legislators regarding student tuition and university appropriations. Popovich at the time had served eight years as a state representative and was the head of the House of Representatives subcommittee appropriating money for the university. He was not at all generous to the university, and university administrators in private reviled him as their "public enemy number one."

Nevertheless, I liked Popovich even then, and over the years we always got along well. The problem for the *Cohen* case was that one of Popovich's biggest clients as a lawyer and lobbyist had been the same *Pioneer Press* that was fighting this lawsuit.

To make matters worse, Popovich was not just a titular chief justice. He dominated the Minnesota Supreme Court by the force of his personality and his political acumen.

Personal admiration is one thing, but I did not want Popovich to be sitting in judgment on a case of such importance to his past client. The question was what, if anything, I could do about it. No independent authority in Minnesota may compel the removal of a chief justice from a case, no matter what the cause. An attorney who feels strongly can only make a request to the chief justice himself and hope for the best. Of course, the risk is that such a plea could antagonize Popovich and exacerbate an already touchy situation. Needless to say, few bother.

The only safe course seemed to be a brief and respectful letter addressed to Chief Justice Popovich alone, without copies to any other justices and certainly not to the media. It seemed a reasonable risk. If Popovich ignored the request and participated in a decision favoring his former client, at least I could have an additional ground for seeking review by the U.S. Supreme Court.

I sent the letter to the chief justice in November 1989, four months before the scheduled oral argument. Week after week went by with no reply. The day for the oral argument arrived, and still nothing from Popovich. I steeled myself for the worst.

I got to the courtroom an hour in advance of the argument. As I was looking over the briefs one last time, Popovich came into the courtroom and sat next to me. He was jovial and reminisced about our association at the legislature.

"Hi, Elliot, I got your letter. You know I worked for the newspaper a long time ago, but it doesn't affect me now. If you're bothered about it, I suppose I'll have to take myself out of the case. I won't take part in the decision, but if it's okay with you, I would like to stay today and preside over the argument. It's an interesting case."

"Sure, Mr. Chief Justice. I hope that you did not take any offense at my request."

"Nah. We go back a long way."

With that, the chief justice laughed and went back to his chambers. A few minutes later, he and the other justices entered the courtroom to convene the oral argument.

John Borger began. "The central error which permeates this entire case is that the court below perceived no constitutional dimension to the case. Yet contract theory interferes with three First Amendment rights of the press. It interferes with news gathering, because under this theory the court and jury will second-guess the manner in which reporters deal with their sources. It interferes with the editing process, because under this theory courts and juries will decide what information editors should have left out and what they should have included in the story. Finally, it interferes with the publication of truthful, newsworthy information and it suppresses or punishes that publication."

Borger concluded, "You must reverse the judgment below, because the trial court gave no consideration to the First Amendment and allowed the jury to give no consideration to the First Amendment."

Justice John Simonett asked several questions of Borger.

"Doesn't the fact that the newspaper put a self-imposed restriction of not revealing the source weigh in the balance?

"I tell you what's bothering me. What's newsworthy about revealing Cohen's name?

"The paper was free to say that the source was a source close to the Whitney campaign, right?

"What was the purpose in publishing Cohen's employer's name?"

All these questions were encouraging.

In my presentation, I tried to convince the justices that the reporters' desire to keep their promises should not shield the newspapers for misrepresentation through the conduct of their editors. Simonett, the most active questioner, kept coming back to the good intentions of the reporters. He also had a question on contract law.

"Let's take up your contract theory. For how long would this promise have to be kept, under this contract?"

"However long it should have been kept," I replied, "certainly it should have been kept longer than the few hours or the few minutes it took them to violate that contract."

The only justice who manifested hostility to Cohen's entire case was Rosalie Wahl, Perpich's first appointment to the Supreme Court and the first woman on the court.

"Why shouldn't the decision on whether a promise is honored or not be an editorial decision, rather than a decision of the court?"

"This would create a privilege for newspapers which no one else in society has. Newspapers ought not to have the right to dishonor and violate promises which were voluntarily entered into," I said.

"But the public interest that's involved to me," Wahl declared, "the greater public interest than even individual contract rights, is the right of the public to have accurate information and, particularly, to have information with regard to their elective processes."

Concluding his rebuttal, Borger returned to his old argument that a reporter's promise of confidentiality in exchange for information should not constitute a contract to begin with. This time Borger asserted that a reporter's promise of confidentiality to obtain information was akin to a promise not to identify to others the source of "backyard gossip." Justice Simonett shot back, "This is more than backyard gossip, though. Don't you think it's within the business of news gathering between the source and the reporter?" That was precisely the point. I thought that Justice Simonett had finally killed that claim for good.

At the end of the oral argument, Chief Justice Popovich praised all the attorneys. He then came down from the bench and bantered with Bernard Casserly and me in the hallway outside the courtroom. Whatever his views on the powers of the press, he was just a great guy.

Winter turned to spring and then summer. There was no word from the Supreme Court. What was the cause of the delay? Were the justices preparing a weighty dissertation on the relationship of the First Amendment to the law of contracts worthy of immortalization in constitutional law treatises?

Meanwhile, Marlene Johnson and Rudy Perpich were campaigning for their third term as lieutenant governor and governor of Minnesota. The timing of the current Minnesota Supreme Court proceeding was not exactly opportune for Johnson and Perpich. Needless to say, they did not welcome any highly publicized court decision reminding voters of Johnson's criminal record. There were degrees of embarrassment, though; the better a decision for Cohen, the worse for Johnson and vice versa. The case became an even hotter political potato as Election Day drew closer.

Two months after the oral argument, the Minnesota Supreme Court decided another contentious press case in a manner not encouraging to

Cohen's case. In *Diesen* v. *Hessburg*, Chief Justice Popovich wrote the decision overturning a $700,000-plus libel judgment against the *Duluth News Tribune*, which happened to be owned by the same company that owned the *Pioneer Press*.

It was good that Popovich was out of the *Cohen* case. I asked the plaintiff's attorney in *Diesen* whether he had similarly sought Popovich's withdrawal. He said that he had thought about it but decided against it for fear of offending Popovich and big-shot local lawyers.

Popovich's decision in that case went out of its way to emphasize that while "First Amendment and other policy [sic] considerations" would support it, "our decision is rooted in state defamation law." That effectively eliminated any chance for getting the U.S. Supreme Court to take the case. In the event, the high court denied plaintiff's request to review the decision.

In early July 1990, Governor Perpich announced that he intended to appoint Justice Alexander M. (Sandy) Keith, a former Democratic legislator and lieutenant governor as chief justice when Popovich was due to retire in November because of Minnesota's mandatory retirement statute.[2] Publicly dangling a promotion to a sitting justice so long in advance was extraordinary, to say the least. Did it have anything to do with the election campaign and the looming decision in the *Cohen* case? While the Supreme Court was still considering its decision, Justice Keith gave an exclusive interview to the *Star Tribune* that the newspaper published on July 9. The idea of so cooperating with a party in a case before his court was dubious in itself, but one comment was particularly interesting. Keith expressed a preference for basing decisions on state law rather than the U.S. Constitution, in order to thwart review by the U.S. Supreme Court.

Q. As the U.S. Supreme Court of Presidents Reagan and Bush becomes more conservative, some states are expected to take the initiative in protecting civil liberties and preserving the legacy of the liberal Warren court. Will Minnesota be one of them?

A. I just bought a book dealing with this subject, and I think this is continually going to come up. It's going to be a very interesting trend. In the old days we all followed the U.S. Supreme Court as it applied the Bill of Rights. Now, with decisions changing the thrust of the Warren court on issues like free speech and exercise of religion, there may be room to take a different tack (on the basis of state constitutions).[3]

It was the same approach as Chief Justice Popovich's in the *Diesen* case.

This was not the first time that state officials had contrived a states' rights doctrine to use state law to defy the authority of the U.S. Supreme Court. The objectives were new but the means were not original. Decades earlier, Southern politicians and judges concocted the doctrine of "interposition" of state law over the U.S. Constitution to flout the U.S. Supreme Court and perpetuate segregation. It did not work then. In the 1958 decision of *Cooper* v. *Aaron*, the Supreme Court ruled that it is a "permanent and indispensable feature of our constitutional system" that the federal judiciary "is supreme in the exposition of the law of the Constitution." It reminded state officials that Article VI makes the Constitution "the supreme law of the land." The Court rebuked state judges for not honoring the supremacy of the Constitution. "No state legislator or executive or judicial officer can war against the Constitution without violating his oath to support it."

Nevertheless, state judges again were promoting currently fashionable, politically correct ends through dubious judicial means to circumvent the Supreme Court. This time, though, they were the very people who had condemned the earlier assertion of states' rights. Whatever the euphemism employed, it was again defiance of the law.

What, if anything, did Keith's interview portend for the *Cohen* case? Plenty, as I would find out soon enough.

The state Supreme Court finally issued its decision on July 20, 1990, eleven days after the publication of Keith's interview and more than four months after the oral argument.

In two paragraphs, the decision written by Justice John Simonett agreed with the Court of Appeals that the newspapers did not commit misrepresentation against Cohen, and that as a result Cohen could not obtain punitive damages.

That was bad enough, but worse followed. The section on contracts started out conventionally enough. Justice Simonett's decision found that Cohen's agreement with the reporters had all the elements required for a contract—offer, acceptance, and consideration. It also declared that "unquestionably" the reporters and Cohen intended to keep their promises.

So far, so good. The jury had found that the newspapers had made and broken contracts with Cohen. Judge Knoll, who presided at the trial, in denying the newspapers' posttrial motions had similarly found that they had "entered into a contract with the plaintiff where the hornbook elements of offer, acceptance, and consideration were unmistakably present." All three judges on the Court of Appeals had agreed that there was a contract, but one thought the First Amendment should invalidate it.

Then—in the face of the verdict of the jury, the opinions of all the judges who had previously heard the case, the testimony of the reporters and Cohen at the trial, and Simonett's observations during the oral argument—the majority declared that Cohen and the reporters did not intend to create a contract "in any business sense," but only a "moral obligation." That was news to Cohen, Sturdevant, and Salisbury. It also contradicted Ismach, who had testified that confidentiality agreements are common business practices by which newspapers obtain information to publish at a profit. To the surprise of everyone, Justice Simonett accepted the newspapers' argument that the promises to Cohen had the same legal effect as promises to marry.

Justice Simonett dismissed the confidentiality promises to Cohen as an "I'll-scratch-your-back-if-you'll-scratch-mine" accommodation. He concluded that contract law is "an ill fit for a promise of news source confidentiality" and that a contract claim is "inappropriate for these particular circumstances."

It took all of one page. In contrast to the painstaking constitutional analyses of Judge Knoll and the three judges of the Minnesota Court of Appeals, the Minnesota Supreme Court decision on contract law was bereft of any mention of the First Amendment or any U.S. Supreme Court decision.

But there was method to what was on the surface a brusque and superficial ruling. Behind the opinion's brevity and paucity of legal exegesis was a thinly veiled objective: to block any review by the U.S. Supreme Court.

It was a master stroke of interposition, 1990s style. The Minnesota Supreme Court arbitrarily had taken the First Amendment out of a case that since 1982 had been the focus of a landmark conflict between rights under contract law and rights under the constitutional guarantee of freedom of the press. The state court did not resolve the conflict; it just buried it.

Then, the decision went off on a curious tangent. After rejecting Cohen's contract and misrepresentation claims, the court's majority added that Cohen was not entitled to relief under promissory estoppel. Neither Judge Knoll nor the Minnesota Court of Appeals had mentioned promissory estoppel.

The theory of promissory estoppel creates an implied contract, in the absence of something bargained for in exchange for a promise, where someone relying upon a broken promise takes action causing him injury. No one had regarded promissory estoppel law as relevant to Cohen's case because Cohen had given the newspapers something of value that they wanted—the court documents—in exchange for their promises of confidentiality. As Judge Knoll had pointed out, Cohen's agreement was a classic example of a contract.

The state Supreme Court decision ruled that even though the newspapers had made and broken promises to Cohen, and Cohen relied on these promises to his detriment, he could not recover under promissory estoppel unless "injustice can only be avoided by enforcing the promise. Here Cohen lost his job; but whether this is an injustice which should be remedied requires the court to examine a transaction fraught with moral ambiguity. Both sides proclaim their own purity of intentions while condemning the other side for 'dirty tricks.' If the court applies promissory estoppel, its inquiry is not limited to whether a promise was given and broken, but rather the inquiry is into all the reasons why it was broken." It sounded as if all the newspapers had to do was to come up with the right excuses—like the other guy's supposed "dirty tricks"—for breaking their promises.

But at the very end of its decision, when all had seemed lost, the court gave the tiniest of openings for a petition to the U.S. Supreme Court. It suggested that the First Amendment was one among other reasons why Cohen could not prevail on a promissory estoppel claim.

"Under a promissory estoppel analysis, there can be no neutrality towards the First Amendment. In deciding whether it would be unjust not to enforce the promise, the court must necessarily weigh the same considerations that are weighed for whether the First Amendment has been violated. The court must balance the constitutional rights of a free press against the common law interest in protecting promises of anonymity. . . . Of critical significance in this case, we think, is that the promise of anonymity arises in the classic First Amendment context of the quintessential public debate in our democratic society, namely, a political source involved in a political campaign."

Was the court talking about the actual First Amendment or some sort of philosophy of state law akin to the purpose behind the First Amendment?

One sentence in the final paragraph of the decision would be the key to getting U.S. Supreme Court review. "We conclude that in this case enforcement of the promise of confidentiality under a promissory estoppel theory would violate defendants' First Amendment rights."

The First Amendment was back. But was it too little and too late? The court clearly rejected Cohen's contract and misrepresentation claims solely on the basis of state law. As for promissory estoppel, the language was less than precise. The spin of the newspapers and their supporters was that, as far as promissory estoppel was concerned, the court ruled against Cohen just on a general notion of "justice" and merely threw in the First Amendment as a rhetorical flourish.

Whatever, the First Amendment was in the decision and was the only hope for getting the case to the U.S. Supreme Court. It was grasping for straws, though. But at least I had a straw.

Why did the justices bring the First Amendment in through the back door after they seemingly had banished it? And why did they take more than four months after the oral argument to hand down their brief decision?

The justices would not talk about it. An inside court source, however, revealed that the reason was an internal court dispute over the integrity of the judicial process. According to the source, one justice refused to sign the opinion if it did not acknowledge the constitutional issue of freedom of the press that all the lower court judges and all the parties had recognized as the heart of the case from the very beginning. The other three justices had no choice. Without a fourth vote, no majority would exist to reverse the Court of Appeals.

Had Chief Justice Popovich not withdrawn, he could have supplied the fourth vote for a ruling in the newspapers' favor on state law alone, without a mention of the First Amendment. More than that, Popovich had the political and legal moxie to craft a decision, as in the *Diesen* case, that was appeal-proof. Getting the chief justice off the case changed the balance of the court. I would not know how decisive it was to the case until later.

Two justices wrote furious dissents. They not only disagreed with the decision, they were outraged. Unlike the majority decision, there was real passion in these dissents.

Justice Lawrence R. Yetka rebuked the decision, which

carved out yet another special privilege in favor of the press that is denied other citizens. The news media should be compelled to keep their promises like anyone else.

I find the consequences of this decision deplorable. First, potential news sources will now be reluctant to give information to reporters. As a result, the public could very well be denied far more important information about candidates for public office relevant to evaluating their qualifications than the rather trivial information disclosed here. Second, it offends the fundamental principle of equality under the law.

This decision sends out a clear message that if you are wealthy and powerful enough, the law simply does not apply to you; contract law, it now seems, applies only to millions of ordinary people. It is unconscionable to allow the press, on the one hand, to hide behind the shield of confidentiality when it does not want to reveal the source of its information; yet, on the other hand, to violate confidentiality agreements with impunity when it decides that disclosing the source will help make its story more sensational and profitable.

Far from being finished, Justice Yetka fired another salvo about press hypocrisy regarding the rule of law. "During the Watergate crisis, the press published many pious editorials urging that the laws be enforced equally against everyone, even the President of the United States. Nevertheless, the press now argues that the law should not apply to them because they alone are entitled to make 'editorial decisions' as to what the public should read, see, or hear and whether the source of that information should be disclosed."

As if all that were not enough, Justice Yetka did something bordering on sacrilege by challenging the very foundation of modern First Amendment law.

The decision in New York Times v. Sullivan has not resulted in a more responsible press. Perhaps it is time in these United States to return to treating the press the same as any other citizen. Let them print anything they choose to print, but make them legally responsible if they break their promises or act negligently in connection with what they print—free of any special protection carved out by New York Times v. Sullivan or any of its progeny. The decision of this court makes this a sad day in the history of a responsible press in America.

Justice Glenn E. Kelley in his dissent lamented that the majority decision "affords to the commercial media immunity from liability from an unmistakable breach of contract, although any other corporate or private citizen of this state under similar circumstances would most certainly have been liable in damages for breach of contract."

Justice Kelley scorned "the majority's analysis that, notwithstanding that all of the elements of a legal contract and its breach are here present, the contract is unenforceable because 'the parties intended none.' It reaches this conclusion even as it concedes that the promises given by the agents and employees of these defendants was [sic] intended by them to be kept."

In obvious anger, Justice Kelley condemned "the perfidy of these defendants, the liability for which they now seek to escape by trying to crawl under the aegis of the First Amendment, which, in my opinion, has nothing to do with the case."

Justice Kelley ended his dissent with an almost 300-word footnote in which he termed the newspapers' position in the *Cohen* case "indeed ironical in light of the extensive efforts of each to promote enactment of the Minnesota Free Flow of Information Act." This law protects the media from compelled disclosure of sources in court and other proceedings. With barely concealed relish, Justice Kelley described in detail how an unnamed "attorney-lobbyist" for the *Pioneer Press* engineered passage of the bill. The anonymous "attorney-lobbyist" was, of course, Peter Popovich before he became a justice. One wonders if Justice Kelley would have been so recalcitrant in naming him if Chief Justice Popovich had refused to withdraw from the case.

On the same day as the state Supreme Court's decision, Justice William J. Brennan retired from the U.S. Supreme Court. Brennan had written the decisions in *New York Times* v. *Sullivan* and *Time, Inc.* v. *Hill.*

To observers of the litigation, there was no mystery why the Minnesota Supreme Court majority avoided the U.S. Constitution in quashing Cohen's contract claim. As University of Minnesota journalism professor and media law textbook author Donald Gillmor saw it, the Minnesota Supreme Court majority "made the only decision it could have made without providing strong grounds for appeal to the U.S. Supreme Court. The Minnesota Supreme Court had to slam the door on that." Gillmor had no doubt that the court had succeeded. It proved the prescience of his original prognostication, he said, that Cohen's case "was doomed to fail from the beginning."[4]

Even some media organization lawyers faulted the Minnesota Supreme Court's ruling that promises of confidentiality were not contracts. For example, Harry Johnston, legal counsel for *Time* magazine, said that "if I make you a promise not to use your name, then it's a contract."[5]

A reporter for a local station came to the house and interviewed me about the decision for the evening television news. "Surely," she said, "you must have kept something from the verdict."

"No, the Supreme Court took it all away."

Walking out the door and thinking I was out of earshot, she said to her cameraman, "That poor slob."

Several other media organizations asked my opinion of the state Supreme Court decision. I bit my tongue. My only comment was that I would ask the U.S. Supreme Court to hear the case.

The conventional wisdom was unanimous that the Minnesota Supreme Court decision had finished the *Cohen* case off for good. My talk of an appeal was ludicrous. It was one more quixotic effort, if I would even stick with it.

One attorney approached me in the county law library. "Hey, Rothenberg, I see you're appealing the *Cohen* case."

"Yeah. I know it will be uphill."

"Ha! It's more than uphill. You've got as much chance as a fart in a whirlwind."

Another lawyer wanted to talk about the case. "What are your odds, Elliot?"

"On getting cert or winning the case?"

"On carrying through with writing the petition."

The promotional mailing for the Practising Law Institute's November 1990 Communications Law Seminar, in effect the annual national convention of media lawyers, announced that one of its principal topics would be the newspapers' "win" in the *Cohen* case and how good that was for the media as a whole. John Borger would be on the seminar's faculty. Borger told the national weekly *Media Law Reporter* that the U.S. Supreme Court would not take any appeal because the decision was based upon state law only.[6]

The newspapers suddenly were anxious to eject the First Amendment from the very case in which for the previous three years they had berated Judge Knoll and then the Court of Appeals for allegedly failing to give it proper obeisance as the fundamental law governing the litigation.

Others boasted that the Minnesota Supreme Court's slamming of the doors on Cohen's case would have a big domino effect benefiting the press in suits across the board for various wrongdoing or dissuading people from challenging media misconduct in the first place. Media lobbyist Jane Kirtley exulted, "I would be surprised if this does not pretty much shut off litigation in this whole area."[7]

Pat spoke to the Minneapolis Kiwanis Club about the state Supreme Court decision, razzing me about winning what she called the final battle in our big case together. "I always knew who was the better lawyer in the family." The audience guffawed, but Pat wasn't laughing. She did not intend it as a joke.

Professor Lucas Powe hailed the state Supreme Court's decision for ending the case in *The Fourth Estate and the Constitution* (1991), a leading scholarly treatise on the First Amendment. "Initially, two lower Minnesota courts ruled that each of the papers violated a valid contract and should pay for the harm it caused. That conclusion is simply wrong. A mere common law label—'contract' rather than 'libel'—does not make the Constitution disappear. The Minnesota Supreme Court corrected the errors."[8]

I could not help agonizing that if the newspapers' lawyers were serious a few months earlier, I could have settled the case for somewhere between $250,000 and $300,000. Now, the newspapers and their supporters gloated, I was shut out for good.

My whole legal career was riding on this case, and I had made what now seemed a catastrophic error by not agreeing to a settlement in the hundreds of thousands of dollars.

Most nights, I could not sleep at all. Those nights when I was able to doze off, I would wake up, in a cold sweat, after a couple of hours.

My only hope for vindication was the petition to the U.S. Supreme Court.

Public television's *Almanac* had a panel of newspaper supporters giving a postmortem of the *Cohen* case. No one took seriously my appeal to the U.S. Supreme Court. One panelist said the only thing Cohen had to show for all his years of litigation was the large bill the lawyers sent the newspapers.

Paul Hannah quipped, "It took 200 years to get Cohen's case. We won't see its like again for another 200 years." The moderator riposted, "We'll all get back together then."

Everyone chortled. The timing of the repartee was perfect, but Hannah's prediction was somewhat off.

It turned out to be closer to 200 days.

Notes

1. Richard J. Tofel, "Under Inspection," *National Law Journal*, March 12, 1990, 13.

2. Betty Wilson, "Perpich Names Keith Next Chief Justice of Supreme Court," *Star Tribune*, July 7, 1990, 1A.

3. Dane Smith, "Keith Brings Expertise in Family Law to Chief-Justice Post," *Star Tribune*, July 9, 1990, 1B.

4. Margaret Zack, "News Sources May Be Less Eager to Talk After Ruling," *Star Tribune*, July 21, 1990, 1B

5. Cary Peyton Rich, "Decision Could Chill Newsgathering," *Folio*, October 1, 1990, 42

6. "NewsNotes," *Media Law Reporter*, July 31, 1990, 1.

7. Zack, "News Sources . . . Ruling."

8. Lucas A. Powe, Jr., *The Fourth Estate and the Constitution: Freedom of the Press in America* (Berkeley: University of California Press, 1991), 189.

The Court Granted the Cert, the Court Granted the Cert!

Parsifal: Who is the Grail?

Gurnemanz: That may not be told. But if you are chosen for it, you will not fail to know.[1]

EACH YEAR, LAWYERS in more than 8,000 cases beseech the Supreme Court to give them the chance to show that a U.S. Court of Appeals or state Supreme Court decision was wrong. They do this even though the process typically costs thousands of dollars in filing fees and expenses of professionally printing the petitions, not to mention massive amounts of attorneys' time. The Supreme Court agrees to hear less than 1 percent of these cases.

Arguing before the U.S. Supreme Court is the pinnacle of the practice of law. Some have compared a Supreme Court appearance in an important case to the World Series or Super Bowl. If anything, that's an understatement. With the World Series and Super Bowl, at least there is a known and precisely defined way of getting there—win more games than anyone else. For the Supreme Court, the process is as inscrutable as the response of Gurnemanz.

Why does the U.S. Supreme Court take a case? How can a lawyer ensure that the justices will bestow their favor upon him or her? The Supreme Court orders granting or denying certiorari do not specify the justices' reasons or even the votes on the petitions.

The published Supreme Court rule on criteria for review does not shed much light. It states that review "is not a matter of right but of judicial discretion" and "will be granted only for compelling reasons." The rule lists some factors the Court may consider but cautions that these are "neither controlling nor fully measuring the Court's discretion."

Justice Felix Frankfurter once said, "In my old age, when I shall have attained wisdom, I plan to write a book entitled 'The calculus of certiorari or how the Supreme Court determines when to grant and when to deny.' "[2] Frankfurter never wrote the book.

There is one procrustean requirement for certiorari, however. A case must present issues implicating the U.S. Constitution or federal law. No matter how unjust a lower court decree, the Supreme Court may not review a decision involving issues of state law only. The Minnesota Supreme Court majority framed its decision with that in mind.

My first task was to persuade the justices that the First Amendment was the basis of the state Supreme Court's decision. Here I got some help from a most unlikely source, *Star Tribune* executive editor Joel Kramer.

In praising the Minnesota Supreme Court decision, Kramer said in a prepared statement to the *New York Times*, "We are especially pleased that the court has ruled that the decision to publish true facts relating to the activities of a political source in a political campaign is one that is protected by the First Amendment."[3] At the same time, *Star Tribune* attorney John Borger was issuing his own statements telling everyone that the First Amendment had nothing to do with the state Supreme Court decision. I reprinted Kramer's statement in the petition.

Even if that gave me a boost on the jurisdictional issue, U.S. Supreme Court review still was very much a long shot. The *Cohen* case was unprecedented. Its sui generis nature may have made the case more interesting but was a hindrance to Supreme Court acceptance of it.

Nine justices on the Supreme Court cannot correct every lower court decision that wrongly interprets the Constitution. Justices who have spoken publicly on the matter have said that they look for splits in decisions of U.S. Courts of Appeals as the most important determinant of whether a case is worthy of review by the Supreme Court. The justices like to see an issue "percolate" in lower courts before deciding it definitively. Individuals like Cohen with early cases are out of luck while the "percolation" is going on. That individual hardship is an unavoidable consequence of the Supreme Court's functioning as an arbiter of constitutional and federal law, and not as a universal guarantor of justice in every case decided by a lower court.

In a 1994 speech at Harvard Law School, Justice Ruth Bader Ginsburg, who joined the Court in 1993, said that 70 percent of the cases the Supreme Court takes are "based on splits of authority among federal courts of appeals or state supreme courts. We take cases primarily to keep federal law fairly uniform throughout the country, to resolve deep splits among federal or state tribunals over the meaning of a federal legislative, executive, or constitutional prescription. The Court usually does not take the first case to raise a particular question. We wait for a split unlikely to heal. Returns from several courts can advance our understanding of an issue, the frequency with which it occurs, the settings in which it arises, and the range of opinions on the proper resolution. A further reason why we resist early grants is the genuine respect we have for the able judges across the country. They strive to get it right, and they generally do."[4]

Splits between federal courts of appeal or state Supreme Courts do not guarantee certiorari. Even there, the Supreme Court turns down many more cases than it accepts.

Cohen's case did not meet the conventional requirements as Justice Ginsburg described them.

Only one approach would have any chance of success.

My strategy was to attempt to convince the justices that they must grant certiorari because the *Cohen* case—even though the first of its kind—raised especially important constitutional questions relating to the validity of the media's claims of powers to injure persons with impunity. I also wanted to make the justices aware of how essential confidential sources are to the flow of information to the public.

I stated on the first page of my petition that the central question before the Court was "Does the First Amendment of the U.S. Constitution grant newspapers immunity from liability for damages caused by dishonoring promises of confidentiality given in exchange for information on a political candidate?"

Every working day, the mail and private delivery services deposit more than thirty petitions for certiorari, on the average, at the Supreme Court clerk's office. Disposing of them requires an assembly line type of operation.

Writing a successful petition to the Supreme Court is just about the toughest challenge a lawyer can face. The justices and their clerks are not about to spend much time plowing through convoluted and turgid tomes of interminable length. Concise and well-reasoned argument expressed in chiseled prose is imperative. Every word, every punctuation mark is critical. The lawyer must prepare a document that is comprehensive but short—one that is logically compelling with precise legal argument and persuasive English composition. No matter how complicated the case, the petition had better be no longer than fifteen pages. It is a lot harder to prepare an effective short brief than a longer one.

But all this is just the bare minimum. The petition must stand out from the crowd to such an extent as to impel the Supreme Court to pluck it from the 99 percent of those it will summarily reject.

The petition's first paragraph has to seize the attention of the justices and their clerks. Otherwise, they could ignore the rest of it and go on to the next petition.

Mine began, "This case raises the question of whether the First Amendment empowers newspapers to inflict injuries with impunity by deliberately breaking promises of confidentiality given for the purpose of obtaining desired information. No previous decision of this Court has specifically addressed this issue. Minnesota Supreme Court Justice Lawrence Yetka in his dissent said that the First Amendment 'is being misused' to enable the press to avoid liability for the consequences of broken promises. Should the press be allowed to employ the Constitution to thwart a remedy for acts, assailed as unethical even by media supporters, which would be unlawful when committed by others?"

I cited a comment in the *New York Times* by Floyd Abrams, who had represented media organizations in several cases before the Supreme Court, calling the *Star Tribune*'s and *Pioneer Press*'s behavior "reprehensible and damaging to all journalists."

The petition stressed that the central question of the Minnesota Supreme Court decision was whether or not the media have an obligation to obey laws that bind all others. The press, I said, should not have a special privilege to infringe the rights and liberties of other citizens.

The First Amendment, I said, "does not allow the media to escape the consequences of violating promises made voluntarily with no governmental compulsion whatsoever."

Other cases had made a distinction "between consensual conduct and governmental coercion. It is the latter which implicates the First Amendment. The present case involves no governmental coercion over editorial judgment but, rather, the exercise of that judgment through a voluntary promise of confidentiality in return for desired information."

"This case," I told the Court, "presents explicitly the question of whether the First Amendment permits a media organization to deliberately violate an undisputed and unambiguous promise.

"It also has implications beyond the violation of agreements. If it is impermissible to hold the press liable for dishonoring voluntary promises to obtain information, is it also to be granted a right to commit torts or crimes in gathering news?"

The importance of offering and honoring promises of confidentiality to acquiring information for the public also made Supreme Court review of the Minnesota decision imperative.

I stressed that "confidential sources are an essential component of news gathering. They are used in reporting on almost all news areas, but are relied upon most heavily in reporting about the subject of government.

"Legalizing the violation of promises of confidentiality would deter other potential sources, resulting in the denial of important information to the public."

The petition referred to several studies showing how ubiquitous confidential sources are in news stories. For example, 80 percent of newsmagazine articles and 50 percent of wire service stories rely on confidential sources.

One survey the petition discussed found that more than 40 percent of federal officials in high positions admitted having given the press information on condition of anonymity while in office.

I pointed to a study showing that two-thirds of stories nominated for Pulitzer Prizes used confidential sources. "Several nominees agreed that the more important the story, the more likely the need for confidentiality." One scholar wrote, "When it comes to stories that count, i.e., those that are embarrassing to government officials and politicians, the use of confidential sources is a necessity."

I quoted journalism executive and educator Richard M. Clurman that abandoning the use of confidential sources would carry a price "so high as to be unacceptable, not only to the press but to the public." It would deprive the public of "a large percentage of the valuable, accurate, and important stories that appear in print and on the air." On a typical day, the *Washington Post* and *New York Times* attribute information to confidential sources more than 100 times, and the *Wall Street Journal* did it 42 times in one story alone.

I did not mention that Supreme Court justices themselves have been confidential sources.

The petition pointed out that the Minnesota Free Flow of Information Act and many similar state statutes, which the press lobbied for, protect the news media from compelled disclosure of sources. The Minnesota statute's section titled "Public Policy" states that the public interest and free flow of information require protection of the confidential relationship between reporter and source.

Allowing newspapers to break these promises—voluntarily and without court compulsion—would discourage other sources from providing material, and thus reduce the amount of information available to the public.

In concluding the petition, I referred the justices to Judge Knoll's holding that to deny an injured person recovery for demonstrated harm caused by the breach of an otherwise valid contract would deprive him of the protection of the law without any countervailing benefit to the public in being informed. Instead, it would have the opposite effect of impeding the free flow of information.

Finally, I wrote, "As Justice Yetka declared, no one, including the news media, should be above the law."

After trumpeting claims of constitutional rights under freedom of the press ever since the case began, the newspapers now were running away from the First Amendment. The *Star Tribune* brief in opposition to the petition, written by Borger, pronounced my "entire discussion" of the First Amendment "an exercise in obfuscation."

Borger urged the justices not to take the Minnesota Supreme Court's allusions to the First Amendment literally. "The court's references to 'First Amendment considerations' are broad enough implicitly to include state as well as federal constitutional guarantees, together with state common law interests in protecting public debate on political campaigns."

He also claimed that I "overstated" a "narrow" state Supreme Court decision that would not necessarily rule out claims by others to enforce media promises of confidentiality. Why make a U.S. Supreme Court case out of something where only one person was hurt?

At the end, however, Borger's brief confirmed that there was an important constitutional dimension to the case. Borger argued that my petition presented "at base, yet another attempt to evade the protections of common law and of state and federal constitutions for truthful newspaper reports of matters of public interest. This is the first case in which a breach of contract claim arising from media newsgathering activities resulted in a jury verdict for plaintiff and even partially survived initial appellate review. The petition's legal theory has an audacious scope. The breach of contract claim left no room for consideration of free press interests or of the public's interest in obtaining full and accurate information about an upcoming election." Borger then quoted from an article I had written that "potential claims for breach of contract, or fraud, are not limited to violations of promises of confidentiality."

Paul Hannah, for the *Pioneer Press*, reiterated the claim that the Minnesota Supreme Court decision was based solely on its interpretation of state law. Anyway, said Hannah, like Borger in his brief, the Supreme Court should not waste its time with Cohen's case. "The importance of this decision is grossly exaggerated." The case concerned "a highly unique set of facts which had not previously occurred and was unlikely to reoccur." Hannah concluded that my petition simply did not "present a cert-worthy issue."

Neither newspaper brief commented on editor Kramer's statement to the *New York Times*.

One day after receiving the newspapers' briefs, I had a reply at the printer and had it shipped to the Supreme Court that afternoon. Time was of the essence, because there was no guarantee that the Supreme Court would wait for a reply brief before deciding on certiorari. For this, at least, it was an advantage being a sole lawyer and not having to go through layers of bureaucracy at a large law firm.

I emphasized once again that the state Supreme Court had held that the jury verdict violated the First Amendment rights of the newspapers. I also cited a quotation from Borger in the *Media Law Reporter* confirming that the scope of the state Supreme Court decision was much broader than he let on in his brief opposing the petition. "The circumstances of this case presented some strong arguments on the plaintiff's side. If the court doesn't recognize a promise in this situation, I don't think they'll recognize it in many others. I think it's safe to say that it'll be a very rare occurrence when a promissory estoppel gets very far."

Pat's name was not on the *Star Tribune*'s brief. She would have no further role in the case. Indeed, she no longer was working for the newspaper. The long-serving chief counsel for the paper had departed to pursue a new career as a psychologist. Pat would have been his logical successor. However, the *Star Tribune* instead hired a lawyer from Faegre & Benson, the firm that was handling the *Cohen* litigation for the newspaper.

In November, Rudy Perpich and Marlene Johnson lost their bid for reelection to the Republican ticket headed by Arne Carlson. Johnson's defeat of course was not legally relevant in the U.S. Supreme Court's consideration of our petition. However, I thought it was a stronger psychological position with Johnson being a defeated politician rather than a current holder of an important public office.

Better still, Perpich and Johnson's defeat happened to get a lot of national media coverage. Carlson had become governor in a most unorthodox fashion. The Republican party's endorsed candidate, business executive Jon Grunseth, had crushed Carlson in the primary. Grunseth, however, withdrew in late October because of *Star Tribune* "revelations" of alleged sexual escapades that Grunseth and his campaign claimed were lies surreptitiously planted by Carlson.[5] Carlson replaced Grunseth as the Republican nominee. The newspaper, by the standards it applied to the Johnson court records, could have deemed the late charges against Grunseth a "dirty trick." This time, though, the *Star Tribune* honored its promises.

What got even more national publicity were the antics of Carlson's first wife. Barbara Carlson, a local politician, hosted a zany and popular Minneapolis talk-radio show. After Arne won the election, Barbara regaled her listeners about the new governor's penis, which she had named Oscar. As Barbara put it, "Oscar was the talk of the town, a celebrity in his own right."[6] Arne added to the media frenzy by threatening to sue Barbara for invasion of privacy, a tort that Minnesota courts did not then recognize.[7] Arne and Oscar never did sue, but all the controversy and the reminders of Johnson's defeat could only help the petition's chances.

Shortly after the election, Pat and I happened to share an elevator going down fifty floors in downtown Minneapolis's tallest building. Pat told me that she had sent in a general application for a job in the new Arne Carlson state administration. She asked if I would give her a recommendation. I told her yes.

We got off the elevator and went our opposite ways. It turned out to be our adieu. We have not seen each other or talked since.

Pat did not go to work for Carlson but wound up with a Minneapolis law firm.

Would the Supreme Court regard Cohen's case as one implicating the First Amendment or merely state law? Even if there was a First Amendment issue, would it consider the case in the top 1 percent of importance among petitions for certiorari? The Court does not take long to dispose of requests for review.

The lawyers in the case knew that the Supreme Court would decide on the petition around the second week of December. John Borger joked, "One of us is going to get a nice Christmas present."

At 9:45, central time, on the morning of December 10, 1990, I got a phone call from Tim O'Brien, the chief legal affairs correspondent of ABC television news, who wanted to know how I felt about the Supreme Court's action in my case. I panted that I did not know what the action was. He was the first to give me the news that the Supreme Court agreed to take the case.

I called Cohen and screamed, "The Court granted the cert, the Court granted the cert, the Court granted the cert! . . ."

Apprehension was the order of the day in the media industry. To put it mildly, victory no longer was a sure thing. American Society of Newspaper Editors lawyer Richard Schmidt put it most pithily: "I have a gut feeling that this isn't good."[8]

I ran into John Borger a couple of days later. He was stunned that the Supreme Court had agreed to take the case. Still, he was gracious. "You're a magician, Elliot."

Notes

1. Richard Wagner, *Parsifal*, act 1, scene 1.

2. Bernard Schwartz, *Decision: How the Supreme Court Decides Cases* (New York: Oxford University Press, 1996), 13.

3. Alex S. Jones, "Newspaper Wins Appeal on Lawsuit," *New York Times*, July 21, 1990, 6.

4. Carol Rose, "Ginsburg on the Supreme Court's Inner Workings," *Harvard Law Bulletin*, Winter 1995, 27; Jeff Bucholtz, "Justice Ginsburg Answers Students' Questions," *Harvard Law Record*, December 2, 1994, 1.

5. Bob von Sternberg, "Bitter Day for Grunseth Camp; Fallen Candidate Launches New Charge at Carlson," *Star Tribune*, November 7, 1990, 10A. Also see David Hoium and Leon Oistad, *There Is No November* (Inver Grove Heights, Minn.: Jeric Publications, 1991).

6. Barbara Carlson, *This Broad's Life* (New York: Pocket Books, 1996), 242–244.

7. Robert Whereatt, "Governor Had Reason to Worry," *Star Tribune*, June 14, 1996, B1.

8. Tony Mauro, "High Court Handpicks 1st Amendment Dispute," *USA Today*, December 11, 1990, 11A.

The Karen Silkwood Rejoinder

LIKE ALL THE thousands of orders each year granting, or mostly denying, petitions for certiorari, the order in the *Cohen* case did not disclose the vote of the justices. For all anyone in the case knew at the time, all the justices had agreed to grant review.

Later, Justice Thurgood Marshall's donation of his papers to the Library of Congress lifted the veil of secrecy over Supreme Court deliberations during his tenure. Marshall retired at the end of the 1990–1991 Supreme Court term, and the *Cohen* case was one of the last he considered.

We know now that four justices, the bare minimum, voted to grant my petition. It was one more victory—like the jury verdict and Minnesota Court of Appeals decision—with no votes to spare.

One of the Supreme Court's law clerks, who screened certiorari petitions for the justices, had recommended that the Court refuse to hear the case even though "this question is quite interesting. First, the issue is one of first impression so the Court would not have the assistance of a body of lower court decisions. Second, because news organizations have a vested interest in keeping their promises of confidentiality, cases like this are likely to be rare. Third, the state Supreme Court's reasoning is inextricably entwined with state law. Fourth, the state Supreme Court's reasoning presents no direct conflict with rulings of this Court or other circuits."

It was a cogent summary of all the arguments that the case did not satisfy the traditional criteria for Supreme Court review. The clerk's recommendation likely would have had even greater influence because of the justices' inability to devote much time to personal scrutiny of any particular petition in the daily flood. Five justices agreed with the clerk and voted not to consider the *Cohen* case.

Chief Justice William Rehnquist and Justices Byron White and Antonin Scalia voted to review the case. I had thought that they would be receptive to my arguments. Justice Sandra Day O'Connor cast the fourth vote for certiorari.

Not knowing all this at the time may have been fortunate. Awareness of the vote would have made me more terrified.

It is hard enough to win a Supreme Court case. If the majority of the justices refused even to review a decision, how would it be possible to convince one or more of them to vote to reverse it? Worse, a vote for certiorari did not guarantee a vote to reverse on the merits, so one or more of those who voted for certiorari could in the end opt to affirm the Minnesota Supreme Court decision.

Nothing ever came easily in this case. The important thing was that it had a new lease on life. I was back on a level playing field.

I had forty-five days from the order granting certiorari to submit my brief on the merits.

The statement of the facts in the brief may seem of secondary importance compared with the legal arguments that follow. Quite the contrary obtains in a case before the Supreme Court. The brief must persuasively marshal the facts to show that the law and justice require the result the attorney desires.

Indeed, the fulcrum of my brief was its statement of facts. I had summarized them in the petition. The more comprehensive statement of facts in my new brief comprised more than 30 percent of the document. The First Amendment precedents were no mystery to anyone; the justices were familiar with all the cases. But the law stated in the abstract was bloodless. It told nothing about the consequences to real people in real cases.

What the justices did not know in detail were the facts of this particular case. How the brief presented them would go a long way to determining who would prevail in the Supreme Court. The newspapers' deliberate violation of voluntary agreements through which they obtained information to be published for their profit, the injuries they inflicted on another with brazen disregard for his rights, their harping on the source's identity while refusing for many days to disclose that they made and dishonored promises to him, and their abuse of the Constitution to evade any responsibility for their conduct—all were egregious. The newspapers' arrogance of power had infuriated the jury, trial Judge Knoll, and state Supreme Court Justices Yetka and Kelley.

I would use this background to demonstrate the danger of expanding once again the powers of the press, under the logic of *New York Times* v. *Sullivan* and *Time, Inc.* v. *Hill*, to create a new and far-reaching privilege to injure private individuals by the calculated violation of voluntary agreements. It was time to call a halt to the continuing aggrandizement of the special privileges of the press against ordinary citizens.

Freedom of the press makes a great slogan in the abstract. It sounds a lot less noble when the press uses it to harm others by violating their rights. This case was not about a conventional infringement of freedom of the press. There was no censorship or other lawless action by government. Instead, the newspapers themselves had acted with contempt for another's rights and had targeted him for real damage. They now were attempting to escape the consequences by hiding behind the First Amendment.

Trying to eschew hyperbole and adjectives in describing what the *Star Tribune* had done, I quoted Judge Knoll and Justices Yetka and Kelley rather than assert my own indictments of the newspapers' behavior.

The argument section of my brief began, "This case raises the issue of whether the First Amendment empowers newspapers to inflict injuries with impunity by deliberately breaking undisputed and unambiguous promises of confidentiality in conducting their business of acquiring information."

I contended that the First Amendment does not abrogate voluntary agreements by newspapers. "The First Amendment protects the press from governmental action only. It is not a tool to undo bargains agents of media corporations entered into with private persons. Contract law allows the press to choose—without governmental interference—the material to be the subject of its promise in exchange for something it wants from another party."

Clothing themselves in the robes of defenders of freedom of the press, the newspapers in reality were demanding powers against private citizens far beyond anything the Supreme Court had previously sanctioned. "Defendants are asking, in effect, for an unprecedented interpretation of the First Amendment to convert it into a regulatory instrument to rewrite or supersede agreements bargained for by media organizations, to the prejudice of those who have relied upon voluntary promises of the media and have fully performed their part of these agreements."

The Court already had held, continued my brief, that the First Amendment "does not bestow a right to publish information in violation of obligations willingly incurred through an agreement or through the acceptance of conditions by which the information was obtained."

I gave special emphasis to the 1980 case of *Snepp* v. *United States*. There the Supreme Court held that a voluntary agreement not to publish was enforceable over claimed First Amendment rights. Frank Snepp, a former CIA official, had published a book about certain CIA activities in Vietnam without submitting his book to the agency for prepublication review. In his employment agreement with the CIA, Snepp had specifically promised not to publish anything about the agency before getting its approval. Like the *Star Tribune* and *Pioneer Press*, Snepp claimed that he was free to violate the agreement because of the First Amendment.

The Supreme Court gave Snepp short shrift. It upheld an order stripping him of all profits from his book and an injunction against future violations of his agreement with the CIA. In no uncertain terms, the Supreme Court held that Snepp was bound by his voluntary agreement. "When Snepp accepted employment with the CIA, he voluntarily signed the agreement that expressly obligated him to submit any proposed publication for prior review. He does not claim that he executed this agreement under duress."

I stressed that the right to obtain what one bargained for in a contract is a fundamental right that must be protected by the Court. Agreements between newspapers and sources to obtain information are nothing other than commercial arrangements and should be subject to the laws governing commercial relationships in general. "The First Amendment does not render newspapers immune from the law for violating commercial contracts for goods and services. They should not be exempt from liability when they break promises for the purpose of gathering news."

The Court, I continued, has "recognized the importance of protecting expectations based on promises in return for goods or services provided in reliance upon them." The 1978 decision in *Allied Structural Steel Co.* v. *Spannaus* acknowledged "the high value the Framers placed on the protection of private contracts. Contracts enable individuals to order their personal and business affairs according to their particular needs and interests. Once arranged, those rights and obligations are binding under the law, and the parties are entitled to rely on them."

I quoted Judge Knoll's findings that the newspapers' behavior was especially egregious because they had dishonored their agreements "after thoroughly considering what they were about to do." He held that no

First Amendment interest exists in protecting "the knowing and willful breach of a legally sufficient contract after hours of thought and discussion by corporate officers," conduct that "can fairly be characterized as a calculated misdeed." This was a powerful indictment by the judge who tried the case.

The linchpin of my argument was that the First Amendment does not give the press immunity from laws everyone else must obey, such as the law of contracts. As in the statement of facts, I could rely on others to supply the outrage. "Dissenting Minnesota Supreme Court Justice Lawrence Yetka wrote that the opinion below 'offends the fundamental principle of equality under the law' by exempting newspapers from rules by which ordinary people are bound. Dissenting Justice Glenn Kelley agreed and reproached 'the perfidy of these defendants, the liability for which they now seek to escape by trying to crawl under the aegis of the First Amendment, which, in my opinion, has nothing to do with the case.' He said that any other person under similar circumstances 'would most certainly have been liable in damages for breach of contract.' "

"The Court," I wrote, "already has indicated that wrongdoers cannot employ the First Amendment to thwart a remedy for acts which would be unlawful when committed by others."

The brief then quoted from the Supreme Court's 1972 decision of *Branzburg* v. *Hayes*, which held that the First Amendment does not invalidate the enforcement against the press of laws of general applicability, despite the possible burden that may be imposed. Writing for the Court, Justice Byron White declared that a publisher "has no special immunity from the application of general laws. He has no special privilege to invade the rights and liberties of others."

Branzburg was especially important as the only previous Supreme Court case adjudicating the relationship of the First Amendment to newspaper promises of confidentiality to sources. There, ironically, the *New York Times* and others claimed that requiring disclosure of sources to a grand jury would impose an unconstitutional burden on news gathering. The identification of sources promised confidentiality, the press argued there, would deter them and others from providing publishable material, all to the detriment of the free flow of information protected by the First Amendment.

Four justices agreed with the *New York Times*. A dissent of Justice Potter Stewart, joined by Justices Brennan and Marshall, saw a First Amendment right to preserve confidentiality deriving from "the broad societal interest in a full and free flow of information to the public. A corollary of the right to publish must be the right to gather news. The full flow of information to the public protected by the free press guarantee would be severely curtailed if no protection whatsoever were afforded to the process by which news is assembled and disseminated. The right to gather news implies, in turn, a right to a confidential relationship between a reporter and his source. Confidentiality is essential to the creation and maintenance of a news-gathering relationship with informants."

Of particular pertinence to the newspapers' accusations of "dirty tricks" against Cohen, the dissenters observed: "The First Amendment concern must not be with the motives of any particular news source, but rather with the conditions in which informants of all shades of the spectrum may make information available through the press to the public."

The beauty of the *Branzburg* case was that it did not matter which opinion the current Court would embrace—both the majority opinion and the dissents supported my position.

The brief continued with the argument that the First Amendment does not give newspapers a right to gather news through intentional wrongdoing. The decision of the Minnesota Supreme Court went far beyond *New York Times* v. *Sullivan* "by validating a wrongful means of gathering news through the deliberate dishonoring of promises. *New York Times* gave protection to journalists from liability for inadvertent errors committed in the course of doing their jobs honestly. It did not free them from the consequences of knowing and deliberate misconduct like the calculated violation of a clear-cut promise."

I returned once again to the point that the issue of the case was not some academic definition of freedom of the press but the intentional harming of an individual with whom the newspapers made an agreement. "The infliction of injury by the knowing and deliberate violation of clear-cut and undisputed promises is unworthy of constitutional protection. The First Amendment should not be construed to authorize lies in any form."

Next, I challenged the newspapers' claim of an unlimited right to publish truthful information. To begin with, their "publication of truthful information was selective; the articles identifying Mr. Cohen did not disclose that the newspapers had made and had broken promises to him. That notwithstanding, the publication of truthful information does not automatically afford immunity from liability."

From the summary motion judgment before Judge Knoll through all the appeals, this was a crucial issue of the case. The cases the newspapers relied upon, I contended, protected the publication only of lawfully obtained information and refused invitations to hold more broadly that newspapers could publish without penalty what they had acquired unlawfully.

I pointed out that truthful, but illegally obtained, information is excluded from criminal trials to protect the rights of individuals during investigations. "Newspapers should not be granted greater rights than judges, juries, and law enforcement officials to obtain information by violating the rights of others."

In the final section of the brief, I argued that no First Amendment interests would be served by protecting newspapers from the consequences of breaking promises of confidentiality. In a 1945 decision, *Associated Press v. United States*, the Supreme Court stated that the First Amendment "rests on the assumption that the widest possible dissemination of information from diverse and antagonistic sources is essential to the welfare of the public."

Naming sources despite promises of confidentiality would discourage others from providing information and curtail the flow of news to the public. The *Star Tribune* took exactly that position in a brief filed in a 1978 New Jersey case, *Matter of Farber*, in which it opposed court-ordered disclosure of confidential sources. According to the newspaper in that case, "Much information would never be forthcoming to the news media unless the persons who were the sources of such information could be entirely certain that their identities would remain secret." The result, said the *Star Tribune*, would be "a substantial lessening in the supply of available news on a variety of important and sensitive issues, all to the detriment of the public interest."

The newspapers had several valid options consistent with their agreement with Cohen. They could have run a story like that of the Associated Press, which did not reveal the name of the source. Like the television station, they could have declined to run any story at all. If they wanted to inform readers of the source's motivations, they could have described him by type, such as "Republican activist," without naming him.

I repeated the warning in my petition that the case had implications beyond the violation of agreements. "If the press is not liable for dishonoring voluntary promises to obtain information, is it also entitled to commit torts or crimes in gathering news?" *Star Tribune* witness David Anderson in his textbook acknowledged that this concern was not merely hypothetical. Anderson began his chapter "Ethics of Investigative Reporting" thus: "Many fundamental techniques of investigative reporting involve actions some would label dishonest, fraudulent, immoral, and perhaps even illegal."

I discussed U.S. Court of Appeals decisions, like that affecting Jacqueline Kennedy Onassis, which rejected claims that the First Amendment vests the press with immunity from liability for torts committed while gathering news. The same should apply to media claims that they should be free to break agreements.

My brief concluded, "No one, including the news media, should be above the law."

The newspapers brought in a new heavy artillery team of lawyers. Stephen M. Shapiro became lead counsel for the *Pioneer Press*. Shapiro specialized in arguing cases before the Supreme Court. More than that, he was an author of the bible of Supreme Court litigation, *Supreme Court Practice*, now in its seventh edition. Joining Shapiro on the *Pioneer Press* team was Kenneth S. Geller, another of the textbook's authors. Eight lawyers signed the *Pioneer Press* brief.

John French, chairman of the Minneapolis firm of Faegre & Benson, was the new chief lawyer for the *Star Tribune*. French had had a brilliant legal career. He, too, had previously argued before the U.S. Supreme Court, and had been Justice Felix Frankfurter's law clerk after graduating from Harvard Law School. Four lawyers signed the *Star Tribune* brief.

Shapiro's and French were not the only blue-ribbon lawyers joining the case on the other side. In fact, a battalion of the nation's leading lawyers and most prominent media organizations entered the Supreme Court appeal supporting the *Star Tribune* and *Pioneer Press*. Nineteen attorneys from leading law firms in New York, Washington, and Los Angeles filed a third brief opposing mine. Their amicus curiae brief represented the big leagues of American media: Advance Publications, the Newhouse publishing conglomerate; the American Newspaper Publishers Association; the American Society of Newspaper Editors; the Associated Press; Copley Press; Gannett Company, which publishes *USA Today* and other newspapers, and operates many television and radio stations; the Newsletter Association; the *New York Times*; and the Times Mirror Company, which publishes the *Los Angeles Times*, the *Baltimore Sun*, and other newspapers.

No one offered any support to Cohen's side despite the huge stake reporters had in the outcome of the case. Even before the trial, University of Minnesota journalism professor Ted Glasser had told the *Washington Post* that "this is not as much a trial between the plaintiff and defendant as it is between reporters and editors."

Neither the newspapers nor any of their numerous supporters would acknowledge that the *Star Tribune* and *Pioneer Press* had done anything wrong in their conduct toward Cohen. Far from expressing any regret over their broken promises, they claimed a constitutional right to treat sources like Cohen in any way they choose, without hindrance from the courts. The amicus brief could have admitted that the *Star Tribune* and *Pioneer Press* had made a mistake, but taken the position that the First Amendment should still immunize the newspapers from liability in the higher interest of protecting freedom of the press. If anything, however, the amicus brief was the most bellicose of all.

Of the three opposing briefs, only the amicus one directly confronted the essential issue of the case: whether laws applicable to everyone else also bind the media. Regardless of its appeal to fairness, the legal answer was not at all obvious, despite the categorical language in *Branzburg v. Hayes*. After all, *New York Times v. Sullivan*, *Time, Inc. v. Hill*, and *Hustler Magazine v. Falwell* gave media organizations First Amendment privileges enjoyed by no one else to perpetrate libel, invasion of privacy, and emotional distress.

Said the amicus brief, "Petitioner's entire argument is based on the premise that, because the media are not exempt from the application of general laws, understandings between reporters and sources also must be subjected to the application of general promissory estoppel principles without any consideration of the First Amendment. That premise is fatally flawed. It *only* applies when the state action is a nondiscriminatory regulation of commercial activities. Here, however, petitioner seeks to restrict directly the media's ability to gather and disseminate information to the public by transforming what is, at most, an ethical obligation to maintain the confidentiality of a source's identity into a legally enforceable promise. That restriction on the media falls within the First Amendment's protections. The First Amendment has particular force here, because the information sought to be restrained is truthful information about the conduct of government affairs."

The amicus brief claimed that even though the newspapers broke their promises to Cohen, they did not unlawfully obtain the information on his identity. The Minnesota Supreme Court held that they did not violate the state law of contracts. "Moreover, empirical evidence indicates that the methods employed by respondents to obtain information from petitioner were far from unorthodox, let alone illegal. Respondents' acquisition of information from petitioner was simply a newspaper reporting technique."

The amicus media organizations ridiculed as "untenable" my point—which was only a variation of their own oft-repeated argument—that allowing newspapers to unilaterally dishonor promises of confidentiality would discourage sources from giving the press information in the future, and thus dry up the flow of news to the press and the public. "Petitioner has not presented any evidence whatsoever which even remotely suggests that those relationships will not continue, without a civil remedy by sources against reporters. In any event, it is not the province of the courts to 'improve' the relationship between sources and reporters, any more than it is the province of the courts to 'improve' editorial judgments."

These media organizations threw down the gauntlet to the Supreme Court. "A responsible press is an undoubtedly desirable goal, but press responsibility is not mandated by the Constitution."

According to the media brief, media organizations have it both ways, depending on their whim—no court has the authority to compel a newspaper either to honor promises of confidentiality or to disclose the name of a source promised confidentiality. "The government is not permitted to intrude into the relationships between reporters and their sources in this manner, any more than it should be allowed to interfere with that relationship by attempting to compel reporters to reveal the identities of their confidential sources. It is simply not up to the courts to improve relationships between sources and reporters."

Moreover, said the amicus brief, "no important state interest would have been furthered" by enforcing the newspapers' agreement with Cohen because the latter was responsible for a "smear campaign" and "attempted to use the media to disseminate misleading information" about Johnson. The parties to the brief did not explain how official criminal court records are "misleading."

The brief argued that courts must not suppress the dissemination of truthful information to the public. Like the *Star Tribune* and *Pioneer Press* in 1982, the zeal for disclosure was selective. The *New York Times* every day trumpets on its front page, "All the News That's Fit to Print." Nevertheless, in the course of its coverage of the case in the U.S. Supreme Court, the *Times* never deemed fit to print the news that the newspaper itself had entered the litigation as a party supporting other newspapers. The same applied to the *Los Angeles Times* and the *Baltimore Sun*.

Shapiro's and French's principal argument was that the Supreme Court made a mistake in granting its writ of certiorari and should now dismiss the case. They expanded the arguments opposing certiorari in Borger's and Hannah's briefs. Shapiro quoted from his textbook: "If the Court is convinced after the case has been fully briefed and argued that a juris-dictional fault exists, it will be compelled to dismiss the case despite the expenditures of time and energies."

Failing that, they also sought a ruling in their favor on First Amend-ment grounds.

French's brief claimed that Cohen sought and won damages for injury to his reputation resulting from publication of the newspaper articles. Citing *Time, Inc. v. Hill* and *Hustler Magazine v. Falwell*, French said that Cohen's damages "are indistinguishable from the claims of injury to rep-utation, humiliation and embarrassment which give rise to most defa-mation actions." French continued that Cohen could not satisfy the elementary prerequisite of a defamation case because the newspapers ac-curately reported that he was the source of the information on Johnson. "Truth always has defeated claims for these types of damages, and it should do so here." Similarly, Shapiro argued, "This Court's decisions conclusively establish that the right to publish truthful information re-garding an imminent political election lies at the core of the First Amend-ment's protections."

It was an argument the newspapers had made from the beginning of the suit. Would publication of the truth free the newspapers from the obligation everyone else had under the law of contracts to honor prom-ises? French and Shapiro posed what could be the critical issue of the case.

The Supreme Court rules gave me a last shot via a reply brief. I couldn't wait to hoist with their own petard the *New York Times*'s and cohorts' huffing that no "evidence whatsoever [exists] which even remotely sug-gests" that sources will not continue to give information to the media if the Court grants journalists a right to unilaterally violate promises of confidentiality.

"Amici's argument contradicts the position of many of these same or-ganizations in cases where they sought to protect their confidential sources. For example, amicus New York Times Co. as an appellant in *Matter of Farber* argued that if confidential sources were to be exposed through a court order, 'newsgathering and the dissemination of news would be seriously impaired, because much information would never be forthcoming to the news media unless the persons who were the sources of such information could be entirely certain that their identities would remain secret.' Amici supporting the *New York Times* in *Farber* who are also parties to the amicus brief in this case include the Times Mirror Co., Associated Press, Gannett Co., the American Society of Newspaper Editors, and the American Newspaper Publishers Association."

I also rebutted the amicus brief's claim that agreements with sources to procure information are in a category different from general commercial contracts and should not be subject to laws of general applicability. Information is just one of the goods and services for which newspapers regularly contract in the course of their business.

"The First Amendment does not justify a distinction between general commercial agreements and agreements with sources of information. To obtain much of the news, the press must promise confidentiality to sources of information. The competitive pursuit of information is integral to the business operations of newspapers. Journalism School Dean Arnold Ismach testified that media organizations 'are in the business of acquiring information. That is their trade.' The trial court found that the relationship between journalist and source of information is a commercial one; the Minnesota Court of Appeals held that newspapers should no more be exempt from the law for violating promises to sources than for violating agreements for other goods and services."

The reply brief also addressed French's argument that Cohen's damages made the case indistinguishable from a defamation suit. I pointed out that the jury awarded Cohen compensation for purely financial injuries.

"Respondent erroneously claims that the jury awarded Mr. Cohen damages for 'injury to reputation, humiliation and embarrassment.' In fact, the jury awarded nothing for such injuries. The trial court specifically instructed the jury that damages for emotional distress were not recoverable in this case. Mr. Cohen was fired from his job the day the newspaper articles identifying him—and in the *Star Tribune*'s case his employer as well—were published. The Minnesota Court of Appeals held that the loss of Mr. Cohen's employment was a reasonably foreseeable consequence of the dishonoring of promises to him. The jury in its special verdict awarded compensatory damages in an amount of $200,000 to 'fairly and adequately compensate the plaintiff Dan Cohen for his loss.' An expert witness testified that Mr. Cohen's financial losses resulting from respondents' wrongful conduct exceeded $725,000."

That was supposed to have been the last written argument. As in the trial and the Minnesota Supreme Court appeal, however, the newspapers and their supporters again managed to get the last word. Less than a week before the oral argument, the editor of the *Rutgers Law Review* dispatched by overnight Federal Express, to each justice individually, galley proofs of a Miami law professor's 123-page article—with 418 footnotes—on the case. The journal would not actually publish the article until three months later. It was a thinly disguised brief for the newspapers. After 118 pages, the author concluded that this was an "easy case" and that the Supreme Court should rule against Cohen, not out of general principle but because he was a bad fellow.

Because the approach suggested here is a context-sensitive model, it cannot abstractly be used to predict the results of particular contract actions by sources. However, it does suggest that there will be some easy cases. If classic whistleblowers Karen Silkwood and Ernest Fitzgerald were to sue the press for a breach of promise of confidentiality, the various factors listed above would make it easy for courts to find their agreements enforceable. If Henry Kissinger were to have sued the press for breaching the anonymity ground rules of a backgrounder in which he lied about United States military intervention in Cambodia, however, the social policy considerations underlying the decisional guidelines would clearly dictate that he lose. Those are the easy cases, in which real life closely parallels the idealized prototypes of the sympathetic whistleblower and the despicable manipulator. . . .

A fact-sensitive look at *Cohen* suggests a close-to-prototypical "sourceristic" [*sic*] situation. Confidentiality was sought strategically and misleadingly by a sophisticated source whose political partisanship was critical to the story. Keeping the promise of confidentiality would have resulted in skewed public debate and would have misled voters as to the tactics and character of the Republican candidates on the eve of the election. Because the specific identification of Cohen lent needed credibility to the report and diverted suspicion from other possible leakers, because disclosure gave the public the "full" story, and because Cohen's interest in seeking anonymity for an authorized "dirty trick" was not particularly worthy of protection, I would suggest that the *Cohen* situation is closer to that of Kissinger than that of Silkwood.[1]

If only Cohen were more like Karen Silkwood and less like Henry Kissinger! It was the newspapers' "dirty trick" defense apotheosized to self-caricature.

Note

1. Lili Levi, "Dangerous Liaisons: Seduction and Betrayal in Confidential Press-Source Relations," 43 *Rutgers Law Review* 609, 727–729 (1991).

Thank You, Justice O'Connor. Thank You, Justice Scalia

IN FEBRUARY 1991, I warmed up for the Supreme Court by arguing another case, *Ruzicka* v. *Conde Nast Publications*, with the same issue before the Eighth Circuit U.S. Court of Appeals in St. Paul. A few months before the Minnesota Supreme Court's *Cohen* decision, Minnesota U.S. District Judge Harry MacLaughlin dismissed a suit by another source claiming violation of a promise of confidentiality, this time by *Glamour* magazine. Judge MacLaughlin at least was forthright. He did not pretend that there was no contract but held that the First Amendment barred the enforcement of such agreements. I urged the Court of Appeals to await the U.S. Supreme Court decision in the *Cohen* case, which likely would resolve the constitutional issues.

Glamour magazine attorney Tom Tinkham, heading the litigation department of the Minneapolis firm of Dorsey & Whitney, a counterpart of Faegre & Benson, responded that even a U.S. Supreme Court victory ultimately would not make any difference for Cohen. Tinkham said that the best Cohen could expect was a remand to the Minnesota Supreme Court for what the legal argot calls proceedings consistent with the U.S. Supreme Court decision.

In other words, the most the U.S. Supreme Court would do would be to rule that the First Amendment did not give newspapers immunity from the consequences of broken agreements. It would then send the case back to the Minnesota Supreme Court for a determination solely on the basis of state law.

The Minnesota court, said Tinkham, then would rule against Cohen

again, but for a different reason. It would cite only the state law of promissory estoppel, without any reference to the First Amendment. Eighth
Circuit Chief Judge Donald Lay agreed, and remarked that even a victory
for the source at the U.S. Supreme Court would have no effect on the
final outcome of his litigation. It would only delay the inevitable. Coming
from a senior U.S. Court of Appeals judge, it was not an encouraging
comment.

To get acclimated, I attended several Supreme Court oral arguments
in January. The most important was *Masson v. New Yorker Magazine, Inc.*,
which was the other big freedom of the press case before the Court that
term. Charles Morgan, a respected trial lawyer from San Francisco, had
persuaded the Court to review a U.S. Court of Appeals decision dismissing without trial the highly publicized defamation suit his client, psychi-
atrist Jeffrey Masson, had brought against *The New Yorker* and writer Janet
Malcolm for allegedly fabricating quotations in an article about Masson.

Masson was a nationally prominent Freudian scholar. He objected to
several quotes he said he never made. In one, Malcolm claimed he said
he wanted to make a house associated with Freud into "a center for schol-
arship but also a place of sex, women, and fun." In another, Malcolm
quoted him as describing himself as "an intellectual gigolo—you get your
pleasure from him, but you don't take him out in public." Malcolm said
that Masson himself said that a girlfriend had told him, "It is very nice
sleeping with you in your room, but you're the kind of person who should
never leave the room—you're just a social embarrassment anywhere else."

About halfway through his oral argument, Morgan became increasingly
irritated about a line of hostile questions. Finally, he snapped, "If that's
the way you feel, I might as well pack my bags and go home right now!"
I doubt that Morgan had planned to say anything like that. The tension
must be close to unbearable for the lawyers standing up there.

As my own oral argument approached, I began to have recurring nightmares about the upcoming ordeal. All the nightmares were virtually identical. I would find myself standing before nine severe justices in the
intimidatingly formal courtroom unprepared, unshaven, clad in old, less-
than-fragrant running clothes, and generally disheveled; the opposing
lawyers were immaculately groomed and wore expensively tailored suits.

A day before the big argument, I had a moot court practice session
before a group of friendly lawyers. Jordan Lorence, a staff member at the
Minnesota legislature during my terms there, had called me out of the
blue in February with an offer to organize the practice argument. I had
not seen Jordan, who had become a Washington lawyer, for almost ten

years. He explained that he and some colleagues with a lot of constitutional law experience thought that the case was very interesting and important. The leader of the group was Jay Sekulow, a lightning-quick
thinker who had won twice before the Supreme Court. In fact, I cited
one of his cases, *Board of Education of Westside Community Schools* v.
Mergens, decided in June 1990, both in my petition for certiorari and in
my brief to the high court.

I took an instant liking to the whole group. Jay and his pals helped me
clarify some of the legal points. More important, their wit and encouragement put me at ease for what I expected to be a harrowing ordeal the
next day.

After the practice, they took me to lunch at Monocle, a Capitol Hill
watering hole for high-rolling lobbyists and politicians. I sat next to Jay.

"Say, Jay, I hope that you won't be offended, but I'm wondering if
you're Jewish."

The question seemed simple enough; the answer was more complicated.
Jay told me that he had grown up in a Jewish family in Brooklyn. He
wound up attending a Baptist college in Atlanta and had successfully
represented Jews for Jesus before the Supreme Court in the 1987 case
Board of Airport Commissioners of the City of Los Angeles v. *Jews for Jesus,
Inc.* He eventually founded a law firm specializing in protecting freedom
of speech and other constitutional rights.

Jay and I seemed an odd duo—one a former national law director of
the Anti-Defamation League and the other a lawyer for Jews for Jesus. It
was ironic that Jay and his friends were the only people who had ever
offered me any help in the case.

In reality, we had something in common—a passion for advocating the
rights of unfashionable underdogs. Jay had made his mark advocating First
Amendment rights for people even more politically incorrect than Cohen. The *Mergens* case, for example, involved the issue of whether voluntary religious clubs should have the right to meet on school premises
on the same basis as other student groups. Civil rights proponents Anti-
Defamation League and American Jewish Committee, still conspicuously
silent in the *Cohen* case, actually filed amicus briefs opposing these students' rights.

The next morning—March 27, 1991—the enormity of it all hit me as
I was walking up the steps of the Supreme Court building for the oral
argument. Here was a solitary lawyer from the heartland, working out of
a makeshift office in his basement, single-handedly taking on in a landmark constitutional case the cream of the national media and legal es-

tablishments—and, most amazingly, with at least an even chance of winning.

It was not a David against just one Goliath like John French or Stephen Shapiro. Hundreds of superlawyers from the nation's leading law firms were working for the *Star Tribune*, the *Pioneer Press*, and all the other parties, like the *New York Times*, who entered the case on their side.

How, I thought, could I possibly compete with all this talent?

Still, no one was talking Don Quixote anymore.

I thought about my mother, who had cheered me on in the trial and the first state appeal, but had died in 1990 at the bleakest time for me in the case. She did not live to see her son make it to the biggest court of all. My father had died almost twenty years earlier.

In contrast to all the lawyers working for the other side, my big support, besides Jay Sekulow and Jordan Lorence, came from my family. My wife, two daughters, and mother-in-law came from Minneapolis for the big event. So did two cousins.

On the day of the argument, when I had a flock of butterflies in my stomach, my daughters were agonizing about what dresses to wear. It seemed mundane, but then I was worried over whether my deodorant would hold up.

"Equal justice under law," engraved on the Supreme Court building pediment, greets every lawyer walking up those steps to present his or her argument. It was especially appropriate for this case, because equality under the law had been the issue right from the beginning.

Does the same law that binds ordinary people also govern the conduct of arrogant elites, or do we have a two-class society for applying the law? Should favored politicians be given a free ride when it comes to violating the criminal law and ordinary citizens be punished instead for publicly exposing the politician's crime? Does the First Amendment give the media a privilege to flout the law of contracts that every other business and individual must obey? Does equal justice under law mean something or is it only a platitude?

The Supreme Court is unique among American political institutions. Disparity of political and economic power and social class is irrelevant to the legal merits of an argument. Only the justice of the cause matters, not political influence or lack of it. One lawyer may go against an army of powerful lawyers representing clients with unlimited resources and prestige, and have an equal opportunity to persuade the Supreme Court of the justice of his or her cause. A single lawyer for each side will stand alone before the Court—only a few feet from the chief justice of the

United States—for the allotted half-hour, with nobody accompanying the advocate but his or her knowledge of the case and powers of legal analysis.

Would the sole criterion of merit similarly gain equal access to anyone else in the federal government in the executive branch or Congress, or even to less exalted bodies like a state legislature or city council? To ask the question is to answer it.

Whatever the importance of the oral argument compared with the briefs, the oral argument is the most visible manifestation to the public of how the Supreme Court dispenses justice. Adding to the pressure, it tests before a national audience how quick and agile an attorney is on his or her feet.

The oral argument today is not a contest of prepared declamations but a pair of dialogues in which the lawyers answer questions by the justices. The attorney must be fully prepared on the facts and the law, and at the same time be flexible and not adhere slavishly to a scripted presentation.

It was 9:15 in the morning. Lines of spectators were filing into the courtroom. I almost rubbed shoulders with Chief Justice Rehnquist in the Supreme Court clerk's office. He had no bodyguards or other trappings of power. The Supreme Court clerk escorted me into an attorneys' waiting room. John French was there. Stephen Shapiro originally was supposed to have given the oral argument for the newspapers, but he had withdrawn. The story was that Shapiro had hurt his back getting off a train.

I had known French from law and politics but had not seen him for about ten years. He was friendly. "Whatever may happen here, Elliot, you established a new cause of action against the press." John was first class—a nice guy as well as a brilliant attorney.

A few minutes before 10 A.M., the clerk escorted us into the chamber. Spectators had taken every available seat. We took our seats at the counsel tables in front of and below the justices' bench.

The Supreme Court chamber is less a courtroom than a temple, a lot like the Parthenon of Athens, filled with columns that soar to a forty-four-foot-high ceiling. The room, if you can call it that, measures more than thirty yards in length and more than twenty-seven yards in width. The individual human being inside is insignificant by contrast. The whole effect is not calculated to contribute to an attorney's self-confidence.

Still, what struck me the most about the architecture was the huge clock behind the chief justice. It is suspended on a pendant and seems almost free floating. The clock seemed to be alive; it was like a tenth justice—straight out of Kafka or Poe. It is an apt symbol of the evanescence of the high point of an attorney's career. With the brevity of the time allotted, and the constant barrage of questions that would seize upon the slightest error of fact or logic, you cannot recover from any blunder. The infernal clock ticking away is there to remind you.

When the clock struck ten, the chamber went silent. The clerk pounded the gavel. Everyone rose. He recited the ritual incantation, following a tradition two centuries old. "Oyez! Oyez! Oyez! All persons having business before the honorable, the Supreme Court of the United States, are admonished to draw near and give their attention, for the Court is now sitting. God save the United States and this honorable Court."

As the clerk enunciated these words, the justices in their black robes emerged through the red draperies behind the bench. The spectacle sent a frisson up and down my spine.

The Court did not get to the oral argument immediately. The first order of business was the admission of several lawyers to the Supreme Court bar. Like most others, I got admitted by mail application. Some, though, like to appear personally for the blessing of the chief justice. After that, Justice O'Connor read excerpts from a decision the Court issued that day.

I was on the edge of my seat, my heart pounding loud enough for the justices to hear. The wait seemed like an eternity, but the admissions and the reading took less than five minutes.

Finally, Chief Justice Rehnquist said, "We'll hear argument now in No. 90–634, *Dan Cohen v. the Cowles Media Company, Doing Business as Minneapolis Star and Tribune Company*. Mr. Rothenberg."

As I strode to the podium, I resolved not to flinch, no matter what questions the justices hurled at me. Still, bowls of jelly took the place of my knees as I began with the obligatory salutation.

"Mr. Chief Justice and may it please the Court.

"This case is on writ of certiorari from the Minnesota Supreme Court, which held that promises of confidentiality from newspapers to a source of information were unenforceable because it would violate the First Amendment rights of the newspapers. *Cohen* v. *Cowles Media* presents the question of whether newspapers have the right to inflict injuries by dishonoring voluntary promises used to obtain information.

"Honoring promises of confidentiality is critical in ensuring the free flow of information to the public. An expert witness in the trial testified that at least one-third of all newspaper stories and 85 percent of newsmagazine stories come from sources promised confidentiality by the media organizations involved."

I wanted to convince the justices—especially those sensitive to claimed infringements of freedom of the press—that establishing a right to violate promises of confidentiality would cut off the flow of information to the media and public, and thus disserve the interests of the First Amendment. It is the argument media organizations make in every case where someone seeks a court order to compel journalists to identify confidential sources. That was the concern expressed by Justice Marshall and the other dissenters in the *Branzburg* case.

I could not suppress a quaver in my voice. The barrage of questions then hit me. From then on, I was more relaxed.

In spite of the size and formality of the court chamber, once the interplay between justices and lawyer begins, the setting becomes almost an intimate one for the arguing lawyer. The argument becomes a conversation between lawyer and justices rather than a declamatory exercise. The attorney is surrounded by a virtual semicircle of the nine justices and is only a few feet from the chief justice. I was standing closer to Chief Justice Rehnquist than to any of the judges in the Minnesota courts or to the jury when I gave the closing argument. I could almost have shaken hands with him.

The chief justice and Justices Scalia and Anthony Kennedy asked me if I was saying that the First Amendment actually required that these promises be enforceable. I replied, "The Minnesota Supreme Court ruled that the First Amendment barred enforceability of these promises. It's been the position of the trial court and the Minnesota Court of Appeals that the First Amendment simply ought not to allow news media organizations to break promises they voluntarily made in order to obtain information, that the media organization should be subject to the same law as everyone else, every other business, every other individual in keeping their promises."

"Well," said Chief Justice Rehnquist, "then what you're saying is that the First Amendment doesn't accord them any special protection when they break their promises."

"Yes, Mr. Chief Justice."

In response to questions by Justice Kennedy, I refined the answer further. "There is no necessary conflict between the First Amendment and rules of contract law as applied to this case. The Minnesota Supreme Court seemed to believe that the First Amendment required that these promises not be enforceable. It's our position that the First Amendment does not require this. And not only that, but that there are certain values of the First Amendment which are enhanced by honoring these promises rather than allowing newspapers to violate these promises."

Justice O'Connor was not a very friendly interrogator. "Did you argue promissory estoppel? Why did the court even address it?"

I replied that promissory estoppel is closely related to the law of contracts and implies a contract where a contract might not otherwise exist.

"The problem I have is that I don't understand how the court could address it at all if it was never urged below."

"It isn't necessary, Justice O'Connor, in Minnesota to specifically plead promissory estoppel apart from general contract law. Minnesota is a notice-pleading state."

"As a matter of state law," asked Justice O'Connor again, "it's possible to sustain a jury verdict that was presented on a different theory by concluding there was promissory estoppel. That's the Minnesota state law?"

"There is not this distinction between implied contracts on promissory estoppel or conventional contracts. It's based upon section 90 of the restatement on contracts. In the *Christensen* case, the lower court held against the plaintiff, and then the Minnesota Supreme Court reversed the decision on the basis of an implied contract through promissory estoppel when the issue had not been raised below. So in Minnesota state practice, it is possible to do this without specifically pleading promissory estoppel as apart from conventional contracts."

Justice O'Connor then asked a dangerous question implying that the money award to Cohen was equivalent to a prior restraint on the press, barring publication—a classic infringement of freedom of the press. If I did not make the proper distinctions, I could have lost the case right then. I did not dare fumble now.

"Here you sought damages for the disclosure. Had the plaintiff known in advance that there was a danger of disclosure, I take it you would feel you could even go in and enjoin the publication. Is that right?"

"Justice O'Connor, plaintiff did not ask that this publication be enjoined. Plaintiff asked for damages for the violation of the promises made by the newspapers."

"Yes, I know. Is it your position that an injunction could be sought before publication?"

"Plaintiff has not sought an injunction."

"Yes, I know that," said Justice O'Connor. "Is it your view that an injunction could be sought?"

"Could it be sought? That presents the issue of prior restraint, Your

Honor, and it would present a different issue than damages. No, because this case does not involve any attempt at prior restraint, nor would any principle established by the Minnesota Court of Appeals or the trial court involve any issue of prior restraint on publication by the newspapers. It merely involves the issue of whether newspapers should be liable for their promises and whether they should be liable for damages caused by violations of their promises."

I wanted the Court to see the central issue of this case as a violation of an agreement—for which the First Amendment gives no protection—before the newspapers published anything rather than interference with a First Amendment right to publish.

Justice Scalia then entered the discussion.

"You think maybe only the government can get prior restraint of publication? Is that it? The *Snepp* case is all right, but nobody else can get prior restraint except the government?"

(Actually, in a case not involving a contract, *New York Times* v. *United States* prohibited even the U.S. government from seeking prior restraint of the Pentagon Papers.)

"It's our position that the Court doesn't have to even reach the issue of prior restraint. It merely has to allow a plaintiff to recover damages for a violation. . . ." As happens frequently in oral arguments, I did not get to finish my answer.

"You seem very much worried about it," Justice Scalia commented.

Justice David Souter then asked several questions suggesting that the Supreme Court did not have jurisdiction over the case. "Doesn't the state court decision rest on the state Supreme Court's view of good policy by saying, 'Considering the nature of the political story involved, it seems to us the law best leaves the parties here to their trust in each other'? They ought to be left to deal on matters of trust and if that doesn't work, too bad. Isn't that the independent holding of the case, if not the principal holding of the case?"

"No, Justice Souter, any fair reading of the decision would lead one to conclude that this decision was in fact based on the First Amendment. They pointed out that this case presents the classic First Amendment situation of a source providing information in connection with a political campaign, which they called the quintessential First Amendment situation. And then they said that we think that in this situation, the law best leaves the parties to the trust in each other."

Justice Scalia intervened again. "I thought that when they said the law best leaves the parties to the trust in each other, they included within the law the First Amendment. Isn't the First Amendment part of the law?"

"Absolutely, Justice Scalia."

Justice John Paul Stevens, with a reputation for asking tough questions, then began his interrogation. "May I ask you a variation of Justice Souter's question? Supposing you had two statutes, one in one state and one in another. One state had a statute that just said, contracts of this kind shall not be enforceable, period. And in the other state the statute said the same thing, but it had a preamble that said, because the members of the legislature are convinced that it would violate the First Amendment to have such a statute, contracts like these are unenforceable. Would each of those have the same constitutional result? Would they both be valid or invalid, or would you get one result in one case and another in the other case?"

"If the one statute was ostensibly based upon the First Amendment, that would provide jurisdiction for this Court to consider whether the First Amendment actually requires that the. . . ."

I didn't get to complete the sentence.

"Do we review the reasoning that the legislators adopt? Or do we review the end product of their work?"

"Both, your honor. If there are values of the First Amendment involved in this case, these values require that these promises be honored to ensure the free flow of information to the public. That's what the Minnesota state legislature did.

"It would be one thing," I continued, "if you had a statute saying that these promises are unenforceable. Giving notice to all potential sources that they could not trust promises from newspapers. I would assume that the newspapers themselves would not support such a statute.

"A solemn promise was made to the source, Mr. Cohen, as is made to many other sources on a daily basis. He believed that he could trust the promise of the reporter, that the newspapers would honor their promises. They did not do so. He had no notice whatsoever. Had he had that notice, he wouldn't have offered the information to the newspapers, he wouldn't have trusted the promises, and this case wouldn't have arisen. He wouldn't have lost his job as a result."

"Well, I know, but of course in the future the law will be clearer if this is affirmed. The future will be as though a statute like this was on the books."

"Yes, Your Honor," I answered Justice Stevens. "But it's important to point out that in other cases involving court orders of reporters to divulge confidential sources before grand juries, newspapers and other media organizations took the position that if newspapers are forced to expose their sources, that sources will dry up, that the public will be deprived of important information it now gets from confidential sources, and that will disserve the interest of the First Amendment. That's exactly the position they took in the *Branzburg* case twenty years ago."

I continued with an argument that the First Amendment should not interfere with voluntary private agreements. "The First Amendment really ought not to be applicable to this case. You have an agreement between private parties, a newspaper and a source of information. There was no governmental compulsion involved in this case. The case ought to be decided on the common law, on issues of contract law. The First Amendment ought not to be interpreted to give newspapers or other media organizations a right to violate their voluntary promises to another private person."

"But the maximum result you can achieve here is that we remand it to the Minnesota Supreme Court and say, 'You're really not required to reach this result by the First Amendment. But you can reach the same result because you believe in the policy of the First Amendment.' That would be all right, wouldn't it?"

"No, Justice Stevens, because the problem that we have if you open the door for state courts to say that, that's going to give state courts the opportunity to in effect reach final judgments on constitutional issues without allowing litigants the opportunity to appeal to this Court."

This whole interrogation reminded me of my first class on my first day of Harvard Law School thirty years earlier. At 8:30 A.M., Professor Robert Braucher, a big, powerfully built man with a booming voice, convened his class of contract law. Without so much as a welcome-to-my-class, he began screaming impossibly complicated questions on the first cases in the casebook and summoned bewildered class members by name to attempt to answer them. Braucher's face was bright red; he was terrifying. After a few weeks of this, we realized that he was putting on an act, and Braucher became much beloved by his students.

The difference was that this was no act by Justices O'Connor, Souter, and the others.

I emphasized again the inapplicability of the First Amendment to private agreements to which all parties consent. "The issue comes down to whether an agreement between private individuals, a newspaper on the one hand and a source of information on the other, ought to implicate the First Amendment at all and whether the Minnesota Supreme Court acted in error, as we submit it did, in holding that the First Amendment makes these promises unenforceable. We have here, again, a private agreement—no governmental compulsion forcing the newspapers to make this agreement with a private person. But an ordinary business prac- tice of the newspapers, a practice that is indulged in frequently by all. . . ."

Chief Justice Rehnquist then interrupted and brought up *New York Times* v. *Sullivan* for the first and only time in my oral argument. "You have government compulsion just as you have in a libel case, don't you? There's no government compulsion that a paper print a story about some- one that may libel them. But if a court organized by the government gives a judgment for damages, that's thought sufficient to invoke the First Amendment, to invoke the *New York Times* v. *Sullivan* doctrine. And here, too, if the court gives a judgment for damages, that is sufficient government activity to raise the First Amendment question if the First Amendment properly applies."

"Mr. Chief Justice, there is a difference between the *New York Times* v. *Sullivan* type of situation and this type of case. *New York Times* v. *Sullivan* protected a newspaper from inadvertently publishing defamation about someone else. It did not involve a situation where a newspaper made an agreement with a private person to obtain information. It ob- tained this information, and then the newspaper decided that it was going to violate the agreement."

"Well, there are many differences, I agree," said the chief justice. "But I don't think there's a difference in the extent of government involve- ment in the two."

I then argued that the newspapers waived any claim of a First Amend- ment right. "There are many other ways of looking at the issue. For example, the issue of waiver. When a newspaper makes a promise of confidentiality to a news source or makes a voluntary promise of any sort, does it then have the right to say that we're going to violate that promise because we have a First Amendment right to do so? Once that promise is made, the newspaper has in effect waived the right to make any First Amendment claim of a right to violate the promise. Otherwise, promises of newspapers or media organizations would be virtually worthless, not only to news source confidentiality but to any individuals or businesses that newspapers deal with."

"You had a similar type of situation in the *Snepp* case that Justice Scalia mentioned, where a person promised not to publish any information re- garding his employment at the CIA without first getting approval. He broke the promise. He claimed a First Amendment right to do so. The Court ruled that he couldn't do it—in fact, it established a constructive trust on all the profits from the publication in that case."

This was an argument that was the subject of heated controversy in the Minnesota appellate courts. It also raised fundamental First Amendment issues. Yet, surprisingly, no justice questioned any of my statements on waiver. I then returned to my first theme, urging the Court not to exempt the press from laws applying to everyone else.

"The issue is whether newspapers should have the right to violate agreements, should be subject to the same law as applied to everyone else, every other individual or every other business who makes an agreement with another party. Should newspapers and media organizations who enter into such agreements willingly, in exchange for other types of information they consider valuable, shouldn't they be subject to the same law as applies to everyone else who makes voluntary agreements without being given a special First Amendment right to violate those agreements?

"Finally, in *Branzburg* v. *Hayes*, the journalist argued there that honoring promises of confidentiality was so important to First Amendment values as to require constitutional protection. The Court rejected that request and ruled that the First Amendment was simply inapplicable to these types of agreements. This Court should not now accede to respondents' demand to create a special First Amendment right to dishonor their agreements."

I reserved my remaining time for rebuttal.

John French began his argument. Rather than starting with the claim that the Minnesota State Supreme Court had based its decision on state law only, as he did in his brief, French right away challenged my First Amendment arguments. Publishing the truth, he said, should immunize the newspapers from liability.

"The issue before this Court on the merits, if the Court reaches the merits, is whether a reporter's oral promise to a source is sufficient reason to punish the publication of truthful information on a matter of public significance where the promise does not satisfy the standards for waiver of a constitutional right, and as a matter of state law does not even amount to a legally binding contract."

Justice White asked a question for the first time. "Would you be making the same argument if the contract was in writing and there was consideration on both sides?"

"I would be making the same argument," answered French, "but this is an easier case, I think. The two facts that are beyond dispute are that the publications at issue are entirely true, and that they involved matters of public significance. As the Minnesota Supreme Court observed, this was the quintessential public debate in our democratic society. The decisions of this case say that it is clear that there should be protection accorded to the publication of truthful information about matters of public significance. The point I'm making here is that plainly it was truthful information."

Justice Stevens began boring in. "May I ask what is public significance? About the candidate or about the person who gave the information?"

"The election campaign in toto," French answered.

"You could have published the information that she'd been arrested or whatever it was, and that would have satisfied the requirement without identifying the source, couldn't you?"

"The information about Mr. Cohen was information that was a part of a story about matters of public significance. It is possible for news organizations to print the name of Mr. Cohen in a situation like this or to leave it out. Our two clients here today printed his name. The Associated Press did not print his name. WCCO Television didn't carry the story at all. That's the point," French argued.

Justice Stevens did not see it the same way. "Apparently, that indicates that reasonable news editors could differ as to the public significance of the information. And we should say—we should choose between the two views on that."

"You should choose to allow reasonable editors to differ, Your Honor. That is our point. This is subject for editorial judgment. If there is any basis for a challenge such as that leveled by Mr. Cohen, that basis pales to insignificance when the subject is truthful information about a matter of public significance."

"Such as there was involved in the *Snepp* case."

It was interesting that Justice Stevens should bring up that case, because he had written a dissent in it.

French responded, "But in the *Snepp* case what the Court had before it was, number one, protecting national security, and number two, as the Court said, a fiduciary relationship of the highest order. Also, in *Snepp*, the Court did not hold that the information could not be published. It simply held that the prepublication review agreement was valid."

"He had to pay the consequences for what he did. But this is not a prepublication case. You could go ahead and publish and pay damages and publish anything you wanted to."

I was relieved that Justice Stevens did not embrace O'Connor's linkage of the damages awarded Cohen after publication to a prior restraint on that publication. French tried to revive it, though.

"It is not a prepublication case, but I think the case comes so close to being prepublication. The newspapers have had to live now for nine years with a lawsuit which at the trial stage appeared to be going to cost them $700,000 in compensatory and punitive damages. And of course, over the course of nine years cost them countless thousands in attorneys' fees. That kind of sanction can be just as chilling on free speech as the sanction imposed by prepublication injunction."

Justice Stevens came back. "It's still something that they could weigh in the balance when they decide whether or not to breach their agreement."

French was adamant. "It's something they should not have to weigh in the balance."

Chief Justice Rehnquist suggested that litigation for causing damage is part of the normal course of business for all large enterprises, including newspapers. "Mr. French, any number of large concerns which have the potential for doing damage to people, whether they're trucking companies or making asbestos—and newspaper companies have the potential for doing damage—have to live with a certain threat of litigation. That's part of doing business in our economy, isn't it?"

French tried to make a distinction between Cohen's case and previous Supreme Court decisions which held that generally applicable laws also bind media organizations.

"That's absolutely right, Mr. Chief Justice. And these newspapers live with it. They live with it under the antitrust laws. They live with it under the labor laws. They live with it under the laws of taxation. Here we are talking about the core business protected by the First Amendment, the business of publishing the truth. And in that area, they should not have to live under this. Justice Frankfurter has a nice phrase in his concurring opinion in *Associated Press*, where he talks about the business of the press being truth and understanding, not the sale of wares like peanuts and potatoes. This is a case in which Mr. Cohen and his counsel are arguing that it is appropriate by agreement to suppress the publication of truthful information about a matter of public significance. They are not suing because they sold a product or a service to these newspapers and didn't get paid. They are suing because a piece of truthful information came to light in the course of a heated political campaign."

Justice Stevens asked if a reporter lawfully could deliberately mislead a source. "Suppose the newspaper reporter had known that her editor would countermand her promise, but the reporter made the promise anyway?"

"You'd have a different case," French answered, "because I think you'd get closer to fraud and there would be more to weigh in the balance on Mr. Cohen's side. There's nothing in the balance on his side right now. I do not suggest that Mr. Cohen ought to win that case."

"Well, then, it's the degree of wrong, the egregiousness of the press misrepresentations that controls the case?"

"No, they do not control the case."

"How should the case come out, the case that I put to you?"

"The case that you put to me should, in my judgment, still be a case in which the First Amendment is relevant. Mr. Rothenberg argued here today before this Court, as he argued in his briefs, that the First Amendment is irrelevant. It has no weight. It doesn't count. All this Court has to do in order to affirm the Minnesota Supreme Court is to decide that that's wrong. And plainly that has to be wrong. If this Court's decisions protect, under the First Amendment, the utterance of defamatory speech, surely this Court must find some room under the First Amendment to protect the utterance of honest, accurate speech."

Justice Marshall then pounced on French. "Mr. French, on that word 'honest,' did you publish that you promised not to publish that?"

"The two reporters gave Mr. Cohen a promise that they wouldn't. . . ."

"Did you publish that the deal was made not to release it?"

"They did not, Your Honor."

"Well, now you're talking about truth. You didn't publish the truth," Justice Marshall insisted.

"The entire truth about everything did not get published."

"You didn't publish all the truth."

"That's absolutely right, Your Honor," French said. "What the Court has said, however, is that that is a subject to be left to editorial judgment. This Court has said that editorial judgment is a part of the free press publication process that is entitled to constitutional protection."

It was the only participation of Justice Marshall in the oral argument.

In my briefs, I told the Court that the articles, columns, and editorial cartoon the *Star Tribune* and *Pioneer Press* published in the few days after they had identified Cohen did not inform their readers that they had made and broken promises to him. I was careful not to state that the newspapers never made such a disclosure. Indeed, after the 1982 elections, Lou Gelfand's *Star Tribune* column talked at length about the reporters' promises to Cohen and the editors' decision to dishonor their promises.

The disclosure was belated, to be sure, but a response of "better late than never" would have taken a lot of the sting out of Justice Marshall's questions.

I had expected the newspapers to respond in their briefs that they had come clean with the public about their broken promises in articles they had published only a few days later. They never did, and left themselves open to Justice Marshall's strike.

As far as recalling specific facts like this, French was at a disadvantage in not having participated in the trial. Reading and trying to remember thousands of pages of trial transcripts and exhibits almost three years after the fact was not nearly as good as having been there.

Chief Justice Rehnquist hit French again. "So what you're asking us to vindicate is publication of the truth as truth is determined by the editors."

"What I am asking the Court to do," French answered, "is to conclude that the editors are the repository of First Amendment–bestowed rights to make judgments about what to publish and not to publish. There was so much to publish in this case. But what this Court has said is that whether the decision is fair or unfair, the decision belongs to the editors, not to judges."

Round and round the justices turn the lawyers. Tough as it may be, it is not even enough to try to satisfy the justice who asked the original question. Every question and its answer take on a life of their own. The response to one justice's question is grist for the mill of the next justice. Each exchange between justice and lawyer becomes a pirouette in an intricately choreographed ballet. There is a logic more of music than of speech.

Justice Scalia, the Court's George Balanchine, drew French out further. "You're saying more than that. You're saying contract obligations can't stand in the way. What if a reporter for a newspaper—in violation of his contractual obligations to his employer—is for money leaking scoops to a competing newspaper? Don't you think that the newspaper that hires him should be able to sue him for that breach of his agreement?"

"Yes, I do, Your Honor."

"Even though he's turning over the most newsworthy material in the world."

"I do believe it should be able to sue. First, what the reporter is doing is turning over proprietary information. And this Court has said that people who create proprietary information have a right to reap the reward of having created it. Second is. . . ." French did not get a chance to complete the sentence.

"Well, wait, wait, wait—excuse me. Why is that proprietary information? It is confidential information that the paper received. Right?"

"Yes, that's correct."

"Well, why is that any different from the confidential information that was transmitted to the reporter here?"

"The reporter obtained that information in the course of performing services for the newspaper. The right to his services belongs to the newspaper. Moreover, there is a fiduciary relationship between the reporter and his newspaper, which is another that this Court has said deserves protection," French argued.

"All important contract rights."

"Important contract rights which do not suppress publication of the truth," French said. "The difference here is simply the difference in whose newspaper will the truth be published."

Justice Kennedy did not accept the claim that the newspapers should have stronger contractual rights over the control of information than Cohen. "It's a very odd calculus that the person closest to the truth, in this case the source, cannot protect his ability to divulge or not to divulge, but that as you get further away from the sources of truth, i.e., in the newspaper room, you say, 'Oh, then the newspaper has a right to protect its information by a contract suit.' It seems to me the calculus should be just the other way around."

French did not agree. "I think not, Your Honor. The press in our country stands in the role of the surrogate for the public. The public has no way of knowing many things that it ought to know. The press goes and ferrets out the information and publishes it. In the course of that process, reporters find facts, evaluate them, and write stories. Editors decide what to print and what not to print. And in the end, what we're trying to do is to protect the public's right to know. And that's what this case is about. Mr. Cohen wants, by contract, to restrict the ability of editors to do their job and decide what is important to convey to the public as part of its right to know."

Justice O'Connor questioned French's position as being contrary to the major precedent on the subject. "It seems to me that your argument would lead the Court to reach a different result in *Branzburg* v. *Hayes* as well, where the Court held that reporters are not exempt from a generally applicable duty to appear and respond to questions before a grand jury even though they might be asked to reveal confidential information. You would say that decision rests with the editors, and apparently that case would have to come out the other way."

"No, I would not say that, Your Honor," said French. "When a private citizen attempts to assert a right under contract law—which by the way, the Minnesota Supreme Court said doesn't exist—to suppress publication of a piece of information, and that information is truthful and has to do with a matter of high, public significance, then under all the decisions of this Court decided under every other rubric—right of privacy, protection of emotional distress, and so forth—the press prevails."

The oral argument, which had become an interrogation, was turning into an inquisition.

Justice White wanted to return to the newspapers' claims that the Court should not have taken the case because it lacked jurisdiction. "Because of the First Amendment," said Justice White.

"Because of the First Amendment," said French.

Justice White continued, "And so you think we really do have a First Amendment question before us. And we certainly have jurisdiction to decide it, is that it?"

"I think the Court could have had the First Amendment before it if that's what the Minnesota Supreme Court had decided."

"Well, I know," said Justice White, "but what's only been argued now is that the paper has a First Amendment right not to live up to this contract. I don't know why you're arguing it if the issue isn't here."

"I believe the issue is not here, but Mr. Rothenberg says the issue is here, and I think I'm obliged to respond to Mr. Rothenberg."

"Why don't you tell us why we don't have to decide it?"

"I would be delighted to."

"Tell us why we don't have jurisdiction to decide it," reiterated Justice White.

"I would be delighted to do that, Your Honor," repeated French.

"Well, that's always usually the first part of a question."

"It is indeed. The petitioner in this case had two theories at trial, breach of contract and fraudulent misrepresentation. The Court of Appeals took away the fraudulent misrepresentation claim on the ground that it didn't apply to the facts of this case. The Minnesota Supreme Court also took away the breach of contract recovery. In both instances, those decisions were made under state law. And the Minnesota Supreme Court made it very clear that the First Amendment had no part to play in those rulings. The claims have been lost under Minnesota state law, and there is no way that they can be retrieved."

Justice O'Connor asked French the same question she had of me. "Well, how is it that the court got into its discussion of promissory estoppel?"

"There is not, Justice O'Connor, and with respect I have to dispute

Mr. Rothenberg's representation of Minnesota state law. No one thought about promissory estoppel until, on rebuttal argument in the Minnesota Supreme Court, Justice Yetka, one of the dissenting justices, raised it as a possibility. The Minnesota Supreme Court did indeed address it, but it is not essential to the decision to vacate the judgment that petitioner won in the trial court level on contract and fraud."

Justice White resumed his questioning. "But surely there's a strong intimation in the part of the majority opinion of the Supreme Court of Minnesota dealing with promissory estoppel that that theory could sustain the judgment. Otherwise, why would they talk about it?"

"It is difficult in the context of Minnesota state law to understand why Justice Simonett talked about it, Your Honor."

"No, it was the court talking about it, wasn't it?"

"It was the court, Your Honor," French said. "It was the court talking about it."

"And they talked about it. I wouldn't think that there was any principle of Minnesota law that would prevent them from doing that. We'd have to second-guess the Minnesota Supreme Court. They said to enforce the promise under promissory estoppel would violate the defendants' First Amendment rights. I would think you're defending that. You've been defending that judgment most of the morning."

"May I focus, Justice White, the Court's attention on this sentence? In deciding whether it would be unjust not to enforce the promise, the court must necessarily weigh the same considerations that are weighed for whether the First Amendment has been violated. That sets forth the thought process of a court thinking about federal principles and incorporating them into its analysis of state law. That is looking to federal principle for guidance rather than compulsion."

"Yes, Mr. French, but in the next sentence they use the word 'must.' "

"The case could still have been decided under Minnesota promissory estoppel law without a decision on the First Amendment but with a decision that concepts germane under the First Amendment should inform the decision."

Justice Scalia asked French the final question on the issue of jurisdiction. "Justice Yetka's dissent at least seemed to think that the decision of the majority of the court was based upon the First Amendment. And his dissent was joined by the other dissenter, Justice Kelley. He said the First Amendment is being misused to avoid liability under the doctrine of promissory estoppel."

"He could have said that two ways. He could have said the First Amendment is misused or it is a misuse of the First Amendment to think about First Amendment principles when you're thinking about promissory estoppel. So it's not clear to me that he is there saying this is a federal First Amendment case or we're not thinking about the First Amendment right when we're applying state law."

Justice Souter posed a hypothetical case about the newspapers' contract rights in relation to the First Amendment similar to that of Justice Scalia a few minutes earlier. "Assuming we get to the First Amendment issue, would the result be any different in this case, or would the First Amendment significance be any different in this case if the editors of the newspaper had said, 'We agree that the promise ought to be kept and yet the reporter had changed his own mind and said I shouldn't have made the promise, the informant is a rat, and I should expose him.' And the reporter then went out, contrary to the newspaper's judgment, and revealed the identity. Would the First Amendment protect the reporter against damages, too?"

"I suppose the reporter would have an argument that the First Amendment applies to me," French said. "If I were judge, it would be very thin."

"Well, how can you say it would be very—he goes to another newspaper and sells the information and they publish it."

"Well, I'm back to the other hypothetical," French said. "If he goes to another newspaper and publishes it, then once again, he has acted contrary to his fiduciary duty to his employer and has sold a piece of information that doesn't belong to him. He obtained the information in the course of performing services for the first employer."

Justice Stevens followed up. "Does it make it easier for you to answer if we assume also that the newspaper is liable for the misdeeds of its agents, so you're stuck for the damages? Does that change your answer?"

"I believe that in this context, since we are talking about assessing damages with respect to the act of publication, the newspaper should not be stuck for the damages, as you put it."

Justice Kennedy exclaimed, "But the reporter is?"

"No—the First Amendment always counts. I have to come back to that. Mr. Rothenberg. . . ."

Justice Kennedy did not let French finish. "But most of all when it's the newspaper that's involved."

"What this Court has said is that it is protecting the public's right to know and it is protecting the process of editorial judgment. What I am defending here is the right of these editors in the context in which they found themselves, having received substantial information that the reporters did not know."

Justice Kennedy was not satisfied with French's answer. "But you're not sure as to what happens with the reporter. You're also not sure as to what happens in the hypothetical of when the reporter deliberately misleads, knowing that his promise is going to be countermanded. And it seems to me that that's a very, very difficult position. We're asking what the First Amendment consequences are. And you haven't explained this in a coherent theory."

"I'll try again, Your Honor. What the Court must do is, at a minimum, say that the Minnesota Supreme Court was right in concluding that First Amendment interest should be balanced. Now, the Court could go far beyond that and erect a much more absolute rule that says the First Amendment interest is so paramount that we cannot think of a circumstance in which the promise must be kept. I don't ask the Court to do that here today, because I don't have to. If the Court will apply its own prior holdings that with respect to the publication of truthful information of matters of public significance, the First Amendment interest is paramount. And it is possible to balance something against it. It is possible, as this Court has said many times, to balance a state interest of the highest order. But I haven't seen one of those yet."

Justice Stevens had a final question for French just as his time ran out. "That depends on what you mean by balancing. And there are two ways that this opinion might be understood. I suppose you might say, and this is your position, that all it's saying is that you have to take into account First Amendment considerations. But it might also be saying that the First Amendment, not in all circumstances but in some circumstances, prohibits the penalty for the contractual breach. I'm sorry if I went over your time."

"That's all right, Your Honor. I'm here at your disposal." French had a wry sense of humor.

"I think the Chief Justice will let you. . . ."

Chief Justice Rehnquist was eager to hear the answer. "By all means answer the question."

"Your Honor," said French, "if we had 100 of these cases and we could see enough fact situations, I think we would find some instances in which we would say if this is the interest that the claimant is trying to protect, it is insignificant in comparison with the First Amendment interest, and the First Amendment interest always overrides. But there might also be some cases in which the interest advanced by the claimant is regarded by this Court as a state interest of the highest order. And under the particular facts of the case, the Court might hold it was appropriate for the press to honor the promise."

I had five minutes left for rebuttal. To begin with, I reminded the Court of the language of the Minnesota Supreme Court, showing that "there can be no question that the Minnesota Supreme Court regarded that its decision was required by the First Amendment." Second, how the promissory estoppel arose in the Minnesota Supreme Court and who first raised it was irrelevant. "The fact that the Minnesota Supreme Court did consider First Amendment issues is sufficient to give this Court jurisdiction under the long-standing practice of the Supreme Court."

I wanted to challenge the notion that newspapers should have a right to break agreements in order to publish what editors determine is the "truth."

"Mr. French says the issue is whether the promise is kept, this is going to prevent the publication of truth. But the question is quite different. To obtain the truth in many cases, up to 75, 80 percent of the cases in terms of certain news media, the media organizations must make these promises of confidentiality to induce sources to give them information. Without these promises, they would not have the truthful information to convey to the public. The public would be deprived of information."

Justice O'Connor then asked a question that no one had raised since the summary judgment motion. "Well, that troubles me a little, because Mr. Cohen could have sent the information in an unmarked envelope, and the paper would still have had it, right?"

"Mr. Cohen, as many other confidential sources, felt that he could trust the promises of the reporters," I answered.

Justice Scalia and Justice O'Connor began arguing with one another while I was looking on at the podium, trying to maintain a poker face.

Scalia: "Of course, you can't say it comes from a reliable source if you get it in an unmarked envelope, and I assume no responsible reporter would use it if it just came—unless it was independently verifiable somehow."

O'Connor: "Well, I guess if it was—the question here was just a court record of an earlier prosecution which then the paper could possibly check it."

Everyone said not to try any humor in the Supreme Court, but I could not resist. "Thank you, Justice O'Connor; thank you, Justice Scalia, on that one."

That broke the tension. The courtroom audience erupted in laughter. Justice Scalia joined in. Even Justice O'Connor had a smile.

I pointed out again that broken agreements by newspapers may cause serious injuries and do not just raise abstract questions of interpretation of the Constitution.

"Your Honor, the issue is raised by Justice Yetka below, where he pointed out that the real issue of this case is the fact that the newspapers made a promise to Mr. Cohen. Mr. Cohen relied upon that promise and provided information that the newspapers consider valuable, in fact, published on the first page of the *Star Tribune*. As a result of their violating their promises to him, they caused him damage—considerable damage—in the form of getting him fired from his job and subsequent financial damages. Any other person, any other business, in a similar situation would be liable for breach of contract."

Justice Harry Blackmun, originally from Minnesota, asked his only questions of the argument. I had met him a quarter-century earlier, when he was a judge on the Eighth Circuit U.S. Court of Appeals. While on the Supreme Court, Justice Blackmun wrote a character reference letter to support my admission to the New York State bar. I didn't know if he remembered me.

Before meeting with the court clerk that morning, I stopped in the Supreme Court's cafeteria with my wife and daughters. Justice Blackmun was sitting at a table a few feet away, with his law clerks. I wanted to go and say hello to him but was afraid that he wouldn't appreciate it with the oral argument coming up a little later.

Justice Blackmun's questions helped highlight Cohen's damages. There was a hint of a smile on his face. "Why did he get fired from his job as a consequence?"

"He got fired from his job precisely because of the newspaper articles," I responded. "When those articles came out the next day, the *Star Tribune* article not only identified Mr. Cohen but also named his employer—gratuitously named his employer, Justice Blackmun."

"Who was his employer?"

"Martin-Williams Company, a major Minneapolis advertising company which does work for political figures and for government. They felt that because of what had happened—because of their being named—that they had to fire Mr. Cohen. That was found by the jury, the Minnesota Court of Appeals, and the Minnesota Supreme Court and that was conceded by the newspapers."

The red light went on. The oral argument was over.

"Thank you, Mr. Chief Justice."

"Thank you, Mr. Rothenberg."

As I walked out of the Supreme Court building, Judge Knoll was the first to greet me at the top of the steps. He had come to Washington for the argument and brought his son with him.

In fact, the courtroom was packed with players in the case for the past decade. Among others present were former top officials of the newspapers, including past *Pioneer Press* executive editor Deborah Howell and former *Star Tribune* general counsel Norton Armour. It was like old home week.

John Cowles, Jr., the chief executive officer and publisher of the *Star Tribune* at the time the newspapers' editors broke their reporter's promises to Cohen, also happened to be in Washington when the U.S. Supreme Court heard oral argument in the case. His purpose, however, was not to express support for his former newspaper.

Instead, he was there to exercise another claimed First Amendment right that was the subject of controversy. Cowles and his wife, both in their sixties, were featured dancers—in the nude—at George Washington University's Lisner Auditorium in an entertainment called *The Last Summer at Uncle Tom's Cabin—The Promised Land.* A few days before the oral argument, the *Washington Post* ran a profile on Cowles on page 1 of its trendy Style section, titled "The Nude Paper Man."[1]

I had met Cowles in the spring of 1982, when I was running for Minnesota attorney general. We got along well. Despite his prominence, he was a humble, modest guy; there was nothing of the pompous stuffed shirt about him. Unlike his newspapers' editors, whose editorial positions he made no attempt to control, he supported my candidacy and contributed financially to it.

Cowles left the *Star Tribune* in 1983, after twenty-two years as editor in chief and then chief executive officer. He just got tired of the media business. The nationally prominent media mogul launched a new career as an aerobic dance instructor at a St. Paul establishment named The Sweatshop. Cowles was bitten by the performing artist bug. He became, with his wife, a dancer with or without clothes in various productions performed before audiences around the country. The reviews were mostly favorable. As far as appearing nude on stage, Cowles said, "It's a minor issue compared to remembering lines. Other people, though, think we've gone around the bend."

The *Cohen* and *Masson* cases were not the only First Amendment cases on the Supreme Court agenda during Cowles's performances. The issue in *Barnes v. Glen Theatre, Inc.* was whether state and local laws prohibiting nude dancing infringed the free speech rights of something calling itself the Kitty Kat Lounge of South Bend, Indiana. Cowles apparently had not performed there.

After the *Cohen* oral argument, there was pandemonium on the Supreme Court steps. Reporters, camera people, and a busload of high school students from New York were all trying to do interviews. Deborah Howell ran around imploring reporters, "Talk to John French, talk to John French."

A Supreme Court oral argument is a stupendous public spectacle. But is the interchange between justices and lawyers a good predictor of the outcome of a case?

The first indication would come a couple of days later.

Note

1. Lloyd Grove, "The Nude Paper Man; Ex-Publisher John Cowles Jr.'s Dancing Career," *Washington Post*, March 22, 1991, F1.

We Shall Not Be Moved

ON MARCH 29, two days after the oral argument, the justices met and took a preliminary vote on the *Cohen* case. Seven justices—the four who supported certiorari and Kennedy, Souter, and Stevens—voted to reverse the Minnesota Supreme Court. Chief Justice Rehnquist assigned the writing of the decision to Justice White. Justice White had written the decision in *Branzburg* v. *Hayes* two decades earlier.

Justice White circulated his first draft to the justices on April 17. That same day Justice O'Connor—who did not manifest much support of my position at the oral argument—sent a memo joining Justice White's opinion. Two days later, Justice Stevens sent a memo joining the opinion of Justice White. Justice Souter also was supportive, and announced that he would be writing a concurring opinion. (Justices Stevens and Souter, unlike Justice O'Connor, had opposed the grant of certiorari.) As expected, Chief Justice Rehnquist and Justice Scalia also signed on to Justice White's opinion. Justice Kennedy agreed to join Justice White's opinion, too, but not until May 22, three weeks later than any other justice.

On the other hand, Justice Marshall—who at the oral argument roughed up French in indignation that the newspapers did not tell the whole truth—was adamant about protecting the rights of the press. In the Marshall papers is an 8 1/2-by-11-inch sheet of paper with just these words in bold handwriting: "We shall not be moved!"

On May 1, Justice Marshall sent a memo to Justice Blackmun: "You and I are in dissent here. Will you take on the dissent?" Justice Blackmun responded that he would dissent, but was undecided about writing an opinion.

Meanwhile, in April and May another controversy involving a reporter and a source was getting a lot of coverage in Washington, D.C., newspapers, legal periodicals, and the *New York Times*. In *Wheeler* v. *Goulart*, the *Washington Post* and a reporter were resisting a subpoena to a reporter to disclose a news source in a drug abuse case. The *Washington Post* had not entered the *Cohen* case.

But the *New York Times* and others—who were taking the position in the Supreme Court that the press has a constitutional right to identify sources, notwithstanding any contracts to the contrary—were arguing in the D.C. Superior Court and Court of Appeals a few blocks away that newspapers have a First Amendment privilege *not* to disclose to a court any sources, whether or not they are confidential. They claimed in their brief: "The reporter's privilege protects information—published or not— even if it is not confidential." Contrary to their denigration of my free-flow-of-information argument in their Supreme Court amicus brief, they now were demanding that courts not compel reporters to identify sources because of "the important public interest in the free flow of information to the public, covering not only confidential sources and information but the entire newsgathering process. . . . A reporter cannot hope to gather controversial information if sources fear that the reporter will testify about sources despite promises to the contrary."

The hypocrisy was too much even for supporters of the press. Harvard Law School visiting scholar Gary McDowell said that the media's position was "preposterous" and "one of the most blatantly self-interested campaigns on the part of the press."[1] Both D.C. courts ruled against the reporter.

In a May speech in Washington and in an op-ed column, Floyd Abrams, who has frequently represented media organizations before the Supreme Court, blasted the Minnesota newspapers for dishonoring their agreements and their strategy in the *Cohen* case. "In doing so, they acted in a fashion contrary to core principles of journalistic ethics. They also invited the lawsuit now awaiting decision by the Supreme Court, one that offers enemies of the press a particularly inviting target. What the Minnesota newspapers did was wrong; they should have said so. Why is any defender of the press unwilling to say as much?"[2]

The timing of all this could not have been better.

With a comfortable 7–2 majority I seemed headed for the most lopsided victory yet of this litigation. That was before the maneuvering began.

On June 17—only ten days before the Supreme Court would end its term and go on summer vacation, and almost three full months after the oral argument and the Court's initial vote—Justice Souter announced to the Court that although he originally had voted to support Cohen, "I argued myself to the other view while writing what I had originally meant to be a concurrence." He added that he would join Justice Blackmun's dissent as well.

The next day, Justice O'Connor declared that she, too, would switch her vote and join Justice Souter's dissent. "I dislike late in the Term shifts, but, nevertheless, I am persuaded by David's writing that we should not dispense with the balancing test in this case."

Neither Souter nor O'Connor gave any further explanation for their switch.

In the final hours of the Court's term, after nine years of hard-fought litigation, would one more justice change his mind and snatch defeat from the jaws of victory?

Week after week went by with no decision in the other big freedom of the press cases, *Masson v. New Yorker Magazine, Inc.*, either. The Court usually leaves its toughest and most contentious decisions until late June.

Finally, on June 20, the Court handed down its decision in *Masson v. New Yorker Magazine, Inc.*, authored by Justice Kennedy. The *Masson* ruling reversed a decision of the Ninth Circuit Court of Appeals dismissing a suit by the plaintiff, Jeffrey Masson. The Supreme Court gave him a right to a trial of a claim of libel for deliberate alteration of quotations by writer Janet Malcolm that made him the subject of ridicule.

Malcolm was notorious for beginning her 1990 book, *The Journalist and the Murderer*, with this paragraph:

Every journalist who is not too stupid or too full of himself to notice what is going on knows that what he does is morally indefensible. He is a kind of confidence man, preying on people's vanity, ignorance, or loneliness, gaining their trust and betraying them without remorse. Like the credulous widow who wakes up one day to find the charming young man and all her savings gone, so the consenting subject of a piece of nonfiction writing learns—when the article or book appears—his hard lesson. Journalists justify their treachery in various ways according to their temperaments. The more pompous talk about freedom of speech and "the public's right to know"; the least talented talk about Art; the seemliest murmur about earning a living.[3]

The Supreme Court ruled that journalists did not have a First Amendment right to materially change the meaning of quotations. The Kennedy opinion warned of the consequences to the press itself of giving journalists a privilege to materially alter quotations.

Not only public figures but the press doubtless would suffer under such a rule. Newsworthy figures might become more wary of journalists, knowing that any comment could be transmuted and attributed to the subject, so long as some bounds of rational interpretation were not exceeded. We would ill serve the values of the First Amendment if we were to grant near absolute, constitutional protection for such a practice.

That was the very point I was seeking to make in oral argument about the adverse consequences to First Amendment values of allowing the press to break promises of confidentiality. The Court's embrace of this logic in the *Masson* decision was a good sign.

The Court ruled that Masson still must satisfy the *New York Times* v. *Sullivan* standard of knowing falsity or reckless disregard for the truth. The decision seemed to be a defeat for the press, but lawyers and others representing media organizations were fulsome in their praise for Justice Kennedy. Media attorney Bruce Sanford, for example, said that Justice Kennedy was "very impressive" and showed a "depth of knowledge and appreciation for the journalists' profession."[4] Jane Kirtley said the Court in its decision displayed "a remarkable sensitivity to journalism." Floyd Abrams called the decision "rather supportive" of the media.[5] Justice White, joined by Justice Scalia, filed a partial dissent, taking the position that the standard announced by the majority was unworkable and too favorable to the press. The two justices and the media lawyers proved to be right. In two later trials, both the *New Yorker* and Janet Malcolm won jury verdicts. Despite his Supreme Court victory, Masson got no financial recovery.

When I read the *Masson* decision, I hoped that mine would be authored by White or Scalia. Four days later, I learned that I had gotten my wish.

Whatever may have been the lobbying in the Court, the Marshall papers do not disclose any wavering by any of the remaining majority of five.

The Supreme Court ruled that the First Amendment did not free the newspapers from the obligations of their agreement with Cohen. The law of contracts and promissory estoppel is applicable to all citizens, and the First Amendment does not bar its enforcement against the press. "Generally applicable laws do not offend the First Amendment simply because their enforcement against the press has incidental effects on its ability to gather and report the news." The Court allowed for no special privileges for the press by the back door—through such phrases as "balancing" of First Amendment interests or "heightened scrutiny" for court rulings and laws regulating the press. "Enforcement of such general laws against the press is not subject to stricter scrutiny than would be applied to enforcement against other persons or organizations."

In other words, the press is subject to the same law as everyone else when it breaks a contract, and the First Amendment gives it no special privileges against individuals or businesses who are injured by press misconduct.

Under the Court's reasoning, newspapers could be liable for publishing the truth if doing so violates an agreement. "Minnesota law simply requires those making promises to keep them. The parties, themselves, as in this case, determine the scope of their legal obligations, and any restrictions which may be placed on the publication of truthful information are self-imposed."

Regarding any suggestion that the Court was "punishing" the publication of accurate information, "compensatory damages are not a form of punishment." On the contrary, it is "a cost of acquiring newsworthy material to be published at a profit. In any event, the characterization of the payment makes no difference for First Amendment purposes when the law being applied is a general law and does not single out the press."

The Court took pains to point out that any protection for the publication of truthful information applies only where the newspaper lawfully obtained the facts. "It is not at all clear that respondents obtained Cohen's name 'lawfully' in this case, at least for purposes of publishing it. Unlike the situation in *The Florida Star*, where the rape victim's name was obtained through lawful access to a police report, respondents obtained Cohen's name only by making a promise which they did not honor. The dissenting opinions suggest that the press should not be subject to any law, including copyright law for example, which in any fashion or to any degree limits or restricts the press' right to report truthful information. The First Amendment does not grant the press such limitless protection."

Justice White's decision held that the law of contracts binds the press just like everyone else. That was eminently fair on its face. But how did the Court deal with *New York Times* v. *Sullivan* and the other cases creating special privileges for the press?

The Court held specifically that an action for breach of promise is not subject to the "strict requirements for establishing" a defamation or infliction of emotional distress claim. The jury did not award damages for "injury to reputation or state of mind," but instead compensated Cohen for "a breach of a promise that caused him to lose his job and lowered his earning capacity. Thus this is not a case like *Hustler Magazine, Inc. v. Falwell*."

The decision mentioned *New York Times v. Sullivan* only once, and only for the point that state court enforcement of promises constituted "state action" within the meaning of the Fourteenth Amendment, and would trigger protection of any First Amendment rights.

The writing was direct—stark, even—and without bloat to it. It was unequivocal in repudiating any claim of a special privilege for the press to break promises. The Court's spare and concise prose had none of the verbosity and convolution that infect many judicial decisions. It was actually readable. There was no hedging in the decision, either. It threw no bones to the newspapers. No one suggested that Justice White's opinion, unlike Justice Kennedy's in the *Masson* case, manifested any "sensitivity" to accommodate the interests of the media.

It was the worst defeat the media had ever suffered in the Supreme Court.[6]

Justices Blackmun and Souter wrote dissenting opinions joined by the other dissenters. (O'Connor joined Souter's but not Blackmun's). Despite all the time spent on the issue during oral argument, there was unanimity that the Minnesota decision had rested on the First Amendment and that Supreme Court jurisdiction was proper.

Justice Blackmun said the court erred in holding newspapers liable for reporting truthful information regarding a political campaign. "I do not read the decision of the Supreme Court of Minnesota to create any exception to or immunity from the laws of that State for members of the press. In my view, the court's decision is premised, not on the identity of the speaker, but on the speech itself. Necessarily, the First Amendment protection afforded respondents would be equally available to non-media defendants." The decision's holding that newspapers had no special immunity from the application of general laws was, he said, "misplaced." *Branzburg v. Hayes* and other cases supporting this principle, said Blackmun, did not impose liability for the content of what a newspaper had published.

What Justice Blackmun did not acknowledge was that any limitation of the newspapers' right to publish Cohen's name was not the result of governmental compulsion but of the enforcement of the newspapers' voluntary agreement to so restrict the content of their articles in exchange for other information valuable to them. The law of contracts was neutral, allowing the newspapers to make whatever agreements they deemed in their interest.

Finally, Justice Blackmun contended that the decision in *Hustler Magazine* v. *Falwell* was "precisely on point" in favor of a First Amendment right of the newspapers to break their promises. "There was no doubt that Virginia's tort of intentional infliction of emotional distress was 'a law of general applicability' unrelated to the suppression of speech. . . . As in *Hustler*, the operation of Minnesota's doctrine of promissory estoppel cannot be said to have a merely 'incidental' burden on speech; the publication of important political speech *is* the claimed violation. Thus, as in *Hustler*, the law may not be enforced to punish the expression of truthful information or opinion."

Justice Souter saw the determinative issue as what would maximize the amount of information available to the press and the public. He did not, however, accept my argument that permitting newspapers to break agreements would hinder the free flow of information.

His dissent said that laws of general applicability "may restrict First Amendment rights just as effectively as those directed specifically at speech itself."

The fact that the newspapers voluntarily agreed to confidentiality should not matter. Souter charged that the decision embraced "a conception of First Amendment rights as those of the speaker alone, with a value that may be measured without reference to the importance of the information to public discourse. But freedom of the press is ultimately founded on the value of enhancing such discourse for the sake of a citizenry better informed and thus more prudently self-governed."

Along with the erudite constitutional analysis, the issue of Cohen's character, which had been so central to the newspapers' strategy in the trial, was back.

The First Amendment, Souter continued, prohibits "limiting the stock of information from which members of the public may draw. . . . There can be no doubt that the fact of Cohen's identity expanded the universe of information relevant to the choice faced by Minnesota voters in that state's 1982 gubernatorial election, the publication of which was thus of the sort quintessentially subject to strict First Amendment protection. The propriety of his leak to respondents could be taken to reflect on his character, which in turn could be taken to reflect on the character of the candidate who had retained him as an advisor. An election could turn on just such a factor; if it should, I am ready to assume that it would be to the greater public good, at least over the long run."

Would it indeed? Granting newspapers a right to break agreements of confidentiality may have "expanded the universe of information" in this one case. The opposite would have obtained "over the long run" had the Souter position prevailed in the Supreme Court. Judicial protection of confidentiality agreements is more likely to ensure and increase the flow of information to the press and the public. That was exactly the media's claim in *Branzburg* v. *Hayes* and all the other cases—including the Washington, D.C., case that was going on when Justice Souter was writing his dissent—where they did not want to disclose their confidential sources to courts.

Creating a First Amendment right to violate promises of confidentiality could only discourage potential sources from trusting media promises in the future. Future informants from the Deep Throats to the Karen Silkwoods—worried about the threat to their jobs or worse from identification—would be a lot less likely to hand over information if editors' decisions to honor or dishonor reporters' promises of confidentiality would depend not on the requirement of law but only on the expediency of what will sell the most newspapers the next day. The result inevitably would be a reduction of the stock of information, contrary to the interests of the First Amendment and an informed public.

In the end, it was another victory with no votes to spare.

The Supreme Court recognized new rights—or resurrected ones dormant more than a quarter-century—for those injured by the media. *Editor & Publisher* magazine attacked the *Cohen* decision for putting "Minnesota, and every other state, in the position of being able to dictate what can or cannot be printed, which is something the First Amendment prohibits them from doing. The Court has taken a step away from unfettered publication."[7]

I was exhilarated. Still, after nine years of litigation and a landmark decision by the highest court in the land, the case was not over.

Notes

1. Daniel Klaidman, "Bad Timing for the *Washington Post*: Protecting Sources Gets Tougher for Reporters," *Legal Times*, April 29, 1991, 6.

2. Floyd Abrams, "Battles Not Worth Fighting," *Washington Post*, June 13, 1991, A21.

3. Janet Malcolm, *The Journalist and the Murderer* (New York: Alfred A. Knopf, 1990), 3.

4. Debra Gersh, "Quote Alterations and Libel," *Editor & Publisher*, June 29, 1991, 7.

5. Linda Greenhouse, "Justices Refuse to Open a Gate for Libel Cases," *New York Times*, June 21, 1991, A1.

6. Professor Burt Neuborne in "Free Expression and the Rehnquist Court," *Communication Law 1998*, vol. one (New York: Practising Law Institute, 1998), 1273, 1297, wrote that the *Cohen* decision was "the media's most serious loss" in the Rehnquist Court. The current author's analysis of pre-Rehnquist Supreme Court decisions reveals none comparable to *Cohen* regarding media liability to the victims of wrongdoing.

7. Editorial, "Decision on Confidentiality," *Editor & Publisher*, June 29, 1991, 4.

Turnabout Is Fair Play

SPEAKING BEFORE THE annual communications law seminar of New York's Practising Law Institute in November 1991, I said that the *Cohen* decision "will cast a glow or pall, depending on one's point of view, over all of media law. When news organizations are sued, they will be subject to the same laws as any other business. This is a sea change from the philosophy that goes back to *New York Times v. Sullivan*. The *Cohen* decision represents a fundamental change in First Amendment law and will compel the press to make special efforts to protect the rights of people with whom you deal."

The question remained, however, whether Cohen himself would benefit financially from it. The Court did not reinstate the jury verdict for compensatory damages but sent the case back to the Minnesota Supreme Court. "The Minnesota Supreme Court's incorrect conclusion that the First Amendment barred Cohen's claim may well have truncated its consideration of whether a promissory estoppel claim had otherwise been established under Minnesota law and whether Cohen's jury verdict could be upheld on a promissory estoppel basis. Or perhaps the State Constitution may be construed to shield the press from a promissory estoppel cause of action such as this one. These are matters for the Minnesota Supreme Court to address and resolve in the first instance on remand."

The Souter dissent gave further encouragement to the newspapers by maintaining that revelations of political activist Cohen's character were proper in the last days of the campaign. The state Supreme Court could take the hint and rule that, under the criteria of state promissory estoppel

law rather than the First Amendment, "justice" did not require enforcement of the promises to Cohen.

Was that an invitation to use state law to throw out the case again or
just a gesture of respect to a state Supreme Court? The latter made more
sense. I didn't think that the Supreme Court would welcome a flouting
of its decision. The phrase "resolve *in the first instance* on remand" hinted
that the Court would give stricter scrutiny to a second state Supreme
Court ruling favoring the newspapers than an ordinary petition for certiorari. The "experts" did not agree.

The newspapers' supporters crowed that the Minnesota court would
rule the same way it had before; this time, though, it would not make the
mistake of mentioning the First Amendment but would cite only state
law and the Minnesota Constitution. To them it was inconceivable that
the Minnesota court would reverse itself and rule for Cohen.

A signer of the amicus brief, George Freeman (for the *New York Times*),
said he was optimistic about the Supreme Court decision. "The court
paved the way for the newspapers to win the case in Minnesota courts by
leaving wide open the option to use the promissory estoppel analysis."[1]

Professor Donald Gillmor declared flatly, "I can't imagine the state
Supreme Court is going to reverse itself. I can see no reason why they
would do that." Mark Anfinson, the attorney for the Associated Press
and the Minnesota Press Association, was more flamboyant. "If the Minnesota Supreme Court is given a four-lane highway by which to reach
the same conclusion it did before—namely, the Minnesota Constitution—it's reasonable to prophesy they will use the four-lane highway to
do it." The state freedom of speech language, said Anfinson, was "wide
open and the state court can interpret that any way they want to."[2]

Political consultant D. J. Leary, who had not been heard from for three
years, since his forecast of a newspaper victory in the trial, predicted again
that the newspapers would win. Under the banner "ADVICE TO DAN
COHEN: DON'T SPEND THE MONEY YET," Leary's newsletter *Politics
in Minnesota* belittled the Supreme Court decision. "Last week's U.S.
Supreme Court decision made it appear to many that Cohen had finally
won. We doubt it. The Supremes merely sent it back to Minnesota's high
court. We think the Minnesota Supreme Court could find in favor of the
newspapers because Minnesota's Constitution has a much more positive
approach to press freedom than the negatively constructed federal constitution."[3]

Leary had some precedent to back him. Just a year earlier the U.S.

Supreme Court and the state court had been at odds over another case involving claims to a dispensation from laws everyone else must obey. The U.S. Supreme Court had reversed the state court's initial ruling, in *State* v. *Hershberger*, embracing First Amendment freedom of religion claims by some Old Order Amish who had refused to obey a highway safety law. After the U.S. Supreme Court held that the First Amendment did not confer rights to endanger others traveling on highways, the state Supreme Court ruled again for the Amish parties. This time it declared that the state constitution gave more religious rights than the First Amendment.

Adding to the problems, the state Supreme Court was even more partisan than before. Justice Glenn Kelley, the author of one of the two powerful dissents to the first Minnesota Supreme Court decision, had retired. So had Chief Justice Popovich. Outgoing Governor Rudy Perpich had appointed two women justices. Both were close to Perpich and had held appointive posts in the Perpich-Johnson administration and Democrat-controlled Minnesota legislature.

One of the appointments was especially controversial. Sandra Gardebring had been a political jack-of-all-trades for Perpich. I had worked with Gardebring on various environmental cases when I was at the Minnesota Public Interest Research Group. She had begun her career as an attorney with the Minnesota Pollution Control Agency before getting politically active with Perpich. As governor, Perpich had appointed Gardebring to five different positions. In between these various appointments, Gardebring married a Democratic state representative from northern Minnesota, Paul Anders Ogren. Ogren was a distant relative of mine. I was never able to figure out how I became related to someone with such a classic Scandinavian name. Anyway, Ogren and I were not close, and we did not have much contact even when we were both in the legislature. Ogren did not invite me to the wedding. Any family connection was so tenuous that it probably would do more harm than good.

The *Star Tribune* described Gardebring as a "longtime Perpich personal ally and troubleshooter" and "a longtime favorite" of the governor. Perpich delayed until the last minute naming Gardebring to the vacancy created on November 30 by Popovich's retirement. He arranged for Popovich to administer the oath of office to Gardebring in the governor's reception room on the night of January 4, 1991, only hours before Arne Carlson would take over as governor. Popovich, not Perpich, informed the press later. The appointment was Perpich's last act in office.

Stealthy or not, no one could do anything about it. In Minnesota the governor has absolute power over judicial appointments with no need to get the legislature's approval.

Four of the seven justices now were women; Minnesota had the first state high court in the country with a female majority. The *Star Tribune* was elated. It editorialized, "More women on the bench could mean greater court sensitivity to the special concerns of women."[4]

Perpich earlier had appointed sitting Associate Justice Alexander M. Keith to replace Popovich as chief justice.

Like the other appointees, Keith had a strong partisan background. In 1966, Lieutenant Governor Keith was a rising political star. He sought and won, after eighteen ballots in the state convention, the Democratic party's endorsement for governor against incumbent Democrat Karl Rolvaag. Rolvaag refused to withdraw, and overwhelmed Keith in the primary. Rolvaag then lost the election. Keith never ran for office again. Instead, he established a successful private law practice. He did not totally divorce himself from politics, however. He was an early supporter and avid fund-raiser for Perpich.

As chief justice, Keith would get a second chance in this case to apply his theory that the state court could circumvent the U.S. Supreme Court by aggressively interpreting the Minnesota Constitution and laws to find "rights" that did not exist in the U.S. Constitution. The U.S. Supreme Court's decision seemingly invited Keith to do just that. It was not an invitation that the Keith court was likely to refuse, though there was a certain irony in its source.

A Minneapolis attorney and future state district court judge, who had made a crusade of pushing state law to resist Supreme Court review, made no bones about the purpose of the strategy. In late October 1991, Jack Nordby declared the state constitution "the last stand of liberals who think we ought to have some individual freedoms. If others want to call it sour grapes over what has happened at the Supreme Court, I have no quarrel with that."[5] At least he was honest about it.

The momentum was building, too. Less than three weeks before the U.S. Supreme Court's *Cohen* decision and again in August 1991, the Minnesota Supreme Court ruled, in the case of *Friedman v. Commissioner of Public Safety*, that an accused drunken driver had state constitutional rights to consult a lawyer before taking a breathalyzer test. This was contrary to U.S. Supreme Court decisions interpreting the U.S. Constitution. Charging that "the federal courts have eroded the federal Bill of Rights," the state court decision challenged the judicial primacy of the U.S. Supreme Court.

In recent years, as the United States Supreme Court has retrenched on Bill of Rights issues, state courts have begun to interpret expansively the rights guaranteed under their own state constitutions. Commentators have noted and encouraged the trend. State courts must follow the United States Supreme Court in matters of federal constitutional law. They are free to interpret their own law, however, so as to provide greater protection for individual rights than that which the federal Constitution minimally mandates. Rulings which rest on adequate independent state grounds are not subject to review by the United States Supreme Court.

State courts are returning to local protection of individual liberties as intended by the colonists before there was a United States Supreme Court. Whether the state constitution has language similar to that of the federal Constitution or not, states are free to interpret their own constitutions.

The state court did not expect any problems with the U.S. Supreme Court. "The United States Supreme Court has, in effect, encouraged the states to expand their own bill of rights."

Justice Yetka, of all people, wrote the decision.

Jay Sekulow warned, "Settle this thing for whatever you can get. Don't let the state court get its hands on it again." I didn't take Jay's advice. Not that I had any choice about it.

The newspapers no longer were trying to get a settlement for $200,000 plus an unspecified amount of interest. Despite the U.S. Supreme Court decision, they were so confident of victory that they were not offering anything.

The worst that could happen, they thought, would be a new trial, where they would either win outright or get a hung jury. They would make sure that they would have at least two jurors with them the next time around. Jim Fitzmaurice had told me four years earlier, when his firm was appealing the jury verdict, "The next trial we'll do right."

Whatever the state Supreme Court did this time would not necessarily be the last decision in the case. The losing party in the Amish case, a rural county attorney's office, threw in the towel rather than draw down its sparse financial and political resources to challenge the state Supreme Court again.

In contrast, I had no qualms about petitioning the U.S. Supreme Court a second time.

All the talk about using the state constitution to confer "liberties" and "freedoms" rejected by the U.S. Supreme Court sounded very high-minded. The elevation of the state constitution to a moral pedestal became more questionable, however, when its use to expand the privileges of some meant infringing the rights of others. That was exactly the issue in the *Cohen* case.

My brief to the state Supreme Court argued that any interpretation of the state constitution to empower newspapers to break promises to Cohen and other sources would violate the latter's rights under the U.S. Constitution. I reminded the court of the holding of *Cooper* v. *Aaron* that state courts could not use state constitutions and laws to deprive citizens of their rights under the U.S. Constitution.

First I argued that the U.S. Constitution's Fourteenth Amendment equal protection clause requires that newspaper promises be subject to the same law as the promises of other businesses and individuals in Minnesota. In its decision, the U.S. Supreme Court found that the law of promissory estoppel enforcing agreements "is generally applicable to the daily transactions of all the citizens of Minnesota."

The newspapers, I said, were "attempting to deny Mr. Cohen a right enjoyed by all other citizens of Minnesota: the right to enforce voluntary promises and agreements." I quoted previous Minnesota Supreme Court decisions which held that the Fourteenth Amendment "requires equality of application of the laws."

I referred the court to the Minnesota Free Flow of Information Act, which denied courts the power to require journalists to disclose their sources. "Far from granting newspapers permission to break promises to sources, the Minnesota Legislature—at the behest of defendants themselves—enacted legislation protecting promises of confidentiality.

"If anything, then, the Minnesota Legislature has sanctified promises of confidentiality even more than promises in general.

"Defendants demand that Minnesota law empower journalists to protect or expose confidential sources at their sole discretion while allowing no recourse for those injured by dishonored promises. They not only would refuse equal protection to Mr. Cohen but would give him none at all.

"Mr. Cohen should have the same rights as any other Minnesotan to enforce promises made to him; defendants should have the same obligation as any other Minnesota business to abide by their promises."

Next, I argued that interpreting the Minnesota Constitution to grant newspapers an indiscriminate right to break agreements would violate

Cohen's rights under Article 1, section 10, of the U.S. Constitution, which prohibits any law impairing the obligations of contracts.

Citing the trial testimony of Dean Arnold Ismach, the brief stated, "The agreement by which defendants exchanged promises of confidentiality in return for the documents possessed by Mr. Cohen was a typical business transaction of journalists to obtain information. Sources who enter into such agreements are entitled to the same protection of the contract clause as those who enter into other commercial agreements."

By now, despite the 1990 state Supreme Court decision, there could be no question that the agreements between the newspapers and Cohen indeed were contracts.

The U.S. Supreme Court decision described the agreement between the newspapers and Cohen as "the contract between the parties" and held that the promise of confidentiality was "constitutionally indistinguishable" from an agreement to pay money for information. In the latter case, said the Court, "it would be perfectly clear that the payment would represent a cost of acquiring newsworthy information to be published at a profit."

Interestingly, the U.S. Supreme Court in *Allied Structural Steel Co. v. Spannaus*, which I had cited in my brief to the high court, struck down a Minnesota state attempt to invalidate private agreements. There the state legislature imposed on a company leaving the state retroactive pension obligations substantially beyond the terms of its employment contracts. The Supreme Court minced no words in holding the state statute unconstitutional for impairing the obligations of contracts.

Entering a field it had never before sought to regulate, the Minnesota Legislature grossly distorted the company's existing contractual relationships with its employees. That burden was imposed upon the company only because it closed its office in the state. This law was not even purportedly enacted to deal with a broad, generalized economic or social problem. It did not operate in an area already subject to state regulation at the time the company's contractual obligations were originally undertaken, but invaded an area never before subject to regulation by the state. It worked a severe, permanent, and immediate change in contractual relationships. And its narrow aim was leveled not at every Minnesota employer. We hold that if the Contract Clause means anything at all, it means that Minnesota could not constitutionally do what it tried to do to the company in this case.

The state constitution did not give newspapers the power to break promises in the first place, my brief argued. Under the relevant provision,

"The liberty of the press shall remain forever inviolate, and all persons may freely speak, write and publish their sentiments on all subjects, being responsible for the abuse of such right." In this case, no one prevented the newspapers from freely publishing Cohen's name. The award of compensatory damages for violating their promises only held them "responsible for the abuse of such right." It was entirely compatible with the state constitution.

On interpreting the Minnesota Constitution, my brief quoted Justice Frankfurter's concurring opinion in the 1946 Supreme Court decision of *Pennekamp* v. *Florida.*

No institution in a democracy, either governmental or private, can have absolute power. . . . In plain English, freedom carries with it responsibility even for the press; freedom of the press is not a freedom from responsibility for its exercise. Most state constitutions expressly provide for liability for abuse of the press's freedom. That there was such legal liability was so taken for granted by the Framers of the First Amendment that it was not spelled out.

I also argued, as I did earlier in relation to the First Amendment, that the newspapers had waived any claimed rights under the Minnesota Constitution by voluntarily promising that they would not disclose Cohen's identity. They understood that they were waiving the right to publish a potentially newsworthy item in return for obtaining another potentially newsworthy item.

One other issue remained. The state Supreme Court's 1990 decision declared that even if a broken promise injured a party, under its conception of promissory estoppel he or she must establish that "injustice can only be avoided by enforcing the promise."

What was "injustice" supposed to mean? The court did not define what, if anything, limited its or any other Minnesota court's authority to enforce or not enforce a promise. The legal effect of a promise could depend upon which of the parties a judge or jury happened to regard as more "politically correct." Further, the undefined notion of "justice" could invite juries to indulge in the worst kind of injustice by issuing verdicts based on prejudice for or against the parties to a case rather than on uniformly applicable law. Would favored parties have a privilege to dishonor promises under state promissory estoppel law that they did not have under the First Amendment?

The whole idea of an arbitrary enforcement of contracts struck at the principle of equality of treatment under the rule of law. It would be further grounds, under the equal protection clause, for an appeal to the U.S. Supreme Court.

Of course, it would be far better to win at the state Supreme Court level. As I saw it, overcoming the promissory estoppel hurdle required a lot more than a conventional legal argument.

My brief emphasized that many journalists condemned the newspapers' conduct as unjust or worse. They repudiated the newspapers' claim of a right to dishonor agreements as a cardinal sin of the profession.

After the U.S. Supreme Court decision, I visited the Minneapolis public library almost daily to read whatever newspapers came in from around the country. I didn't have the luxury of waiting for indexes to be published. My brief recounted the collection of comments I had gathered. As cited in my Supreme Court petition, First Amendment lawyer Floyd Abrams in the *New York Times* called the newspapers' behavior "reprehensible and damaging to all journalists." *Baltimore Sun* legal affairs reporter Lyle Denniston said that the breaking of promises of confidentiality "is a straightforward, baldfaced ethical violation." Writing in *Legal Times*, Stuart Taylor scorned the newspapers for claiming a license "to engage in grossly unethical conduct." The press's claim, Taylor continued, to a "high mission rings hollow when it presents itself as a privileged caste, demanding the right to violate basic ethical and legal standards that others must obey."

Washington Post ombudsman Richard Harwood, in a column about the U.S. Supreme Court decision, wrote, "We're likely to hear a lot of rhetorical whining by newsroom barons and baronesses about the tyranny of court decrees. Plug your ears until they demonstrate a capacity to clean up their own acts and stop defending the indefensible." The *Washington Post* had refused to join with the *New York Times* and *Los Angeles Times* in their U.S. Supreme Court amicus brief. Said a *Post* editorial, "Policy at this paper is to consider writers and editors morally bound to respect confidentiality agreements." The *St. Louis Post Dispatch* in a lead editorial criticized the Minnesota newspapers' "disregard for the high standards that journalism must subject itself to. News organizations that use the First Amendment as a shield for improper conduct are like the boy who cried wolf: When they want to claim constitutional rights they truly need to do their jobs, no one will trust them." A *Miami Herald* editorial titled "When the Press Errs" said that the U.S. Supreme Court decision "affirms principles that many journalists and much of the public hold dear. This newspaper welcomes the Court's sensitivity."

Harvard law professor Laurence Tribe told the *Boston Globe* that the

U.S. Supreme Court decision was a good one for American journalism. "When the press gets special benefits, it suffers a backlash. And to the extent that promises of confidentiality are taken more seriously, the press can operate more effectively."

Local figures also welcomed the decision. University of Minnesota journalism professor Ted Glasser said, "The newspapers' loss is the reporter's victory."

Most important, reporters for the *Star Tribune* and *Pioneer Press* were outspoken in praising the decision against their own newspapers. *Pioneer Press* reporter Bill Salisbury, who fought from the beginning to protect his promise, was gleeful. "My colleagues in the newsroom are all cheering the decision." *Star Tribune* reporter Joe Rigert, former president of the national organization Investigative Reporters & Editors, called the decision "in the public interest. It should strengthen the watchdog role of the news media by assuring sources that their confidentiality will be protected. Confidential sources often provide the tips and leads that make it possible to find wrongdoing in government, business, and public institutions. But these sources may be reluctant to talk if they fear they will be identified and their jobs jeopardized. This ruling should help make it possible for reporters to give a credible guarantee to sources that these fears are groundless."

David Nimmer, whose television station honored his promise to Cohen, agreed. "The decision of the editors to force the reporters to reveal their source had a more chilling effect on press freedom and the access to information than Cohen's lawsuit against the press. The issue was, and is, keeping a bargain, living up to your word, honoring your commitment."

Sam Newlund, a *Star Tribune* reporter for thirty-one years, wrote, "Newspapers must be believed—and trusted—or else sink to the level of tabloid scandal-rags. To be trusted by news sources, those vital cogs in the newsgathering process, they must demonstrate a simple virtue: That they will keep their promises. On that score, the *Star Tribune* and the *Pioneer Press* failed badly nine years ago. To say that those promises can be abrogated because editors' news judgment is more important than honoring one's word smacks of simple arrogance. Clear black-and-white conclusions about complicated issues are hard to come by. But this is one of those rare cases. Set aside all the legal and procedural arcana and one shining principle stands out in bold italics. If you make a promise, keep it."

These comments suggested that something else was involved here than the *Star Tribune*'s and *Pioneer Press*'s posture of newspaper editors on white horses heroically going to battle for freedom of the press.

University of Minnesota journalism professor Phillip Tichenor wrote, "There is good reason in the journalism community—and in society at large—to rejoice over the Supreme Court's ruling that newspapers may not use the First Amendment as an excuse for breaking promises. This decision is a necessary outcome in a case in which freedom of the press is a smokescreen for another agenda. That other agenda, which has gotten little attention in the *Cohen* case, is the issue of media managerial license to control professional reporters in the field."

In fact, the Twin Cities Newspaper Guild, AFL-CIO, which represents reporters of both the *Star Tribune* and *Pioneer Press*, now urged its members not to disclose the name of a source to their editors unless the source agreed to the disclosure. The Guild told its members that it was better to kill a story than to identify a source to their own employers.

Breaking a promise to a source, then, was worse than a mere mistake in judgment. One court went even further than Nimmer and Newlund and the other critics.

I dug up in the catacombs of the county courthouse a microfilm of an 1878 Michigan Supreme Court case, *Tryon* v. *Evening News*, which held that it actually was libelous to falsely accuse a reporter of dishonoring a promise of confidentiality. The court said that this kind of accusation would be defamatory because anyone who so revealed confidences would be, in the court's words, "a very contemptible creature" and "a public nuisance."

Except for the old Michigan case, this was far from the typical fare of a legal brief, but the state Supreme Court had handled the case as a political as much as a legal one. Much of the journalistic community reviled the *Star Tribune* and *Pioneer Press* as having exercised poor judgment. The state Supreme Court could not expect universal applause from the press—and none from reporters and their unions—if it threw the case out again.

The focus on the labor-management dispute between reporters and editors aimed to create a real dilemma for justices whose political bias supported both the "rights" of the press and the interests of labor versus management. The court could not satisfy both in this case.

Moreover, public policy as defined by the Minnesota legislature required protection of promises of confidentiality. The *Star Tribune* and *Pioneer Press* could hardly credibly claim that permitting them to break these promises was consistent with "justice" when they themselves pushed the state legislature to adopt the Minnesota Free Flow of Information Act. This statute declares at its outset:

In order to protect the public interest and the free flow of information, the news media should have the benefit of a substantial privilege not to reveal sources of information or to disclose unpublished information. To this end, the freedom of press requires protection of the confidential relationship between the news gatherer and the source of information.

As in previous briefs, I quoted testimony from *Star Tribune* and *Pioneer Press* editors about the importance of confidential sources in their business and their frequent use of promises of confidentiality to obtain information they otherwise would not have. According to all the evidence at the trial, the two newspapers had never broken such a promise to anyone else. Most especially, they welcomed revelations about politicians from confidential sources.

"Defendants on many occasions have promised confidentiality late in political campaigns in exchange for revelations regarding financial irregularities, criminal and civil actions, plagiarism, and even nervous disorders of a diversity of candidates including Wendell Anderson, Robert Mattson, Thomas Eagleton, Joseph Biden, Geraldine Ferraro, and numerous others. In Ms. Ferraro's case, the information concerned gaming charges 40 years earlier against her parents.

"In none of these cases did defendants expose confidential sources for a putative 'public interest' or any other reason. Far from criticizing the suppliers of such information, *Star Tribune* editor Mike Finney less than three weeks before he decided to identify Mr. Cohen spoke in an October 10, 1982, column of his newspaper's obligation to subject persons assuming a public trust to a high degree of scrutiny and to report immediately any violations of that trust. A May 30, 1982, *Star Tribune* column by Lou Gelfand took the position that public disclosure of the names of persons, especially public figures, who commit crimes is appropriate regardless of any resulting personal humiliation.

The newspapers had several options under their agreement with Cohen. "They could have run a story similar to that of the Associated Press which did not reveal the name of the source. Or, like WCCO-TV, they could have declined to run any story at all. Alternatively, any interest the newspapers had in informing the public of the motivations of the source could have been satisfied by describing the source by type such as 'Republican activist' without identifying him by name. Mr. Cohen, as an individual, was not even 'newsworthy' because his name would not be recognized by most readers. Regardless of whether Mr. Cohen was 'newsworthy,' defendants had no right to violate their agreement with him. Defendants' reporters knew of Mr. Cohen's background and specifically agreed not to disclose his name, regardless of its 'newsworthy' value, in order to obtain the information he possessed."

This made the newspapers' deliberate violation of their agreements all the more unjust. I again cited David Nimmer's testimony that the newspapers "hung Cohen out to dry because they didn't regard him very highly as a source."

Even if all these arguments persuaded the state Supreme Court to abandon its first ruling against Cohen, one big problem remained: how to avoid a brand new trial and many more years of appeals.

The jury had awarded Cohen $200,000 compensatory damages after finding that defendants had broken contracts with him. There were no jury findings at all regarding promissory estoppel, a concept that neither Judge Knoll nor any of the parties as much as mentioned during the trial. Promissory estoppel did not come up in the state Court of Appeals either. The 1990 Minnesota Supreme Court decision held that there was no breach of contract. Must the state Supreme Court now order a new trial so that the new jury would give a verdict on the issue of promissory estoppel instead of contract law? Even if the second jury found in favor of Cohen, wouldn't the damages under promissory estoppel be different from those under contract law?

I tried to make any divergence of promissory estoppel from contract law a distinction without a difference. The brief argued that promissory estoppel is itself a principle of contract law.

The U.S. Supreme Court had described the agreement between Cohen and the newspapers as a contract. So had the jury. So had the trial judge. So had the state Court of Appeals. So had Justices Yetka and Kelley in 1990. Experts testified that promises of confidentiality were common business transactions by which newspapers obtain information. Judge Knoll held that the newspapers and Cohen made a contract "where the hornbook elements of offer, acceptance, and consideration were unmistakably present." Only the four state Supreme Court justices in 1990 said it was anything different. They made a mistake. The court should not compound the error by forcing another several years of trial and appeals.

It would make no sense to start the case all over again. The court should sustain an original jury verdict if possible to do so on any reasonable theory of the evidence.

Borger was back representing the *Star Tribune* in the state Supreme Court. His brief argued against reinstating Cohen's jury verdict on the grounds that the court "cannot simply assume that damages in this case would be identical under claims for breach of contract and promissory estoppel." But Borger did not ask for a new trial, either. "At some point, litigation must come to an end, and that principle means that, at least once a jury has returned a verdict, the parties can no longer inject new theories into a case. That is what Cohen is attempting to do here. His complaint should be dismissed."

The *Star Tribune* brief also scolded me for "spending many of the pages allowed under the rules as a clipping service of all the commentary critical of (but none of the commentary favorable to) the defendant newspapers. Notwithstanding his approach, this proceeding is *not* about the prudence, ethics or morality of defendants' decisions to identify Cohen." Neither newspaper brief gave any examples of the "commentary favorable" to them.

The *Pioneer Press* brief, written by Paul Hannah, revived the charge of Cohen's "own dirty trick" to excuse the newspapers' violations of their promises.

Both newspapers urged the state court to interpret the Minnesota Constitution to immunize from liability "the publication of truthful information on matters of public significance," no matter how obtained, regardless of the U.S. Supreme Court's contrary interpretation of the First Amendment. They recycled their old arguments that the First Amendment protected their conduct into new claims that if the U.S. Constitution did not allow them to escape liability, the state constitution did. It was déjà vu all over again, as Yogi Berra said.

The *Star Tribune* and *Pioneer Press* briefs, as expected, made a great deal of the *Hershberger* and *Friedman* cases to support their contention that the state constitution conferred more rights of speech, press, and religion than the First Amendment.

Borger and Hannah called upon the state court to repudiate a U.S. Supreme Court decision, as it had in the *Hershberger* case, and to embrace the dissents by Justices Blackmun and Souter. They were trying to turn the judicial hierarchy upside down and to appeal, in effect, the decision of the nation's highest court to a lower state court. Hannah charged that the Supreme Court decision "ignored fundamental protections provided to political speech. The chilling effect of an unrestricted right to sue requires that protection of such speech emanate from the Minnesota constitution itself."

Borger was more reproachful still. "This court in *Hershberger* chose not to follow the simplistic, near-talismanic invocation of 'neutral laws of general applicability' employed by the United States Supreme Court majority and opted instead for a careful balancing of the individual's interest in the free exercise of religion and the public interest in highway safety. This Court should follow the same approach here." He insisted on terming the U.S. Supreme Court decision a mere opinion of a "five-justice majority" that happened to "disagree" with the state Supreme Court's 1990 decision.

The newspapers' briefs gave short shrift to the state constitution's language expressly making them liable for the abuse of any rights. To them, no abuse—on the newspapers' part—existed in this case. Hannah asserted that I was "unable to specify the precise nature of any such alleged abuses, except to recite the fact that the newspapers broke their promises." Borger said that my "invocation" of this provision "begged the central question of whether the activities involved in this case constituted an 'abuse' of freedom of expression."

It was just the latest refusal by the newspapers to acknowledge what was obvious to everyone from the Minneapolis jury to the U.S. Supreme Court, including their fellow journalists.

On the day of the oral argument, December 3, 1991, the judges hearing the case received yet another strategically timed piece outside the regular briefs promoting the newspapers' cause. It was getting to be old hat by now. It had happened before: with the jury, with the U.S. Supreme Court, and with the Minnesota Supreme Court itself in its first consideration of the case.

This time, Pat resurfaced as an advocate for the *Star Tribune*, in the form of author of the featured article in the November–December 1991 issue of the Hennepin County Bar Association's official publication.[6] For two years, she had maintained public silence about the case. She broke it now with a vengeance.

The U.S. Supreme Court decision notwithstanding, Pat wrote, the *Cohen* case was "without any legal foundation" and "should never have become part of the judicial system. Do we really want juries making decisions about journalistic ethics?" She went so far as to asseverate that the Supreme Court "held that the case is *not* about the First Amendment." The justices, she wrote, "did not place any new restrictions on the media."

Having so disposed of the U.S. Supreme Court ruling, Pat urged the Minnesota court to consider promises not legally inviolate but subject only to the arbitrary discretion of those who make them.

This case is about promises. All of us make them and all of us break them. We base our decisions to break them (or not to break them) on the values that we have adopted. People who share our values refer to our decisions as "ethical." The legal system has not concerned itself with most of the promises we make everyday.

Sometimes keeping a promise will mean you have to do something you don't think is fair to someone else. It happens to all of us. To decide what to do in these difficult situations we call upon our values.

In a complex and multicultural society those values will not be the same for all people. Disagreement on what is right or wrong in any particular situation is inevitable.

The *Cohen* case is a classic example of this problem. Thoughtful and principled people have come down on both sides. Others remain puzzled. Should the newspapers have kept their unambiguous and freely given promises to Cohen even if they thought the citizens of Minnesota should know who leaked information about Marlene Johnson's long past and minor brushes with the law?

After years of legal briefs and arguments we will never know.

The morning of December 3, Borger, Hannah, and I gathered for one more oral argument. Pat did not attend. No one dared predict it would be the last court appearance. The three of us bantered while waiting outside the Minnesota Supreme Court chambers. With all the conflict over the case in all the different courts, we had developed a lot of mutual respect and even friendship. As we entered the courtroom to take our places, Hannah said, "We're like three journeymen players going into one more game."

Borger spoke first.

"Last year, this court overturned two jury verdicts in favor of Mr. Cohen based upon breach of contract and fraudulent misrepresentation. It did so purely on state law grounds. All that remains is the nonclaim for promissory estoppel. I call it a nonclaim because the plaintiff did not seek and did not obtain a jury verdict based on that theory. It is too late now for the plaintiff to preserve his jury award based on a theory never considered by the jury."

Borger next argued the Minnesota Constitution protected the newspapers' publication of Cohen's name. "This court has taken an expansive approach to state constitutional provisions in the *Hershberger* and *Friedman* cases. The state guarantee is particularly strong when it comes to protecting truthful political speech. We submit, therefore, that the Minnesota Constitution protects truthful publications on matters of public significance no matter what legal theory is used against those publications. To challenge that protection the plaintiff at least should identify a state interest of the highest order and demonstrate that it is necessary to further that interest by punishing these particular publications. That is something he consistently has failed to do. His only interest is deniability. His interest in launching an anonymous political attack pales to insignificance beside the public's interest in expanding the universe of information available to Minnesota's voters."

Justice Gardebring hit Borger's argument where it was most vulnerable. "If we are to launch into our own interpretation of our constitution, what meaning should we attach to the last phrase that has to do with being responsible for abuse of the right to speak? If we should construe our provision more broadly, we must give some construction to that last phrase as well."

Borger denied any abuse of the newspapers' rights on the ground that their publication of truthful information overrode any interest of Cohen in enforcing the promise.

Gardebring continued her questioning of Borger. "What are we to make of the argument that you waived this right to speak freely by the fact that the reporters freely made this promise? No one compelled them to do that. Should we take this kind of waiver into consideration under our own constitution?"

Borger answered, "They did not anticipate a legal context to their promises. Had they anticipated that their promises would have effected a waiver of any right to assert a constitutional defense to a lawsuit which they never anticipated, they would have had a more cautionary approach."

Gardebring was not supportive. "So you would have us attach none of the normal legal trappings of contract law, but you would have us attach the legal constitutional protection of the First Amendment? You want to have us attach the law for part of it, but not the rest of it?"

Justice Rosalie Wahl had another critical comment. "With regard to the right of your paper to publish the truth, you weren't foreclosed, were you, from publishing the information and saying that it was from a source close to the Whitney campaign? Most people in the state didn't know who Cohen was. Why would that add anything? I can't see that your right to publish has been all that seriously damaged."

Borger responded, "This was one of the options weighed by the editors. They felt that they had been put on the horns of a moral dilemma in terms of being trapped by the little mousetrap that Dan Cohen had set for the press, in coming to them, not telling them the nature of the information, not telling them the precise nature of his relationship with the Whitney campaign, trying to set up a situation in which everyone could deny any involvement in this particular political stratagem, and trying to get the press to come along and buy into that setup. The editors felt that it was necessary to give the public as much information as they had about the circumstances of where this information was coming from. You can disagree with that. A lot of people have disagreed with that, and a lot of people feel that it was the wrong decision to make. Many journalists feel that it was the wrong decision to make. Some members of the public feel that it was the right decision to make. That particular judgment call is one that should be left with the reporters and editors, subject to the professional and public pressures of opinion in the debate as to whether they should have done it, but not to the second-guessing of a jury many years after the fact."

Hannah took the podium. He spoke more briefly than Borger. Far from being commercial transactions, Hannah argued, agreements of confidentiality were of even more trivial import than the promise to marry of earlier argument.

"Mr. Cohen would have this court accept the argument that he must recover damages simply because a promise has been broken. 'You promised not to tell.' We used to use this phrase as youngsters, perhaps to remind one of our siblings that some matter between us was not our parents' business. But this court has already rejected the notion that such a breach should necessarily have legal consequences. It should do so again."

Hannah denied that the newspapers' agreements with Cohen were commercial arrangements. "I would simply refer the Court to its previous opinion in which the commercial aspect of this case was considered and rejected. This was not a commercial case. It was a personal relationship."

No matter how the court ruled on the enforceability of the newspapers' promises, said Hannah, it could not restore the jury verdict. "Mr. Rothenberg has presented no circumstance to this Court which could allow it at this time to reinstate the damage amount under a promissory estoppel theory. To reinstate the damage verdict at this point would be premature because the issue was not raised below."

Now it was my turn. I began by contesting the newspapers' claim that their agreement should carry no legal consequences. "The agreement with Mr. Cohen was not merely an ethical agreement, but was a common business practice of these and many other newspapers and media organizations throughout the country. It was a commercial arrangement. Much of the news is obtained through exactly this type of promise of confidentiality. As the U.S. Supreme Court said, the promise of confidentiality is legally indistinguishable from a promise to pay money to a source of information. These promises do not merely have a moral and ethical backing, they should have a legal backing as well. In fact, this was realized by defendants themselves right at the time these promises were made, because when the *Star Tribune* wanted to reveal Mr. Cohen's identity, they first called him. The editor who made the decision told the reporter to call Mr. Cohen and ask him to release the newspaper from what the editor called their agreement. Mr. Cohen refused. They called him again, two or three times, to ask Mr. Cohen to release the newspaper from the agreement. Mr. Cohen refused each time. The newspaper decided to renege on the promise anyway. So the newspapers themselves realized that they had an obligation to Mr. Cohen to honor their promises."

Justice John Simonett, the author of the state Supreme Court's 1990 decision, suggested a way for newspapers to get out of promises of confidentiality.

"What if the newspapers had not printed Cohen's name, and the day after that news came out, a television station approached Cohen and said, 'Do you know who leaked that?' He says, 'No, I don't.' I suppose he would be lying. Would the newspaper then be freed of its promise?"

"No, it would not," I responded. "When these promises are made, it is understood that the source does not want to be identified, and if he is asked, he certainly is not going to identify himself. There is some testimony on this issue from *Star Tribune* executive editor Joel Kramer, that is, when we make a promise of confidentiality to a source, we don't comment regarding that source."

Justice Wahl asked, "What is the duration of the promise?"

It was the same question Justice Simonett asked in the 1990 oral argument. This time I had memorized chapter and verse from the transcript.

"Your honor, this was addressed in the testimony of Dean Arnold Ismach of the University of Oregon School of Journalism. He testified, page 705, that the practice in the profession of journalism is that newspapers are held to these promises unless released by the source or if the source dies. Other than those two circumstances, the newspaper must abide by the promise to the source."

After all the years of trial and appeals, the "dirty trick" notion still resonated. Justice Simonett asked: "Apparently the reason for the disclosure was concern by at least some part of the public that this leak would be perceived by some as what they call 'a dirty trick' in politics. Is that fair?"

I disagreed.

"With respect, your honor, that would not be fair. I refer you to the testimony of Mr. Finnegan, who said that the breaking of a promise of confidentiality is the dirty trick. These things go on all the time, these promises of confidentiality in exchange for information, particularly in exchange for information on political candidates. David Nimmer testified that in many cases, this is the only way media organizations can get information on political candidates. Oftentimes the information is provided by persons who are opposed to a particular candidate. The *Pioneer Press* in its editorial, entitled 'Relevant Disclosures,' said that this information was relevant, this is the *Pioneer Press* itself talking, that too much was being made of the source of information, and that the candidate herself should have made the information public to avoid this problem.

"The other way they could have dealt with this situation, which makes it even more inexcusable, is that they could have said he is a Republican activist to inform the public about the motives of the source. There are any number of ways it could have been handled without breaking their agreement with him. They could have said he is a source supporting the Whitney campaign, a source opposing the Johnson candidacy, a Republican activist, any one of a number of ways which could have informed the public that the person who provided the information was not supporting the Johnson candidacy. That would not violate the promise given to him. That's the way in which a journalist typically handles situations like this.

"They can either do as the Associated Press did, no identification whatsoever, they can have the veiled source saying Republican activist, or as WCCO-TV did in this case, don't run the article at all.

"But under no circumstances were they justified in making this solemn promise, which is done many thousands of times a day as a common business commercial transaction of newspapers to obtain material to be published at a profit, and then turn around and try to punish a person for relying on an agreement that the newspaper made with him.

"It must be kept in mind that the obligations that the newspapers assumed in this case were self-imposed, they were assumed voluntarily by the newspapers, and they did this to obtain information to be published at a profit.

"Would defendants also argue that if they promised to pay money to somebody for information that they should likewise be absolved from that obligation as well?

"In the Minnesota Free Flow of Information Act, the legislature said that these promises of confidentiality are so important that they must be protected, that journalists should not be compelled to disclose their sources before a court. In other words, in this situation no court could force the defendants to disclose the name of their source. They demand the right, the full right, not to disclose sources of information when they don't want to disclose. Now they turn around and demand the right to disclose at their own discretion sources, regardless of any agreements to the contrary, regardless of the harm they cause a particular individual."

I concluded, "There is simply no justification for giving the newspapers here a special privilege to invade the rights and liberties of other private individuals. There is not any threat to a free press, either under the Minnesota or the U.S. Constitution, to require newspapers to abide by the law or to abide by their voluntary agreements."

By the end of the oral argument, only three of the seven justices had asked any questions. Justice Yetka, so active in the first oral argument, was silent. So was Chief Justice Keith. Whatever that portended, it was hard to identify four justices in my favor, especially with the retirement of Justice Kelley.

The oral argument went well, I thought, but the newspapers' lawyers were confident of the outcome. As we left the courtroom, Hannah smiled at Cohen. "See you at the trial," he said. I turned white.

We did not have long to wait. This time, the state Supreme Court issued its decision only six weeks after the oral argument. It surprised everyone.

The court unanimously decided to restore the entire jury verdict for compensatory damages. Justice Simonett, who wrote the 1990 ruling dismissing the case, wrote the new decision. The experts were shocked.

The court tersely denied the newspapers' request to declare a state constitutional right to dishonor their promises. "We may, of course, construe our free speech provision to afford broader protection than the federal clause; however, we decline to do so in this case."

The rest of the decision dealt with promissory estoppel. First, the court rejected the newspapers' claim that it was too late to allow any recovery for promissory estoppel because the jury awarded damages for breach of contract. "Promissory estoppel is essentially a variation of contract theory, a theory on which the plaintiff prevailed through the court of appeals. The evidence received at trial was as relevant to promissory estoppel as it was to contract, and the parties now have briefed the issue thoroughly."

Next, the court wrestled over whether, under its view of promissory estoppel law, the newspapers' promises must be enforced to prevent an injustice. "The test is not whether the promise should be enforced to do justice, but whether enforcement is required to prevent an injustice. It is easier to recognize an unjust result than a just one, particularly in a morally ambiguous situation. The newspapers argue it is unjust to be penalized for publishing the whole truth, but it is not clear this would result in an injustice in this case. For example, it would seem veiling Cohen's identity by publishing the source as someone close to the opposing gubernatorial ticket would have sufficed as a sufficient reporting of the 'whole truth.' "

The court then agreed that it would be unjust to countenance the breaking of the newspapers' promises. "What is significant in this case is that the record shows the defendant newspapers themselves believed that they generally must keep promises of confidentiality given a news source. The reporters who actually gave the promises adamantly testified that their promises should have been honored. The editors who countermanded the promises conceded that never before or since have they reneged on a promise of confidentiality. A former *Minneapolis Star* managing editor testified that the newspapers had 'hung Mr. Cohen out to dry because they didn't regard him very highly as a source.' The *Pioneer Press Dispatch* editor stated nothing like this had happened in her 27 years in journalism. The *Star Tribune*'s editor testified that protection of sources was 'extremely important.' Other experts, too, stressed the ethical importance, except on rare occasions, of keeping promises of confidentiality. It was this long-standing journalistic tradition that Cohen, who has worked in journalism, relied upon in asking for and receiving a promise of anonymity."

The court disposed of the various "dirty trick" charges. "Neither side in this case clearly holds the higher moral ground, but in view of defendants' concurrence in the importance of honoring promises of confidentiality, and absent the showing of any compelling need in this case to break that promise, we conclude that the resultant harm to Cohen requires a remedy here to avoid injustice."

What would be the amount of the remedy? Would the court—after

agreeing that the newspapers should be liable for breaking their promises—require a whole new trial just to assess damages? Wisdom prevailed.
The justices did the sensible thing and held that a retrial was unnecessary.

The court cited Judge Knoll's instruction to the jury on damages for
breach of contract.

A party is entitled to recover for a breach of contract only those damages which:
(a) arise directly and naturally in the usual course of things from the breach itself;
or (b) are the consequences of special circumstances known to or reasonably
supposed to have been contemplated by the parties when the contract was made.

"This instruction, we think, provided an appropriate damages remedy
for the defendants' broken promise, whether considered under a breach
of contract or a promissory estoppel theory. There was evidence to support
the jury's award of $200,000, and we see no reason to remand the case
for a new trial on damages alone."

The court had come full circle back to contract law, the basis for the
case in the first place.

To media organization advocate Jane Kirtley, the decision was "bad
news" and "smacks of the courts being super editors. This really could
turn into a real nightmare."[7]

The newspapers made some noises about appealing but dropped the
idea. Any attempted appeal to the U.S. Supreme Court would have been
futile anyway, because this time the state Supreme Court actually had
based its decision solely on state law. Paul Hannah told the press, "This
is the end."[8]

We still had to resolve, however, the calculation of interest on the
$200,000 judgment. The Minnesota statute on interest is complicated
and takes into account, among other things, what each side offered to
settle for in advance of the trial. The trial judge would first hear a motion
for interest, followed by possible appeals to the Minnesota Court of Appeals and state Supreme Court. I scheduled another hearing before Judge
Knoll and asked for almost $140,000 in interest as of the end of July 1992,
although it did require some creative accounting to come up with this
figure.

The hearing did not take place. On July 31, we all got together to settle
the case. Hannah was a genial master of ceremonies. It was like a reunion
of old friends rather than the last encounter of a bitter lawsuit. The newspapers' lawyers presented checks totaling $339,830.24. Everyone shook
hands. The case had ended.

The Minnesota State Bar Association organized a seminar on the *Cohen* case for its annual convention that summer. Hannah and I, along with Pat, were to be on the panel.

In the seminar materials, Pat supplied an article she had submitted to *Editor & Publisher*. In it, she decried the attention journalists, lawyers, and scholars were giving the case, which, she wrote, "does not establish any legal precedent for other cases." The article was not published.

Retired Chief Justice Peter Popovich, who had returned to private practice, was in the audience at the seminar. He made his own contribution. "I wanted to be part of the great case, but Rothenberg wouldn't let me." He led everyone in a huge laugh.

Pat did not show up for the seminar.

Chief Justice Popovich died in 1996 at age seventy-five.[9] Jim Fitzmaurice had died two years earlier. He was only sixty-two years old. Jim Fitzmaurice was eulogized "as vigorous a defender of the First Amendment as ever lived."[10]

In 1997, the Cowles family sold the *Star Tribune* and the rest of Cowles Media to McClatchy Newspapers for $1.4 billion.[11]

Pat left her law firm. She no longer lives in Minneapolis.

The end of the *Cohen* case also closed the book on our relationship. After sixteen years of a marriage, a divorce, and legal warfare in a landmark case, not even the conflict was left.

Notes

1. "NewsNotes," *Media Law Reporter*, November 19, 1991, 3–4.

2. Donna Halvorsen, "Case Returned to State Supreme Court," *Star Tribune*, June 25, 1991, 1A, and "Federal Court Revives Minneapolis Lawyer's Suit Against Glamour," *Star Tribune*, July 20, 1991, 2B.

3. *Politics in Minnesota*, 9, no. 22 (July 1991), 4.

4. Donna Halvorsen, "Perpich Has Two Judgeships to Fill Before Leaving Office," *Star Tribune*, November 18, 1990, 4B; Dane Smith, "Gardebring Named to Supreme Court: State Becomes First in U.S. with Female Majority," *Star Tribune*, January 5, 1991, 1A; Betty Wilson, "New Justice Says Appointment Is Tribute to Perpich," *Star Tribune*, January 5, 1991, 12A; Editorial, "Minnesota's High-Court Women," *Star Tribune*, January 8, 1991, 8A.

5. Paul Gustafson, "State Bill of Rights Gains Key Legal Role: Broader Rights Attract Lawyers," *Star Tribune*, October 27, 1991, 1B.

6. Patricia Hirl Longstaff, "Cohen's Confidential Conversation," *The Hennepin Lawyer*, November–December 1991, 4.

7. Jacob M. Schlesinger and William M. Bulkeley, "Award to Newspaper Source Is Upheld," *Wall Street Journal*, February 7, 1992, B2.

8. Virginia Rybin, "Two Newspapers Must Pay $200,000 to Cohen After High Court Reverses Itself," *St. Paul Pioneer Press*, January 24, 1992, 1B.

9. Margaret Zack, "Peter Popovich Dies at 75: He Was Retired Chief Judge of State's Highest Courts," *Star Tribune*, March 30, 1996, 1A.

10. David Chanen, " 'First Class Lawyer' James Fitzmaurice Dies of Cancer at 62," *Star Tribune*, November 22, 1994, 7B.

11. Mark Fitzgerald, "Twin City Slickers: McClatchy's $1.4 Billion Deal Stuns Analysts; Any More Surprises in Minneapolis?" *Editor & Publisher*, November 22, 1997, 8.

Epilogue: New Individual Freedom Honors the 200th Birthday of the Bill of Rights

THE U.S. SUPREME Court issued its decision in the *Cohen* case in the bicentennial year of the Bill of Rights. It was a necessary and overdue restoration of balance in judicial interpretations of the First Amendment. It made clear that the First Amendment freedom of the press does not abridge the freedom of citizens *from* wrongdoing by the press.

The purpose of the First Amendment and the rest of the Bill of Rights was to safeguard the rights of individual citizens by protecting them against overreaching governments. It was not to empower one favored private industry, the press, to injure other persons with impunity.

In the quarter-century before the *Cohen* decision, however, courts used the authority of the First Amendment not to limit the powers of government but to aggrandize the power of private but increasingly monopolistic media organizations to injure and destroy largely helpless men and women with impunity. The media, in their legal arguments to supportive judges, were successfully perverting the Bill of Rights to use the government, through the courts, to deprive people of the rights they had under the law.

From the time of *New York Times* v. *Sullivan*, the press, almost always successfully, demanded that courts interpret the First Amendment so broadly and so absolutely as to trump all other individual rights. Carried to its extreme conclusion in the *Cohen* case, newspapers wanted the Supreme Court to declare that the First Amendment destroyed any rights an individual would have under the law of contracts.

New York Times v. *Sullivan* created for the press the freedom to criticize public officials without fear of libel suits, except in the most extreme circumstances. By the time of the *Cohen* case, however, the Minnesota newspapers and leaders of the media allied with them had so perverted the First Amendment as to demand a right under freedom of the press to muzzle and punish criticism of favored politicians.

In plain English, with no legal convolution, the Supreme Court ruled that media organizations which dishonor their promises are subject to the same law of contracts as everyone else, and are entitled to no special privileges by the First Amendment. The Court promulgated no incomprehensible and unworkable legal standard for citizens to meet before they can redress their grievances arising from media wrongdoing. The decision does not entitle the media to evade liability to an injured person by having any claimed rights under the First Amendment "balanced" against the rights of those harmed by breaches of contract. From now on, a newspaper that breaks a contract is to be treated like any other business sued for the same offense; the Constitution gives it no right to preferential treatment.

Moreover, as the decision made clear, the First Amendment does not give anyone in the media a special right to violate contracts or commit torts in gathering news, even if the wrongdoing produces the publication of a true story. Deliberate misconduct by calculated misdeeds—even if used to acquire the truth—is more contemptuous of the rule of law than the inadvertent defamation that was the subject of *New York Times* v. *Sullivan*.

Media scholar Donald Gillmor, who had opposed the suit from the beginning, predicted in 1992 that the Supreme Court's *Cohen* decision would "determine the course of media law for the foreseeable future."[1] Since the *Cohen* decision, to avoid any *New York Times* v. *Sullivan* vestiges of preferential treatment for the press, persons injured by media misconduct increasingly have framed their court complaints in the language of contract law, or wrongful methods of obtaining material—like trespass, fraud, intrusion on privacy, or endangering human life—not defamation.

Like *Cohen* v. *Cowles Media Co.*, a 1998 case before the U.S. District Court in Maine, *Veilleux* v. *National Broadcasting Co., Inc.* involved media liability for broken promises. There, the plaintiffs claimed misrepresentation rather than breach of contract. To obtain interviews for a "Dateline NBC" story on the trucking industry, NBC had promised the sources not anonymity but that its story would be favorable. Despite these promises, NBC's broadcast attacked the sources for alleged safety violations. Relying on the *Cohen* Supreme Court decision, the court rejected a First Amendment attempt by NBC to dismiss the case. The jury then found negligence and misrepresentation and awarded damages of $525,000. The plaintiffs' lawyer had told jurors, reminding them of *Cohen*, "The press has no special protection under the laws of the United States. If they do something wrong, they can be brought here and held accountable."

Veilleux expanded upon *Cohen*, but media liability for broken promises to sources was just the beginning of what has been called a *Cohen*-produced "state of upheaval" in First Amendment law.[2]

In November 1995, CBS squelched the broadcast of an interview of a former executive of Brown & Williamson Tobacco Corporation because the tobacco company threatened to sue for inducing a breach of the executive's contract not to disclose confidential information. CBS attorneys and other media lawyers feared a court ruling based on *Cohen* that media organizations had no right to violate generally applicable laws against tampering with contracts.[3]

In *Food Lion, Inc. v. Capital Cities/ABC, Inc.*, where the plaintiff's attorneys relied upon the decisions and even the trial court transcripts of the *Cohen* case, a 1997 U.S. District Court jury in North Carolina awarded a supermarket chain punitive damages of more than $5.5 million (later reduced to $315,000 by a judge) against ABC for fraud and trespass. The network had planted its reporters as phony employees to film, using small, hidden cameras, the preparation and sale of allegedly spoiled meat. As in the *Cohen* case, the reports were accurate. At least, Food Lion did not contest them. The issue was the unlawful manner in which the media organization had obtained its information. In several rulings in 1995, 1996, and 1997, the federal court used the *Cohen* decision to reject ABC's claim that enforcing the laws of trespass and fraud against the media violated the First Amendment.

A later federal court case, *W.D.I.A. Corp. v. McGraw-Hill, Inc.*, likewise ruled a national media organization liable for deceptive practices notwithstanding First Amendment claims. In December 1998, a U.S. District Court in Ohio ordered McGraw-Hill to pay damages for breach of contract and fraud for deliberately misrepresenting to an on-line credit reporting firm the purpose for which it sought access to national computer data banks. After agreeing to search credit files for hiring purposes only, McGraw-Hill instead dug up the records of several public figures which it then published in *Business Week*. The court rejected the publisher's claim of a First Amendment right to publish factual information. Citing *Cohen v. Cowles Media Co.* several times, the court held that McGraw-

Hill must answer to the generally applicable law of contracts and fraud for the wrongful manner in which it obtained the information.

In the 1996 case of *Risenhoover* v. *England*, a U.S. District Court in Texas relied on *Cohen* v. *Cowles Media Co.* to hold that the media could be liable in a civil case for wrongful death by effectively tipping off David Koresh and his Branch Davidians in Waco that federal agents were planning to raid their compound and arrest Koresh. The element of surprise lost, many died or were injured in the resulting firefight. A newspaper and a television station claimed they had First Amendment immunity from liability. The court held that media organizations were subject to the general law, and minced no words in chastising the defendants there. A member of the press is "no more free to cause harm to others while gathering the news than any other individual. The media arrogantly descended on the compound as if the First Amendment cloaked them with immunity from acting as reasonable individuals. Their actions are particularly egregious when considered in light of the fact that they knew how dangerous Koresh and his followers were."[4]

That same year, another federal court applied the *Cohen* principle of legal accountability to media invasion of privacy by sophisticated video and recording equipment. The implications of this decision could be enormous as media organizations avail themselves of continuing technological advancements in the tools of their trade.

In *Wolfson* v. *Lewis*, a U.S. District Court in Pennsylvania went so far as to issue an injunction against the syndicated television program *Inside Edition*'s use of aggressive investigative tactics in staking out the homes of the plaintiffs and their parents, and surveilling them with telephoto lenses and "shotgun" microphones. *Inside Edition* journalists also stalked plaintiffs' children in unmarked cars. Relying on the *Cohen* decision, the court ruled that the First Amendment protects only "routine, lawful news-gathering. . . . It is difficult to understand how hounding, harassing, and ambushing" the subjects of a story "would advance the fundamental policies underlying the First Amendment."

The *Cohen* case also has come up in connection with the death of Princess Diana. An editorial essay in *Media Law Reporter*, a weekly survey of developments in communications law for attorneys specializing in the field, posed the hypothetical question of whether stalking paparazzi blamed for causing her fatal car accident could be held liable if it had happened in the United States. The photographers would claim they were exercising a First Amendment right to gather the news.

On the basis of *Cohen* v. *Cowles Media Co.*, *Media Law Reporter* concluded that the First Amendment does not shield the press from torts and crimes committed in pursuit of a story; the press must abide by laws of general applicability.[5]

It is not just Princess Diana and Waco and *Inside Edition* and Food Lion, either. Courts with regularity are using the *Cohen* case to hold that the media must obey the same laws as everyone else.

A November 1997 decision rejected an especially egregious media attempt to claim immunity from the law. In *Rice v. Paladin Enterprises, Inc.*, the Fourth Circuit U.S. Court of Appeals cited the Supreme Court's *Cohen* decision to hold that media organizations are not above the law against aiding and abetting murder. There a contract killer of three persons—a quadriplegic child, his mother, and a nurse—relied upon detailed instructions on how to commit murder in a book called *Hit Man: A Technical Manual for Independent Contractors*. The murder victims' families sued the publisher for civil damages. The publisher claimed that First Amendment freedom of the press barred any liability in connection with the murder. Mainstream national media organizations like the *New York Times*, the Association of American Publishers, the Reporters Committee for Freedom of the Press, and McClatchy Newspapers (the *Star Tribune*'s new owner) filed briefs supporting the *Hit Man* publisher.

In rejecting the assertion of First Amendment immunity, the court called it "breathtaking" that the national media "would feel obliged to vigorously defend Paladin's assertion of a constitutional right to *intentionally and knowingly* assist murderers with technical information which Paladin *admits* it intended and knew would be used immediately in the commission of murder."

The media's claims in *Rice v. Paladin Enterprises* and other cases hearkened back to an argument made in my U.S. Supreme Court brief. "No First Amendment interests are served by protecting the press from the consequences of dishonored promises of confidentiality. . . . This case has implications beyond the breaking of promises. If the press is not liable for breaking promises to obtain information, is it also entitled to commit torts or crimes?"

Relying on the *Cohen* decision, the California Supreme Court, in the 1998 case of *Shulman v. Group W Productions, Inc.*, held similarly to the *Wolfson* ruling that the First Amendment did not immunize the media from tort liability for what the court termed "highly offensive" tactics. In *Shulman*, a television crew wired a nurse with a small microphone to pick up two auto accident victims' confidential conversations with medical personnel at the scene of the accident. A video camera operator accompanied the victims in a rescue helicopter and continued to film them and their conversations with the nurse and others. All this occurred without the permission or knowledge of the victims. They sued for invasion of privacy by intrusion. The media organization claimed First Amendment protection for its conduct.

The California Supreme Court upheld the plaintiffs as to both the nonconsensual recording of their conversations at the accident scene and the filming of them in the rescue helicopter. It observed that, because of *Cohen*, the media had "*no* recognized constitutional privilege to violate generally applicable laws in pursuit of material." The court concluded that the media may not "play tyrant to the people by spying on them in the name of newsgathering."

Cohen v. *Cowles Media Co.* was a civil case, but courts also have relied upon the Supreme Court decision to reject claims of First Amendment immunity from criminal prosecution as well. In the 1998 case of *U.S.* v. *Matthews*, the U.S. District Court for Maryland refused to dismiss an indictment for receiving and transporting child pornography on the Internet. The defendant argued that the First Amendment protected his "newsgathering activity." National Public Radio, Inc., entered the case supporting him. The court rebuked the defendant and his media supporters, concluding on the basis of the *Cohen* case that "the law is clear that a press pass is not a license to break the law."

In less than a decade, then, *Cohen* v. *Cowles Media Co.* has become the most important legal tool against the entire gamut of media wrongdoing. The many court defeats of media organizations since 1991 show, experts have acknowledged, "the degree to which *Cohen* v. *Cowles Media* has come to haunt the press."[6] The decision restored rights of injured persons to compensation for media misconduct. Still, or maybe because of that, many reviled it, competing with each other in hyperbole.

Congressional Quarterly's *Supreme Court Yearbook 1991–1992* called the decision "an assault on the First Amendment."[7] One law review moaned, "The most dangerous aspect of *Cohen* is probably its failure to place *any* First Amendment limits on recovery by sources who claim that reporters have breached promises to them."[8]

A pro-media law professor saw *Cohen* v. *Cowles Media Co.* as the end of an era of preferential treatment represented by *New York Times* v. *Sullivan* and *Hustler Magazine* v. *Falwell*. The *Cohen* decision, he complained, "cut short the natural evolution of First Amendment protection for newsgathering and set the stage for many wrongheaded opinions coming out of the lower courts today." [9]

Another law review was more apocalyptic still. "The Court's reasoning in *Cohen* could threaten to undermine all that has been accomplished in the pursuit of a free press."[10] Getting beyond the euphemism of describing a constant demand for more and more power to injure others with impunity as "the pursuit of a free press," the decision was long overdue.

The Supreme Court gave true cause to celebrate the bicentennial of the ratification of the first ten amendments to the Constitution. It could no better commemorate the 200th anniversary of the Bill of Rights than by giving it back to the people to whom it belongs.

The *Cohen* case arose from a broken promise to a source of embarrassing information about a political candidate. The source won. But the real significance of the case eclipses the subject of confidential sources. The Supreme Court decision reestablished the principle that newspapers and other media organizations are not exempt from the general law.

At least one prominent constitutional law scholar, Erwin Chemerinsky, in his 1997 textbook *Constitutional Law: Principles and Policies*, regarded the Supreme Court's *Cohen* decision as the strongest judicial statement yet for that proposition of media accountability.[11]

That is how it should be. The protection of individual rights depends upon the uniform application of the rule of law by the courts, and not on the arbitrary whims of the media or other institutions who try to set themselves above it.

Finally, returning to the issue that started it all, journalists at the end of the century are observing an anniversary of the paradigm of ethical treatment of promises of confidentiality. Twenty-five years after Watergate, *Washington Post* reporter Bob Woodward took part in an American Bar Association retrospective panel on the debacle. Two of the panelists tried to get Woodward to finally reveal the name of Deep Throat. Former President Nixon was dead. Who could be hurt? It would be very "newsworthy," too. Woodward's simple answer: "No." [12]

Indeed, the protection of sources promised confidentiality once again is de rigueur in the industry. The *New York Times*, which in the Supreme Court supported the betrayal of a source who had merely provided copies of lawfully obtained public records, eight years later excommunicates from the profession a reporter for failing to shield a source who had engaged in far more dubious conduct. The newspaper condemned a Cincinnati reporter for telling a court the name of a source who, in violation of an Ohio criminal statute, had allegedly stolen voice-mail messages of his employers at Chiquita Brands International. An incensed *Times* editorial declared preserving the confidentiality of a source "one of journalism's most hallowed and least flexible rules." The Ohio reporter's "decision to disclose sources betrays the most basic code of what is undoubtedly now his former profession. The contract between a source and a journalist is one of the sacred bonds, and many a reporter has promised to go to jail to protect such an agreement." The reporter, the *Times* concluded, "damaged his former profession by breaking the contract between reporters and confidential sources."[13]

Even the *Star Tribune* at the end of the 1990s demands that journalists honor promises of confidentiality, at least promises to informants the newspaper wants to protect. A British writer who had identified an aide of President Clinton to Congressional impeachment investigators, one editorial column fumed, "committed an unpardonable sin. He broke his promise." The editorial did not stop there. The miscreant "had broken a cardinal journalistic rule: Never give up a source. . . . It is never OK to betray a source except under rare and unusual circumstances. . . . Good sources do not reveal important information if they think that their identities will be bandied about. . . . Some journalists would blow the whistle on a source if, for example, it would save a life. Even under those circumstances, I don't feel comfortable in breaking that bond. I might try to cajole and beg the source to come forward, but I'd not be the one to out him." The editorial concluded, to make sure nobody missed the message, "One area where I hope the rules won't be changed is that we protect our confidential sources no matter what."[14]

In another editorial a short time later, the *Star Tribune* criticized a Georgia judge in a libel suit for ordering reporters to disclose sources who, unlike Cohen, had allegedly lied. Although the newspaper admitted that the reporting in question was "shabby" and had "wronged" the plaintiff there, it charged that compelling disclosure of sources infringes "legitimate First Amendment values" and "undermines a free press."[15]

In all its 870 words on behalf of what it called the "bedrock principle of journalism that you never give up a source," the *Star Tribune* said nothing about the *Cohen* case.

Notes

1. Donald M. Gillmor, *Power, Publicity, and the Abuse of Libel Law* (New York: Oxford University Press, 1992), 200.

2. David A. Schultz, "Newsgathering Litigation 1998: A Changing Landscape," *Libel and Newsgathering Litigation: Getting and Reporting the News*, vol. one (New York: Practising Law Institute, 1998), 9, 11.

3. P. Cameron DeVore, Letter, "In CBS Tobacco Case, Contract Came Before First Amendment," *New York Times*, November 17, 1995, A30; David Kohler, "Blame the Laws, Mr. Wallace, Not the Lawyers," *Wall Street Journal*, November 21, 1995, A18; James C. McKinley, Jr., "CBS Said to Fear Unusual

Legal Challenge to Report," *New York Times*, November 17, 1995, A18; William Bennett Turner, "News Media Liability for 'Tortious Interference' with a Source's Nondisclosure Contract," 14 *Communications Lawyer* 13 (Spring 1996); Joseph A. Russomanno and Kyu Ho Youm, "The *60 Minutes* Controversy: What Lawyers Are Telling the News Media," 18 *Communications and the Law* 65, 81–83 (September 1996).

4. In an aberration from the media's normal anathematization of libel litigation (when directed at them), one of the Waco journalists sued for defamation over criticism of the media's responsibility for the tragedy. The Texas Supreme Court dismissed his suit in September 1998. *WFFA-TV, Inc. v. McLemore*, 978 S.W.2d 568 (Tex. 1998).

5. "Accident Turns Spotlight on Newsgathering Techniques," "News-Notes," *Media Law Reporter*, October 7, 1997, 1.

6. Victor A. Kovner, Suzanne L. Telsey, Suzanne Herbert, "Recent Developments in Newsgathering, Invasion of Privacy and Related Torts," *Communications Law 1998*, vol. three (New York: Practising Law Institute, 1998), 445, 451.

7. Joan Biskupic, *The Supreme Court Yearbook 1991–1992* (Washington, D.C.: Congressional Quarterly, 1993), 7.

8. Susan Allison Weifert, Note, "*Cohen v. Cowles Media Co.*: Bad News for Newsgatherers; Worse News for the Public," 25 *University of California Davis Law Review* 1099, 1133 (1992).

9. Eric B. Easton, "Two Wrongs Mock a Right: Overcoming the *Cohen* Maledicta That Bar First Amendment Protection for Newsgathering," 58 *Ohio State Law Journal* 1135, 1153 (1997).

10. Elizabeth L'Heureux, Note, "Freedom of the Press—Confidentiality—Reporters Are Liable Under Promissory Estoppel for Breach of Source Confidentiality Agreement," 23 *Seton Hall Law Review* 345, 376 (1992).

11. Erwin Chemerinsky, *Constitutional Law: Principles and Policies* (New York: Aspen Law & Business, 1997), 955.

12. "Watergate: Twenty-Five-Year Retrospective," 15 *Communications Lawyer* 1, 27 (Fall 1997).

13. Editorial, "Banana Journalism," *New York Times*, April 7, 1999, A22. Also see Rekha Balu, "Chiquita Brands Ex-Lawyer's Trial Hinges on Key Journalism Principle," *Wall Street Journal*, April 2, 1999, B5; Douglas Frantz, "Word of Honor: For a Reporter and a Source, Echoes of a Broken Promise," *New York Times*, April 11, 1999, section 4, 3; Douglas Frantz, "Reporter in Chiquita Case Reveals a Source in Court," *New York Times*, April 6, 1999, A14; Bryan Lyman, "More Bad Banana: A Burned Source Reaches for a Shield Law," *Columbia Journalism Review*, May/June 1999, 14.

14. Joel Kaplan, "Never Give Up a Source, Even Blumenthal," *Star Tribune*, February 22, 1999, A10.

15. Commentary, "Requiring Disclosure of Reporter's Sources Undermines Free Press," *Star Tribune*, June 3, 1999, A13.

Appendix: U.S. Supreme Court Decision

COHEN *v.* COWLES MEDIA CO., DBA MINNEAPOLIS STAR & TRIBUNE CO., ET AL.

CERTIORARI TO THE SUPREME COURT OF MINNESOTA

No. 90–634. Argued March 27, 1991—Decided June 24, 1991

During the 1982 Minnesota gubernatorial race, petitioner Cohen, who was associated with one party's campaign, gave court records concerning another party's candidate for Lieutenant Governor to respondent publishers' newspapers after receiving a promise of confidentiality from their reporters. Nonetheless, the papers identified him in their stories, and he was fired from his job. He filed suit against respondents in state court, alleging, among other things, a breach of contract. The court rejected respondents' argument that the First Amendment barred the suit, and a jury awarded him, *inter alia*, compensatory damages. The State Court of Appeals affirmed, but the State Supreme Court reversed, holding that a contract cause of action was inappropriate. It then went on to address the question whether Cohen could recover under state law on a promissory estoppel theory even though that issue was never tried to a jury, nor briefed nor argued by the parties, concluding that enforcement under such a theory would violate respondents' First Amendment rights.

Held:

    1. This Court has jurisdiction. Respondents' contention that the case should be dismissed because the promissory estoppel theory was not argued or

presented in the courts below and because the State Supreme Court's decision rests entirely on a state-law interpretation is rejected. It is irrelevant to this Court's jurisdiction whether a party raised below and argued a federal-law issue that the state supreme court actually considered and decided. *Orr* v. *Orr*, 440 U. S. 268, 274–275. Moreover, the Minnesota Supreme Court made clear that its holding rested on federal law, and respondents have defended against this suit all along by arguing that the First Amendment barred the enforcement of the reporters' promises. Pp. 667–668.

2. The First Amendment does not bar a promissory estoppel cause of action against respondents. Such a cause of action, although private, involves state action within the meaning of the Fourteenth Amendment and therefore triggers the First Amendment's protections, since promissory estoppel is a state-law doctrine creating legal obligations never explicitly assumed by the parties that are enforceable through the Minnesota courts' official power. Cf., *e.g.*, *New York Times Co.* v. *Sullivan*, 376 U. S. 254, 265. However, the doctrine is a law of general applicability that does not target or single out the press, but rather is applicable to all Minnesota citizens' daily transactions. Thus, the First Amendment does not require that its enforcement against the press be subject to stricter scrutiny than would be applied to enforcement against others, cf. *Associated Press* v. *NLRB*, 301 U. S. 103, 132–133, even if the payment is characterized as compensatory damages. Nor does that Amendment grant the press protection from any law which in any fashion or to any degree limits or restricts its right to report truthful information. *Florida Star* v. *B. J. F.*, 491 U. S. 524, distinguished. Moreover, Cohen sought damages for a breach of promise that caused him to lose his job and lowered his earning capacity, and did not attempt to use a promissory estoppel cause of action to avoid the strict requirements for establishing a libel or defamation claim. *Hustler Magazine, Inc.* v. *Falwell*, 485 U. S. 46, distinguished. Any resulting inhibition on truthful reporting is no more than the incidental, and constitutionally insignificant, consequence of applying to the press a generally applicable law requiring it to keep certain promises. Pp. 668–672.

3. Cohen's request that his compensatory damages award be reinstated is rejected. The issues whether his verdict should be upheld on the ground that a promissory estoppel claim had been established under state law and whether the State Constitution may be construed to shield the press from an action such as this one are matters for the State Supreme Court to address and resolve in the first instance. P. 672.

457 N. W. 2d 199, reversed and remanded.

WHITE, J., delivered the opinion of the Court, in which REHNQUIST, C. J., and STEVENS, SCALIA, and KENNEDY, JJ., joined. BLACKMUN, J., filed a dissenting opinion, in which MARSHALL and SOUTER, JJ., joined, *post*, p. 672. SOUTER, J., filed a dissenting opinion, in which MARSHALL, BLACKMUN, and O'CONNOR, JJ., joined, *post*, p. 676.

Elliot C. Rothenberg argued the cause and filed briefs for petitioner.

John D. French argued the cause for respondents. With him on the brief for respondent Cowles Media Co. were *John Borger* and *Randy M. Lebedoff*. *Stephen M. Shapiro, Andrew L. Frey, Kenneth S. Geller, Mark I. Levy, Michael W. McConnell, Paul R. Hannah, Laurie A. Zenner, John C. Fontaine,* and *Cristina L. Mendoza* filed a brief for respondent Northwest Publications, Inc.*

JUSTICE WHITE delivered the opinion of the Court.

The question before us is whether the First Amendment prohibits a plaintiff from recovering damages, under state promissory estoppel law, for a newspaper's breach of a promise of confidentiality given to the plaintiff in exchange for information. We hold that it does not.

During the closing days of the 1982 Minnesota gubernatorial race, Dan Cohen, an active Republican associated with Wheelock Whitney's Independent-Republican gubernatorial campaign, approached reporters from the St. Paul Pioneer Press Dispatch (Pioneer Press) and the Minneapolis Star and Tribune (Star Tribune) and offered to provide documents relating to a candidate in the upcoming election. Cohen made clear to the reporters that he would provide the information only if he was given a promise of confidentiality. Reporters from both papers promised to keep Cohen's identity anonymous and Cohen turned over copies of two public court records concerning Marlene Johnson, the Democratic-Farmer-Labor candidate for Lieutenant Governor. The first record indicated that Johnson had been charged in 1969 with three counts of unlawful assembly, and the second that she had been convicted in 1970 of petit theft. Both newspapers interviewed Johnson for her explanation and one reporter tracked down the person who had found the records for Cohen. As it turned out, the unlawful assembly charges arose out of Johnson's participation in a protest of an alleged failure to hire minority workers on municipal construction projects, and the charges were eventually dismissed. The petit theft conviction was for leaving a store without pay-

---

Rex S. Heinke, Robert S. Warren, Jerry S. Birenz, Ralph P. Huber, W. Terry Maguire, Rene P. Milam, Richard M. Schmidt, Harold W. Fuson, Jr., Barbara Wartelle Wall, James E. Grossberg, George Freeman, and *William A. Niese* filed a brief for Advance Publications, Inc., et al. as *amici curiae*.

ing for $6 worth of sewing materials. The incident apparently occurred at a time during which Johnson was emotionally distraught, and the conviction was later vacated.

After consultation and debate, the editorial staffs of the two newspapers independently decided to publish Cohen's name as part of their stories concerning Johnson. In their stories, both papers identified Cohen as the source of the court records, indicated his connection to the Whitney campaign, and included denials by Whitney campaign officials of any role in the matter. The same day the stories appeared, Cohen was fired by his employer.

Cohen sued respondents, the publishers of the Pioneer Press and Star Tribune, in Minnesota state court, alleging fraudulent misrepresentation and breach of contract. The trial court rejected respondents' argument that the First Amendment barred Cohen's lawsuit. A jury returned a verdict in Cohen's favor, awarding him $200,000 in compensatory damages and $500,000 in punitive damages. The Minnesota Court of Appeals, in a split decision, reversed the award of punitive damages after concluding that Cohen had failed to establish a fraud claim, the only claim which would support such an award. 445 N. W. 2d 248, 260 (1989). However, the court upheld the finding of liability for breach of contract and the $200,000 compensatory damages award. *Id.,* at 262.

A divided Minnesota Supreme Court reversed the compensatory damages award. 457 N. W. 2d 199 (1990). After affirming the Court of Appeals' determination that Cohen had not established a claim for fraudulent misrepresentation, the court considered his breach-of-contract claim and concluded that "a contract cause of action is inappropriate for these particular circumstances." *Id.,* at 203. The court then went on to address the question whether Cohen could establish a cause of action under Minnesota law on a promissory estoppel theory. Apparently, a promissory estoppel theory was never tried to the jury, nor briefed nor argued by the parties; it first arose during oral argument in the Minnesota Supreme Court when one of the justices asked a question about equitable estoppel. See App. 38.

In addressing the promissory estoppel question, the court decided that the most problematic element in establishing such a cause of action here was whether injustice could be avoided only by enforcing the promise of confidentiality made to Cohen. The court stated: "Under a promissory estoppel analysis there can be no neutrality towards the First Amendment. In deciding whether it would be unjust not to enforce the promise, the court must necessarily weigh the same considerations that are weighed for whether the First Amendment has been violated. The court must balance the constitutional rights of a free press against the common law interest in protecting a promise of anonymity." 457 N. W. 2d, at 205. After a brief discussion, the court concluded that "in this case enforcement of the promise of confidentiality under a promissory estoppel theory would violate defendants' First Amendment rights." *Ibid.*

We granted certiorari to consider the First Amendment implications of this case. 498 U. S. 1011 (1990).

Respondents initially contend that the Court should dismiss this case without reaching the merits because the promissory estoppel theory was not argued or presented in the courts below and because the Minnesota Supreme Court's decision rests entirely on the interpretation of state law. These contentions do not merit extended discussion. It is irrelevant to this Court's jurisdiction whether a party raised below and argued a federal-law issue that the state supreme court actually considered and decided. *Orr.* v. *Orr*, 440 U. S. 268, 274–275, (1979); *Dun & Bradstreet, Inc.* v. *Greenmoss Builders, Inc.*, 472 U. S. 749, 754, n. 2 (1985); *Mills* v. *Maryland*, 486 U. S. 367, 371, n. 3 (1988); *Franks* v. *Delaware*, 438 U. S. 154, 161–162 (1978); *Jenkins* v. *Georgia*, 418 U. S. 153, 157 (1974). Moreover, that the Minnesota Supreme Court rested its holding on federal law could not be made more clear than by its conclusion that "in this case enforcement of the promise of confidentiality under a promissory estoppel theory would violate defendants' First Amendment rights." 457 N. W. 2d, at 205. It can hardly be said that there is no First Amendment issue present in the case when respondents have defended against this suit all along by arguing that the First Amendment barred the enforcement of the reporters' promises to Cohen. We proceed to consider whether that Amendment bars a promissory estoppel cause of action against respondents.

The initial question we face is whether a private cause of action for promissory estoppel involves "state action" within the meaning of the Fourteenth Amendment such that the protections of the First Amendment are triggered. For if it does not, then the First Amendment has no bearing on this case. The rationale of our decision in *New York Times Co.* v. *Sullivan*, 376 U. S. 254 (1964), and subsequent cases compels the conclusion that there is state action here. Our cases teach that the application of state rules of law in state courts in a manner alleged to restrict First Amendment freedoms constitutes "state action" under the Fourteenth Amendment. See, *e.g.*, *id.*, at 265; *NAACP* v. *Claiborne Hardware Co.*, 458 U. S. 886, 916, n. 51 (1982); *Philadelphia Newspapers, Inc.* v. *Hepps*, 475 U. S. 767, 777 (1986). In this case, the Minnesota Supreme Court held that if Cohen could recover at all it would be on the theory of promissory estoppel, a state-law doctrine which, in the absence of a contract, creates obligations never explicitly assumed by the parties. These legal obligations would be enforced through the official power of the Minnesota courts. Under our cases, that is enough to constitute "state action" for purposes of the Fourteenth Amendment.

Respondents rely on the proposition that "if a newspaper lawfully obtains truthful information about a matter of public significance then state officials may not constitutionally punish publication of the information, absent a need to further a state interest of the highest order." *Smith* v. *Daily Mail Publishing Co.*, 443 U. S. 97, 103 (1979). That proposition is unexceptionable, and it has been applied in various cases that have found insufficient the asserted state interests in preventing publication of truthful, lawfully obtained information. See, *e.g.*, *Florida Star* v. *B. J. F.*, 491 U. S. 524 (1989); *Smith* v. *Daily Mail, supra; Landmark Communications, Inc.* v. *Virginia*, 435 U. S. 829 (1978).

This case, however, is not controlled by this line of cases but, rather, by the equally well-established line of decisions holding that generally applicable laws do not offend the First Amendment simply because their enforcement against the press has incidental effects on its ability to gather and report the news. As the cases relied on by respondents recognize, the truthful information sought to be published must have been lawfully acquired. The press may not with impunity break and enter an office or dwelling to gather news. Neither does the First Amendment relieve a newspaper reporter of the obligation shared by all citizens to respond to a grand jury subpoena and answer questions relevant to a criminal investigation, even though the reporter might be required to reveal a confidential source. *Branzburg* v. *Hayes*, 408 U. S. 665 (1972). The press, like others interested in publishing, may not publish copyrighted material without obeying the copyright laws. See *Zacchini* v. *Scripps-Howard Broadcasting Co.*, 433 U. S. 562, 576–579 (1977). Similarly, the media must obey the National Labor Relations Act, *Associated Press* v. *NLRB*, 301 U. S. 103 (1937), and the Fair Labor Standards Act, *Oklahoma Press Publishing Co.* v. *Walling*, 327 U. S. 186, 192–193 (1946); may not restrain trade in violation of the antitrust laws, *Associated Press* v. *United States*, 326 U. S. 1 (1945); *Citizen Publishing Co.* v. *United States*, 394 U. S. 131, 139 (1969); and must pay nondiscriminatory taxes, *Murdock* v. *Pennsylvania*, 319 U. S. 105, 112 (1943); *Minneapolis Star & Tribune Co.* v. *Minnesota Comm'r of Revenue*, 460 U. S. 575, 581–583 (1983). Cf. *Uni-*

versity of Pennsylvania v. *EEOC*, 493 U. S. 182, 201–202 (1990). It is, therefore, beyond dispute that "[t]he publisher of a newspaper has no special immunity from the application of general laws. He has no special privilege to invade the rights and liberties of others." *Associated Press* v. *NLRB*, *supra*, at 132–133. Accordingly, enforcement of such general laws against the press is not subject to stricter scrutiny than would be applied to enforcement against other persons or organizations.

There can be little doubt that the Minnesota doctrine of promissory estoppel is a law of general applicability. It does not target or single out the press. Rather, insofar as we are advised, the doctrine is generally applicable to the daily transactions of all the citizens of Minnesota. The First Amendment does not forbid its application to the press.

JUSTICE BLACKMUN suggests that applying Minnesota promissory estoppel doctrine in this case will "punish" respondents for publishing truthful information that was lawfully obtained. *Post*, at 675–676. This is not strictly accurate because compensatory damages are not a form of punishment, as were the criminal sanctions at issue in *Smith* v. *Daily Mail*, *supra*. If the contract between the parties in this case had contained a liquidated damages provision, it would be perfectly clear that the payment to petitioner would represent a cost of acquiring newsworthy material to be published at a profit, rather than a punishment imposed by the State. The payment of compensatory damages in this case is constitutionally indistinguishable from a generous bonus paid to a confidential news source. In any event, as indicated above, the characterization of the payment makes no difference for First Amendment purposes when the law being applied is a general law and does not single out the press. Moreover, JUSTICE BLACKMUN's reliance on cases like *Florida Star* v. *B. J. F.*, *supra*, and *Smith* v. *Daily Mail* is misplaced. In those cases, the State itself defined the content of publications that would trigger liability. Here, by contrast, Minnesota law simply requires those making promises to keep them. The parties themselves, as in this case, determine the scope of their legal obligations, and any restrictions that may be placed on the publication of truthful information are self-imposed.

Also, it is not at all clear that respondents obtained Cohen's name "lawfully" in this case, at least for purposes of publishing it. Unlike the situation in *Florida Star*, where the rape victim's name was obtained through lawful access to a police report, respondents obtained Cohen's name only by making a promise that they did not honor. The dissenting opinions suggest that the press should not be subject to any law, including copyright law for example, which in any fashion or to any degree limits or restricts the press' right to report truthful information. The First Amendment does not grant the press such limitless protection.

Nor is Cohen attempting to use a promissory estoppel cause of action to avoid the strict requirements for establishing a libel or defamation claim. As the Minnesota Supreme Court observed here, "Cohen could not sue for defamation because the information disclosed [his name] was true." 457 N. W. 2d, at 202. Cohen is not seeking damages for injury to his reputation or his state of mind. He sought damages in excess of $50,000 for breach of a promise that caused him to lose his job and lowered his earning capacity. Thus, this is not a case like *Hustler Magazine, Inc.* v. *Falwell*, 485 U. S. 46 (1988), where we held that the constitutional libel standards apply to a claim alleging that the publication of a parody was a state-law tort of intentional infliction of emotional distress.

Respondents and *amici* argue that permitting Cohen to maintain a cause of action for promissory estoppel will inhibit truthful reporting because news organizations will have legal incentives not to disclose a confidential source's identity even when that person's identity is itself newsworthy. JUSTICE SOUTER makes a similar argument. But if this is the case, it is no more than the incidental, and constitutionally insignificant, consequence of applying to the press a generally applicable law that requires those who make certain kinds of promises to keep them. Although we conclude that the First Amendment does not confer on the press a constitutional right to disregard promises that would otherwise be enforced under state law, we reject Cohen's request that in reversing the Minnesota Supreme Court's judgment we reinstate the jury verdict awarding him $200,000 in compensatory damages. See Brief for Petitioner 31. The Minnesota Supreme Court's incorrect conclusion that the First Amendment barred Cohen's claim may well have truncated its consideration of whether a promissory estoppel claim had otherwise been established under Minnesota law and whether Cohen's jury verdict could be upheld on a promissory estoppel basis. Or perhaps the State Constitution may be construed to shield the press from a promissory estoppel cause of action such as this one. These are matters for the Minnesota Supreme Court to address and resolve in the first instance on remand. Accordingly, the judgment of the Minnesota Supreme Court is reversed, and the case is remanded for further proceedings not inconsistent with this opinion.

So ordered.

JUSTICE BLACKMUN, with whom JUSTICE MARSHALL and JUSTICE SOUTER join, dissenting.

I agree with the Court that the decision of the Supreme Court of Minnesota rested on federal grounds and that the judicial enforcement of petitioner's promissory estoppel claim constitutes state action under the Fourteenth Amendment. I do not agree, however, that the use of that claim to penalize the reporting of truthful information regarding a political campaign does not violate the First Amendment. Accordingly, I dissent.

The majority concludes that this case is not controlled by the decision in *Smith v. Daily Mail Publishing Co.*, 443 U. S. 97 (1979), to the effect that a State may not punish the publication of lawfully obtained, truthful information "absent a need to further a state interest of the highest order." *Id.*, at 103. Instead, we are told, the controlling precedent is "the equally well-established line of decisions holding that generally applicable laws do not offend the First Amendment simply because their enforcement against the press has incidental effects on its ability to gather and report the news." *Ante*, at 669. See, *e.g.*, *Branzburg v. Hayes*, 408 U. S. 665 (1972); *Oklahoma Press Publishing Co. v. Walling*, 327 U. S. 186, 192–193 (1946); *Minneapolis Star & Tribune Co. v. Minnesota Comm'r of Revenue*, 460 U. S. 575, 581–583 (1983). I disagree.

I do not read the decision of the Supreme Court of Minnesota to create any exception to, or immunity from, the laws of that State for members of the press. In my view, the court's decision is premised, not on the identity of the speaker, but on the speech itself. Thus, the court found it to be of "critical significance," that "the promise of anonymity arises in the classic First Amendment context of the quintessential public debate in our democratic society, namely, a political source involved in a political campaign." 457 N. W. 2d 199, 205 (1990); see also *id.*, at 204, n. 6 (*"New York Times v. Sullivan*, 376 U. S. 254 ... (1964), holds that a state may not adopt a state rule of law to impose impermissible restrictions on the federal constitutional freedoms of speech and press"). Necessarily, the First Amendment protection afforded respondents would be equally available to nonmedia defendants. See, *e.g.*, *Lovell v. Griffin*, 303 U. S. 444, 452 (1938) ("The liberty of the press is not confined to newspapers and periodicals. ... The press in its historic connotation comprehends every sort of publication which affords a vehicle of information and opinion"). The majority's admonition that " '[t]he publisher of a newspaper has no special immunity from the application of general laws,' " *ante*, at 670, and its reliance on the cases that support that principle, are therefore misplaced.

In *Branzburg*, for example, this Court found it significant that "these cases involve no intrusions upon speech or assembly, no . . . restriction on what the press may publish, and no express or implied command that the press publish what it prefers to withhold. . . . [N]o penalty, civil or criminal, related to the content of published material is at issue here." 408 U. S., at 681. Indeed, "[t]he sole issue before us" in *Branzburg* was "the obligation of reporters to respond to grand jury subpoenas as other citizens do and to answer questions relevant to an investigation into the commission of crime." *Id.*, at 682. See also *Associated Press* v. *NLRB*, 301 U. S. 103, 133 (1937); *Associated Press* v. *United States*, 326 U. S. 1, 20, n. 18 (1945); *Citizen Publishing Co.* v. *United States*, 394 U. S. 131, 139 (1969). In short, these cases did *not* involve the imposition of liability based upon the content of speech.[1]

Contrary to the majority, I regard our decision in *Hustler Magazine, Inc.* v. *Falwell*, 485 U. S. 46 (1988), to be precisely on point. There, we found that the use of a claim of intentional infliction of emotional distress to impose liability for the publication of a satirical critique violated the First Amendment. There was no doubt that Virginia's tort of intentional infliction of emotional distress was "a law of general applicability" unrelated to the suppression of speech.[2] Nonetheless, a unanimous Court found that, when used to penalize the expression of opinion, the law was subject to the strictures of the First Amendment. In applying that principle, we concluded, *id.*, at 56, that "public figures and public officials may not

---

[1]The only arguable exception is *Zacchini* v. *Scripps-Howard Broadcasting Co.*, 433 U. S. 562 (1977). In *Zacchini*, a performer sued a news organization for appropriation of his "right to the publicity value of his performance," *id.*, at 565, after it broadcast the entirety of his act on local television. This Court held that the First Amendment did not bar the suit. We made clear, however, that our holding did not extend to the reporting of *information* about an event of public interest. We explained: "If . . . respondent had merely reported that petitioner was performing at the fair and described or commented on his act, with or without showing his picture on television, we would have a very different case." *Id.*, at 569. Thus, *Zacchini* cannot support the majority's conclusion that "a law of general applicability," *ante*, at 670, may not violate the First Amendment when employed to penalize the dissemination of truthful information or the expression of opinion.

[2]The Virginia cause of action for intentional infliction of emotional distress at issue in *Hustler* provided for recovery where a plaintiff could demonstrate "that the defendant's conduct (1) is intentional or reckless; (2) offends generally accepted standards of decency or morality; (3) is causally connected with the plaintiff's emotional distress; and (4) caused emotional distress that was severe." 485 U. S., at 50, n. 3.

recover for the tort of intentional infliction of emotional distress by reason of publications such as the one here at issue without showing in addition that the publication contains a false statement of fact which was made with 'actual malice,' " as defined by *New York Times Co.* v. *Sullivan*, 376 U. S. 254 (1964). In so doing, we rejected the argument that Virginia's interest in protecting its citizens from emotional distress was sufficient to remove from First Amendment protection a "patently offensive" expression of opinion. 485 U. S., at 50.[3]

As in *Hustler*, the operation of Minnesota's doctrine of promissory estoppel in this case cannot be said to have a merely "incidental" burden on speech; the publication of important political speech *is* the claimed violation. Thus, as in *Hustler*, the law may not be enforced to punish the expression of truthful information or opinion.[4] In the instant case, it is undisputed that the publication at issue was true.

To the extent that truthful speech may ever be sanctioned consistent with the First Amendment, it must be in furtherance of a state interest "of the highest order." *Smith*, 443 U. S., at 103. Because the Minnesota

---

[3]The majority attempts to distinguish *Hustler* on the ground that there the plaintiff sought damages for injury to his state of mind whereas the petitioner here sought damages "for a breach of a promise that caused him to lose his job and lowered his earning capacity." *Ante*, at 671. I perceive no meaningful distinction between a statute that penalizes published speech in order to protect the individual's psychological well being or reputational interest and one that exacts the same penalty in order to compensate the loss of employment or earning potential. Certainly, our decision in *Hustler* recognized no such distinction.

[4]The majority argues that, unlike the criminal sanctions we considered in *Smith* v. *Daily Mail Publishing Co.*, 443 U. S. 97 (1979), the liability at issue here will not "punish" respondents in the strict sense of that word. *Ante*, at 670. While this may be true, we have long held that the imposition of civil liability based on protected expression constitutes "punishment" of speech for First Amendment purposes. See, *e.g.*, *Pittsburgh Press Co.* v. *Pittsburgh Comm'n on Human Relations*, 413 U. S. 376, 386 (1973) ("In the context of a libelous advertisement . . . this Court has held that the First Amendment does not shield a newspaper from *punishment* for libel when with actual malice it publishes a falsely defamatory advertisement") (emphasis added), citing *New York Times Co.* v. *Sullivan*, 376 U. S. 254, 279–280 (1964); *Gertz* v. *Robert Welch, Inc.*, 418 U. S. 323, 340 (1974) ("[P]unishment of error runs the risk of inducing a cautious and restrictive exercise of the constitutionally guaranteed freedoms of speech and press") (emphasis added). Cf. *New York Times Co.*, 376 U. S., at 297 (Black, J., concurring) ("To *punish* the exercise of this right to discuss public affairs or to *penalize* it through libel judgments is to abridge or shut off discussion of the very kind most needed") (emphasis added).

Though they be civil, the sanctions we review in this case are no more justifiable as "a cost of acquiring newsworthy material," *ante*, at 670, than were the libel damages at issue in *New York Times Co.*, a permissible cost of disseminating newsworthy material.

Supreme Court's opinion makes clear that the State's interest in enforcing its promissory estoppel doctrine in this case was far from compelling, see 457 N. W. 2d., at 204–205, I would affirm that court's decision.

I respectfully dissent.

JUSTICE SOUTER, with whom JUSTICE MARSHALL, JUSTICE BLACKMUN, and JUSTICE O'CONNOR join, dissenting.

I agree with JUSTICE BLACKMUN that this case does not fall within the line of authority holding the press to laws of general applicability where commercial activities and relationships, not the content of publication, are at issue. See *ante*, at 674. Even such general laws as do entail effects on the content of speech, like the one in question, may of course be found constitutional, but only, as Justice Harlan observed,

"when [such effects] have been found justified by subordinating valid governmental interests, a prerequisite to constitutionality which has necessarily involved a weighing of the governmental interest involved. . . . Whenever, in such a context, these constitutional protections are asserted against the exercise of valid governmental powers a reconciliation must be effected, and that perforce requires an appropriate weighing of the respective interests involved." *Konigsberg* v. *State Bar of California*, 366 U. S. 36, 51 (1961).

Thus, "[t]here is nothing talismanic about neutral laws of general applicability," *Employment Div., Dept. of Human Resources of Ore.* v. *Smith*, 494 U. S. 872, 901 (1990) (O'CONNOR, J., concurring in judgment), for such laws may restrict First Amendment rights just as effectively as those directed specifically at speech itself. Because I do not believe the fact of general applicability to be dispositive, I find it necessary to articulate, measure, and compare the competing interests involved in any given case to determine the legitimacy of burdening constitutional interests, and such has been the Court's recent practice in publication cases. See *Hustler Magazine, Inc.* v. *Falwell*, 485 U. S. 46 (1988); *Zacchini* v. *Scripps-Howard Broadcasting Co.*, 433 U. S. 562 (1977).

Nor can I accept the majority's position that we may dispense with balancing because the burden on publication is in a sense "self-imposed" by the newspaper's voluntary promise of confidentiality. See *ante*, at 671. This suggests both the possibility of waiver, the requirements for which have not been met here, see, *e.g.*, *Curtis Publishing Co.* v. *Butts*, 388 U. S. 130, 145 (1967), as well as a conception of First Amendment rights as those of the speaker alone, with a value that may be measured without reference to the importance of the information to public discourse. But freedom of the press is ultimately founded on the value of enhancing such discourse for the sake of a citizenry better informed and thus more prudently self-governed. "[T]he First Amendment goes beyond protection of the press and the self-expression of individuals to prohibit government from limiting the stock of information from which members of the public may draw." *First Nat. Bank of Boston v. Bellotti*, 435 U. S. 765, 783 (1978). In this context, " '[i]t is the right of the [public], not the right of the [media], which is paramount,' " *CBS, Inc. v. FCC*, 453 U. S. 367, 395 (1981) (emphasis omitted) (quoting *Red Lion Broadcasting Co. v. FCC*, 395 U. S. 367, 390 (1969)), for "[w]ithout the information provided by the press most of us and many of our representatives would be unable to vote intelligently or to register opinions on the administration of government generally," *Cox Broadcasting Corp. v. Cohn*, 420 U. S. 469, 492 (1975); cf. *Richmond Newspapers, Inc. v. Virginia*, 448 U. S. 555, 573 (1980); *New York Times Co. v. Sullivan*, 376 U. S. 254, 278–279 (1964).

The importance of this public interest is integral to the balance that should be struck in this case. There can be no doubt that the fact of Cohen's identity expanded the universe of information relevant to the choice faced by Minnesota voters in that State's 1982 gubernatorial election, the publication of which was thus of the sort quintessentially subject to strict First Amendment protection. See, *e.g.*, *Eu v. San Francisco Cty. Democratic Central Comm.*, 489 U. S. 214, 223 (1989). The propriety of his leak to respondents could be taken to reflect on his character, which in turn could be taken to reflect on the character of the candidate who had retained him as an adviser. An election could turn on just such a factor; if it should, I am ready to assume that it would be to the greater public good, at least over the long run.

This is not to say that the breach of such a promise of confidentiality could never give rise to liability. One can conceive of situations in which the injured party is a private individual, whose identity is of less public concern than that of petitioner; liability there might not be constitutionally prohibited. Nor do I mean to imply that the circumstances of acquisition are irrelevant to the balance, see, *e.g.*, *Florida Star v. B. J. F.*, 491 U. S. 524, 534–535, and n. 8 (1989), although they may go only to what balances against, and not to diminish, the First Amendment value of any particular piece of information.

Because I believe the State's interest in enforcing a newspaper's promise of confidentiality insufficient to outweigh the interest in unfettered publication of the information revealed in this case, I respectfully dissent.

Bibliographical Note

The Taming of the Press is based on the author's notes and the trial transcripts and exhibits, attorneys' briefs, court files, and the decisions of the
Hennepin County District Court in Minneapolis, the Minnesota Court
of Appeals, the Minnesota Supreme Court, and the U.S. Supreme Court.
Court file numbers are 798806 for the District Court, C8–88–2631 and
C0–88–2672 for the Minnesota Court of Appeals and Supreme Court,
and 90–634 for the U.S. Supreme Court.

Justice Thurgood Marshall's papers, source for the discussions in chap-
ters 14 and 16 of internal U.S. Supreme Court deliberations, are on file
at the Library of Congress.

The table of cases gives the legal citations for the six *Cohen* decisions
and the other cases mentioned in the text.

The petition for certiorari, all briefs, and the transcript of the oral
argument before the U.S. Supreme Court are published in Philip B. Kur-
land and Gerhard Casper, eds., *Landmark Briefs and Arguments of the Supreme Court of the United States: Constitutional Law*, vol. 200 (Bethesda,
Md.: University Publications of America, 1992), 353–666.

John Borger, attorney for Cowles Media Company, prepared unofficial
transcripts from tapes of the two oral arguments before the Minnesota
Supreme Court.

Table of Cases

Index

About the Author

ELLIOT C. ROTHENBERG is a Minneapolis attorney with a J.D. degree from Harvard Law School. His briefs and oral arguments before the U.S. Supreme Court are published in *Landmark Briefs and Arguments of the Supreme Court of the United States*, Vol. 200. He has published articles in many newspapers and periodicals, including *The Wall Street Journal*, *Columbia Journalism Review*, and law reviews. He has also served on the faculties of national First Amendment and communications law seminars.